p1/2 The Time on the Orde/St V d..1

p7. N 2 faced with Orde

p15. Genesis England expects

p17 Jervis 61 when he became

p23/24 Cf Nelson + St V.

P27 N's eye, all useful sight h

p29 St V 14/2 tactics N's behaviour p30

p46. Orde

p64. Orde made Post-Capt

p71. John Swinfen Jervis

p84 1795 promoted R. Admiral g White

p89 St V sucks up to Orde

p89 Orde's expectations of 21/c

p92 Ranks, ages, N Parker + Orde

p95 Minto's part.

p97 Prince W+ Lady H?

p97 And Lady S.

p99 St V not open with Orde + Parker.

* p101 Parker + Leonard 2 ca station 1787 as Commodore.
    55 at the time
    + v St V on prize money. N not the first to contest St V.

* p106/108. All passed the parcel when Nelson did not seem to be delivering the goods.

* p107 Reason for not getting a Viscountcy was that he had allowed Nap to land?

* p126/127 Collingwood's view of St V's Command

p147. Navy knew Nap's plan?

p150 Prize money from the Spanish frigates + N v St V.

p151. The new Cadiz Squadron, Orde, Nelson + prize money.

* p167 Orde, tactics + orders

Why did the Fr slip N again at Toulon?

177 what he Collingwood ordered to do. Look at Ad Board minus.

186. Prep of his coffin?

hoist with his own
etard

Nelson's Mediterranean Command

Nelson's Mediterranean Command

Concerning Pride, Preferment & Prize Money

His Honour Judge Denis A. Orde

The Pentland Press Limited
Edinburgh • Cambridge • Durham • USA

First published in 1997 by
The Pentland Press Ltd.
1 Hutton Close
South Church
Bishop Auckland
Durham

British Library Cataloguing in Publication Data.
A catalogue record for this book is available
from the British Library.

ISBN 1 85821 493 9

Typeset by CBS, Felixstowe, Suffolk
Printed and bound by Bookcraft Ltd., Bath

For my wife Jane and my daughters Georgina and Philippa.

CONTENTS

ILLUSTRATIONS

The illustrations on pp. 66, 91 and 194 are reproduced by kind permission of the National Maritime Museum, Greenwich. The remainder are from prints in the author's own collection.

PREFACE

On two occasions only during the Revolutionary and Napoleonic Wars did the French seriously threaten to invade the British Isles, once in the year 1797-8 and again between the years 1803 and 1805.

In the spring of the year 1798 matters were coming to a head in the long war between the two nations for there were reports of great activity by the French. Sources of intelligence told the British Government that an expeditionary force had been massed at Toulon and at other ports in the Mediterranean ready for embarkation. The danger of invasion therefore looked to be imminent but its destination remained unknown. The belief in Britain was that it was headed for these shores and alarm bells had begun to sound in the corridors of Whitehall for Bonaparte was by now all but master of Europe and Britains feared the worst. Clearly the need now was for a squadron of ships to re-enter the Mediterranean which they should never have left, hunt down the French Fleet and destroy it. Command of such a force would very obviously carry with it immense responsibility and great prestige. It called for an officer of outstanding skill and determination. Indeed there can have been few appointments made in the long history of the British Royal Navy of more crucial importance to the defence of the nation, or, even, of Western Europe for at this moment in time Great Britain really stood alone against the French invader and the might of Napoleon Bonaparte's all-conquering army. It is surprising therefore that the provenance of the appointment has been so little explored.

But it is more astonishing to find that several British admirals were at war, not just with the enemy at this time of national emergency, but also with one another. So much so that a duel was challenged in the year 1799 and would have taken place but for the timely intervention of George III. The concern of this work is to trace the events which set these high-ranking officers on collision course and to measure the extent to which, if at all, the advancement of Horatio Nelson to command of the Mediterranean Squadron was the cause of it. It is an account of pride, preferment and prize money, for there was a considerable golden harvest in the countdown to Trafalgar which so exercised the mind and pen of Horatio Nelson.

History can but be written through the lives of those to whom the nation's affairs have been entrusted at any given time, but at these critical moments a small number of naval officers, perhaps driven on by naked ambition, but undoubtedly stiffened by a strong sense of patriotism, succeeded in writing themselves into the pages of history. All were very different characters and of varying achievement. Not all may have shared Nelson's pathological hatred of the French, but throughout their lives the common enemy was France. Many of them no more than walked in the shadow of those giants who strode the national stage at the turn of the eighteenth century, those few men who so dominated the life of the nation at one of the most dangerous periods of its history, amongst them Pitt, St Vincent, Nelson, and, later, Wellington, all men of magisterial greatness. So much so that little is ever written of others who also had a role to play. But at least each one could count himself fortunate to have served in the Royal Navy through what undoubtedly were some of the most glorious years in its long and distinguished history, crowned as they were by Nelson's three great victories at the Nile, Copenhagen and off Cape Trafalgar.

In order to be able to understand and judge the bizarre events of the years 1798, 1799, 1804 and 1805, the year of Trafalgar, it has been necessary in this work to look back a little at the service careers of some of those naval officers who stood at the very centre of the storm which was to be given such prominence in *The Times* newspaper of the day, including that of the autocratic, formidable, austere and thoroughly difficult St Vincent who had dedicated his entire life to mastery of his profession, whose twin contributions to the defence of the Realm were to transform an ill-disciplined and largely mercantile marine into a well organized fighting machine which was to achieve pre-eminence in the waters of the world in the ten years which followed his assumption of command in the Mediterranean in the year 1795, and then to unleash the brilliance of Horatio Nelson and place him at its head, and at the disposal of the British nation. This was his legacy and these were his lasting monuments. He left behind order and purpose where there was none before – that of the flamboyant, theatrical, petulant but inspirational Nelson himself, the ornament of the service of whom so much has been written; of the proud Northumbrian Admiral Sir John Orde, the target of so much of their acrimony until he along with countless others made his way to St Paul's Cathedral on 9 January of the year 1806 to pay homage to Horatio Nelson as a pall-bearer at his funeral; of the apoplectic and courageous Sir William Parker, also a contender for the crown; of the gentle Collingwood, perhaps the noblest sailor of them all; and of many others, much of it as seen through the eyes of those with whom they served.

ACKNOWLEDGEMENTS

The journey has involved striking a path through countless published works, fortunately many of them in my own personal library at Chollerton, but also much correspondence elsewhere, some of it unpublished hitherto, which emerged from the American War of Independence, the troubles in Dominica, the Battle off Cape St Vincent, the Mutinys of 1797, the blockade of Cadiz, events leading to Aboukir Bay, the countdown to Trafalgar, the funeral of Nelson, and, finally, the aftermath, all of which are represented in the narrative. This has only been possible thanks to the unstinting assistance and unfailing courtesy of the librarians and their staffs at the National Maritime Museum at Greenwich, the National Library for Scotland, the Portsmouth City Library, the Bodleian at Oxford University and particularly Mrs Penny Sturgis, the Monmouth Library, the Newcastle upon Tyne City Library, the Hexham and County Libraries in Northumberland and the Records Office at Kew.

The work was conceived many years ago but it was only when appointed a Crown Court Judge when in my mid-forties, and thus relieved of the punishing demands of practice as a barrister, that time became available for the necessary research. There I owe my thanks to two long-standing friends, the late and much loved Hon. Mr Justice Roddy Smith for suggesting and promoting the move, and Peter Taylor QC, then leader of the North-Eastern Circuit and later to be Lord Chief Justice of England, for giving it his support, although not, I suppose, with the thought that work would be done elsewhere!

Much of the groundwork was thus covered several years ago, but, alas, within a very few years of appointment the ever-growing burden which comes with increasing seniority began again to occupy all waking moments so that my project was put to one side once again where it remained until, mercifully, respite of a few weeks became available for the work in recent times.

I am grateful too for the assistance I received from the Rt. Hon. Sir Patrick Nairne MCPC who, amongst many positions held in both Oxford and London, as a trustee of the Greenwich Maritime Museum arranged for me to use the Museum outside Court hours when sitting on occasion at the Law Courts in the Strand, London and at the Central Criminal Court and for his general encouragement for the book. My thanks are due also to our dear friends of many years, the Viscount and Viscountess Dilhorne, for introducing me when staying to the advantages of computer literacy which made compilation of the book so much easier; to the Reverend Canon Halliburton MA, D.Phil. Chancellor of St Paul's Cathedral who granted me sight of Nelson documents in the Cathedral Library together with a private view of Nelson's last resting place, and much of his time on a visit which he so kindly took over from the Very Reverend Eric Evans KCVO MA Hon DD, Dean of St Paul's, a friend made in my student days at Oxford University to which he had come as a mature student to read theology but who died so tragically but a few weeks before my visit to the Cathedral; to Admiral Sir John Kerr, then Admiral of the Home Fleet, and Lady Kerr for their kind hospitality to my wife and myself at the Trafalgar Night dinner on board HMS *Victory* and at Admiralty House in the year 1993; to the Hon. Fiona Rippon, daughter of yet more old friends, the Rt. Hon. Lord Rippon of Hexham QC and Lady Rippon OBE for arranging urgent assistance with my computer technology at one stage when the script was in its final stages; to our very good friends the Rt. Hon. Dame Elizabeth Butler-Sloss, Lord Justice of Appeal and Mr Joe Butler-Sloss for their generous assistance; to Lord Plant of Highfield MA, D.Phil, D.Litt, to the Hon. Mr Justice Mervyn Davies, to Lady Wakeham, to Lieutenant Commander Jeremy Pett RN and to Mr Paul Batty QC for the contributions they so kindly volunteered; to His Honour Judge Fox QC, ex-RN, and Mrs Kate Fox; to Mr Tom Bowles; to Mrs John Fenwick and her family; to Mrs Cynthia Thompson; and to Mr Robert Milne-Tyte for their great support; and to those many Instructors of Gunnery who attempted to teach me, when a young Artillery officer, the rudiments of their craft which has been of such assistance when writing some parts of this book, a fairly superficial knowledge later advanced somewhat by gunnery *obiter dicta* dropped unknowingly by General Sir Martin Farndale KCB, formerly Master Gunner, in a conversation with him over dinner at Woolwich held for Founders of the Royal Artillery Heritage Appeal. Of the many letters written to Sir John Orde or by him which I have mentioned in the text, a dozen or so are on long-term loan to the National Maritime Museum from Sir John Campbell-Orde Bt., to whom I owe my thanks. I owe my thanks also to my publishers, in particular Mrs Jill Rowena Cole, Executive Editor, and Mrs Mary Denton, Publishing Manager, for demonstrating such enthusiasm for the whole project that I was much encouraged.

Finally and chiefly I offer my grateful thanks to my wife Jane for her great patience and forbearance throughout the research and composition stages of this work and in particular for the valuable assistance she has rendered with her own inquiries as to the dates and places of births and deaths of some of those

Northumbrians referred to in the text. It has been a happy escape from the trial of company fraud, violent rape, QBD claims for damages, drug offending and much else which has been my daily diet now for so many years.

Denis Orde,
Chollerton, Hexham, Northumberland
January 1997

CHAPTER I

A DUEL IS CHALLENGED

Set honour in one eye, and death in the other,
And I will look on both indifferently:
For, let the Gods so speed one, as I love
The name of honour more than I fear death.

Shakespeare

In the dying moments of the last year of the eighteenth century, the year in which Napoleon Bonaparte seized absolute power in France, a leader on the front page of *The Times* newspaper in London brought drama to the breakfast table with the astonishing news that two British admirals were at war, not just with the enemy at this time of national emergency, but also with one another. So much so that a duel had been challenged, as it reported on 5 October 1799:

The public will recollect with regret the serious misunderstanding which prevailed between some of our commanders on the Cadiz station, about the period when Lord Nelson was sent up the Mediterranean with a detached squadron. It was conceived by the senior Admirals that Lord St Vincent had treated them with some disrespect by appointing a junior officer to a separate command. Several distinguished officers were much disgusted upon that occasion, which also laid the foundation of subsequent misunderstandings and quarrels of a very serious description. Sir John Orde, brother to Lord Bolton, was amongst those who felt themselves most insulted or aggrieved . . . the second in command conceived himself to have received some personal affronts, which he found it irreconcilable with his high feelings of honour to forgive or to dissemble. He caused the correspondence which had taken place between him and Lord St Vincent to be printed, and distributed it amongst his private and professional friends immediately . . . and it was but too clearly understood, or too justly apprehended, that he would seek another kind of satisfaction

1

whenever it would be consistent with the rules of military subordination to do so. This unfortunate event has actually taken place. A challenge was sent to the noble Earl who was hastening up to town yesterday in consequence. Happily the activity of the Magistrates of Bow Street has been able to frustrate an intention, which in every event would have proved fatal to their country. Sir John Orde was arrested about 4 o'clock yesterday morning at Durrant's Hotel in Jermyn Street by Townshend and Sayers, who waited with him till Mr Ford's arrival about 11 o'clock, when, entering into a proper security for keeping the peace, he was liberated. Mr Ford, attended by Townshend, then set off for Earl St Vincent's seat in Essex, and met the Noble Lord on the road, on his way to town. On acquainting him with their purpose, his Lordship also gave bail to keep the peace, himself in £2000 and two sureties in £1000 each, being the same security as given by Admiral Orde. Earl Spencer and Mr Dundas were two of their sureties.[1]

The quantum of bail fixed by the magistrate suggests that he at any rate saw this challenge as a real one, as indeed it was, for this was the act of a man who had already exhausted every recognized channel of complaint after his personal reputation and record of long and distinguished service with the Royal Navy had been called into question. His good name was at stake and he saw this as the only way now left open to him of clearing it.

In fact Sir John Orde had actually travelled out to St Vincent's home in Essex before that day in search of revenge, but without obtaining any sort of satisfaction. This had been his first opportunity for although St Vincent had quit the Mediterranean and returned to England suffering from a dropsical condition many months earlier in the hope of achieving a cure before he returned to active service, Sir John had thought it only fair and honourable that he should bide his time until his adversary had been restored to full health before he confronted him lest an unfair advantage be obtained. Now the opportunity to bring matters to a head seemed to have arisen for news of St Vincent's recovery was beginning to reach him. It was reported in late September that he had been seen moving about in society once more, well enough to dine out at the houses of friends and to visit the Admiralty seeking another command. And then came a message that he was preparing to go down to his country home, Rochetts near Brentwood in Essex. Sir John therefore judged that the time had arrived to seek redress for wrongs done to him twelve months before out in the Mediterranean Command.

Travelling up to town from his home in Tunbridge Wells on 30 September, armed with the necessary pistols to do the business and bringing with him one

Captain Wellrond who was to act as his second, he booked into Dorant's Hotel in Jermyn Street. From there he sent the Captain round to Colonel Barré's house in Stanhope Street, the house in which St Vincent had been staying, as an emissary carrying with him Sir John's carefully worded challenge. It read,

My Lord

The reports I receive from time to time of your Indisposition since your arrival in England have prevented me calling upon your Lordship at an earlier period, as I had wished and intended, for that satisfaction I think due to me from you, for the very illiberal and Injurious treatment I received at your hands whilst serving under your command. As I am now given to understand you are much better, I must require it from your Lordship without delay, more especially as I have business in the country that demands my immediate presence, and will detain me there for some time. Captain Wellrond will deliver this, and who intends me the Honour to act as my Second will settle with your Lordship any person you will appoint respecting time, place etc.

I am my Lord your Lordship's most Humble Servant,
     J. Orde

P.S. I shall wait your answer at this Inn.[2]

The mention of urgent business which allegedly demanded his attention suggests that Sir John had no doubt as to which of them would emerge from a duel still able to fulfil commitments elsewhere! But, alas, the bird had flown before Wellrond could deliver his missile, or so a servant who answered the door represented the case to be. It was therefore on 2 October that, with the challenge still in pocket and armed with weapons and all the paraphernalia needed for the deed they had in mind, they hired a chaise and set out for Brentwood in Essex, heading for the address which had been disclosed to them by a less than discreet servant at Colonel Barré's. Here they took a room at the White Hart Hotel in the town, and there Sir John remained whilst the long-suffering Wellrond was sent further on up the road the mile or two to the house, there to test the water, deliver the challenge and generally act as Sir John Orde's mouthpiece. But here, perhaps not surprisingly, his mission failed for St Vincent, safe indoors, would not receive him, and he sent a footman out to the chaise to tell him so. When asked why, that loyal retainer had replied that his master had given clear orders that anyone calling at the house was to be told firmly that he was 'too unwell to be seen'. The ever resourceful Wellrond had then asked if he was at least well enough to read a letter which he carried with him. The man agreed to go and find out. The reply came 'Yes', and so, eventually, the challenge was issued. However it drew, not St Vincent in person, but a response in writing which pleaded both indisposition and justification. It read,

> In the infirm state of health your letter has found me, I can make no other reply than that I do not feel myself accountable to you or any person that has served under my command for any Military conduct.

That answer the disappointed Wellrond carried back to Sir John. But Sir John was not finished yet. Again he put pen to paper:

> My Lord,
> Had your conduct towards me deserved the name of Military, I never should have addressed you as I did this morning, but deeming it after having been refused a Court Martial judicially to ascertain its true Character to have been Tyrannical and Deceitful, I hold your Lordship responsible to me for it, on every principle of Honour and Justice.[3]

That letter alleging private, not military misconduct, he left with the landlord to be taken up to the house with the message that he would wait at Dorant's Hotel for St Vincent's reply.[4] And with that, after a much needed dinner at the Inn, they left that same evening for London and Dorant's Hotel.

In the meantime, when his servant told him of Wellrond's visit to his house in Stanhope Street, Colonel Barré, then seventy-three years of age and with a long experience of military and political life behind him both as a Member of Parliament and as a one-time Treasurer of the Navy, had promptly reported his suspicions to Lord Spencer, First Lord of the Admiralty, for he rightly sensed that a duel was in prospect.[5] Spencer, in turn, had lost no time mobilizing the assistance of the law in the shape of Sir Richard Ford. Sir John, the while, waited two days and two nights at Dorant's Hotel for a response from St Vincent which never came,[6] and there, as the *Naval Chronicle*[7] of that year was to report, at first light of the day appointed for the duel, Townshend and Sayers found him, in bed and fast asleep! Such was the composure of a battle-hardened veteran of many a naval campaign. Later, when Sir Richard Ford arrived and Sir John had been woken, he was required to give security for the peace. This proud Northumbrian, realizing then that nothing could now come of his challenge, abandoned the enterprise and promptly left at ten in the morning for Tunbridge Wells and the wife who was waiting nervously for him there before going on to the place he had recently acquired at Bognor in the county of Sussex – but not before, as the *Courier* reported it, he had 'requested the officers, if they went to Earl St Vincent's house, to proceed with great caution at such an early hour of the day, and to conceal their business from everyone but his lordship, as Lady St Vincent is dangerously ill and a knowledge of the affair might produce alarming effects', and, he added, embarrassment to guests it had been observed they had in the house.[8] The truth is also that St Vincent was reached before he ever set out from his home in Essex, and there, indisposed and in bed, he too was bound over to keep the peace (*Naval Chronicle*). Hence the report of *The Times* newspaper on 5 October.

On Tuesday 8 October *The Times* pronounced that 'Mr Ford and Townshend have accomplished a greater achievement than the united force of Spain could effect – they have taken two of our best Admirals prisoner!'[9]

However, Lord Spencer, fearing that the challenge had been no more than postponed now sought the intervention of George III so that further trouble might be averted. On 6 October he wrote to the King,

> The expedient ... will only prevail for a certain time, and, consulting with Mr Pitt and others of your Majesty's confidential servants, we have agreed as the only effective means of preventing further mischief, humbly to recommend to your Majesty to permit your Royal Authority to be interposed, by signifying to me your pleasure that the Earl of St Vincent should be commanded by the Board of Admiralty not to accept of a challenge from Sir John Orde on this occasion, which should justify his lordship in refusing to meet the Vice-Admiral and may it is hoped put an end to this very unpleasant business.[10]

The King's response was immediate. From Weymouth on 7 October by return of post he wrote expressing his approval 'of the Earl of St Vincent being in the strongest manner acquainted by the Board of Admiralty, in my name, that I expect he will not accept any challenge from Sir John Orde; but I think Sir John should also be acquainted with the instructions I have given to the Board of Admiralty, that he may not offer any further insult to the Earl St Vincent.' He wrote that Sir John had been 'so absurd as to turn into a personal affront what was only his Commanding Officer's employing that discretional power his station authorised'.[11]

Accordingly, on arrival at Bognor, Sir John received from Evan Nepean, Secretary to the Admiralty, a copy of a letter which the Lords Commissioners of the Admiralty had sent to St Vincent containing the command of the King that 'His Majesty has been pleased to signify his express commands that your lordship should be restrained from accepting any challenge from Sir John Orde, on pain of His Majesty's displeasure . . . their Lordships expect you will pay due obedience to His Majesty's commands on this head.'

And so there the matter had to rest. Sir John had been denied satisfaction and the challenge was never to be raised again, although a final shot was fired by him in a very long letter to the Lords Commissioners of the Admiralty on 7 February 1801 in explanation of his refusal to take up an offer of a further command.[12] In this he referred once more to the disgrace and insult which had been dealt him by St Vincent in the year 1798 for which St Vincent had resolutely failed to atone, and there followed in the year 1802 a document setting out his own version of events which had already been circulated privately but held back from a wider audience until peace had been signed and the emergency had been abated by the Treaty of Amiens.[13] But what had set these two Admirals on collision course and to what extent had the advancement of Horatio Nelson been the cause of it? Sir John thought not at all, and, as a pall-bearer, he was to be the officer who stood closest to Nelson at the moment of his interment in St Paul's Cathedral in January 1806. Nelson, after all, whether the cause of it or not, had remained throughout at a distance of several thousand miles on the Mediterranean station.

The Editor of *The Times* judged it in these terms in an editorial published on 8 October 1799.[14] He wrote,

> it appears that he [Sir John Orde] has never been able to brook what he conceived to be a slight on his professional character, by the appointment of Sir Horatio Nelson, his junior in the fleet, to the command of the squadron which was sent in search of Buonaparte on the shores of Egypt. Earl St Vincent's reply to Sir John Orde's remonstrance on this occasion was that the particular service on which Sir H. Nelson had been sent required that no larger ships should be employed than two-deckers, and that to place Sir John Orde in a ship of inferior force to that which he then commanded, would be disrespectful to the high character he bore in the Navy . . . Sir John wrote to the Admiralty, and received an answer similar to that given by the Commander-in-Chief, at the same time expressive of the high respect which the Board entertained for his abilities. Sir John Orde then requested to be recalled . . . Deeply as we enter into the high and honourable feelings of this distinguished officer, we cannot but congratulate the country at large upon his disappointment. The general voice of the British Public bears ample testimony to his high character. Nothing can add to the opinion he has so well deserved; and the issue must have proved injurious to the kingdom, and to the service, of which these brave officers are ornament and support.

Self evidently it requires great tact and diplomacy to promote a man over the heads of those senior to him in rank. If he owes his promotion to proven superior ability it will be accepted with good grace, but if not, it will forever be resented.

But the judgment of *The Times* was but a fraction of the truth. The Lords Commissioners of the Admiralty were to report that Sir John had been treated unjustly at the hands of St Vincent and there followed an offer of high command, but the squabble of 1798 between St Vincent and Sir John Orde was destined to run on and on and to remain for ever unresolved. St Vincent was to continue in naval command and then in political office for many years to come, whilst Sir John, too, returned to active service in the years which followed and was to play a significant role in events leading up to the Battle of Trafalgar whilst all the while acquiring great seniority of rank, albeit won in the general promotions rather than in any field of battle. On two occasions only during the Revolutionary and Napoleonic Wars did the French seriously threaten to invade the British Isles, once in 1797-8 and again between the years 1803 and 1805. Coincidentally it was only in these two periods of national emergency that the name of Sir John Orde achieved any sort of public notoriety – the only officer, as one modern historian has put it, to rumble the genius of Bonaparte at a moment when he was poised to descend on these shores with all the might of his *Grand Armée.*

Yet his very presence on the Cadiz Station in the years 1804 and 1805 gave rise to a flood of acrimonious correspondence and invective from the pen of Horatio Nelson in the distant Mediterranean, although none of it written to Orde personally to whom he always showed courtesy.

St Vincent was to live on for a further twenty-five years and Sir John twenty-six, but the passage of time and advancement in the service did nothing to heal the rift between them or to assuage Orde's feelings which continued to smoulder within him until the day of his death. Although his fellow Northumbrian and Nelson's trusted friend Collingwood at all times spoke of Orde with fairness and affection, and whilst he himself achieved high rank, wealth and a certain degree of notoriety, he continued to feel that the events which had dogged him in 1798 had blighted both his career and his reputation for ever and he carried that sense of grievance with him to the grave.

Indeed the quarrel has since been much misunderstood. Even one hundred years and more later, in July 1914, shortly before the outbreak of the Kaiser's War, Lord Fisher, then seventy-three years of age and about to return to the Admiralty as First Sea Lord, found occasion to use the incident by way of analogy, incorrectly. Winston Churchill, then First Lord of the Admiralty, was seeking to replace Sir George Callaghan as Commander-in-Chief of the Home

Fleet before the outbreak of war because of age. In fact he was then but sixty-two and some two years younger than St Vincent had been in 1798 when commanding the Mediterranean Fleet. But Churchill's judgment, no doubt correct at the time, had been that Sir George would not be equal to the strain of war and should be removed before the Fleet ever went into action. On the advice of Fisher his replacement was to be the reluctant Jellicoe, then Second Sea Lord and a mere fifty-five years of age, even though Jellicoe himself objected most strongly to the arrangement. Clearly this move too called for a tact and persuasion on Churchill's part which was sadly lacking, although the blow to Sir George was later softened to some extent by his appointment to the Nore as Commander-in-Chief in 1915, and then later, at the end of the war, as Admiral of the Fleet. But by letter to A.J. Balfour, former Prime Minister and later to become First Lord of the Admiralty in the Coalition Government, Fisher wrote:

> . . . as to Winston scrapping Admirals 'with a courageous stroke of the pen', I want to mention to you that since being a Midshipman I have adored the English principle of having civilian First Lords of Admiralty, because I read how Lord Spencer, then First Lord, on his own initiative and against the Navy traditions sent Nelson to the Mediterranean over the head of Sir John Orde and others (who had their flags flying) and hence we got the battle of the Nile! The finest of all fights since the World began . . . so now we get Jellicoe as Admiralissimo and there will be a hell of a row among the Admirals (If there is, I've promised Winston to go on the stump)![15]

The assumption made by Fisher in that analogy was to oversimplify the true position for his own purposes, and it is worth noting that when Nelson was given command of the Mediterranean Squadron in 1798 as his first independent Fleet command, Sir John Orde was then but forty-seven years of age and in the prime of life with twenty-six more years ahead of him.

In order to be able to understand and judge the bizarre events of 1799, it is necessary to look back a little in time at the service careers of these naval officers, much of it as seen through the eyes of others with whom they served. Like so many who lived at that time, Orde really walked in the shadow of those giants who strode the national stage at the turn of the eighteenth century, those few men who so dominated the life of the nation at one of the most critical periods in its history, amongst them Pitt, Nelson, St Vincent, and, later, Wellington, that little is ever written of others who also had a role to play. Whether preordained circumstances govern the lives of men, or whether man is master of his own destiny, history can but be written through the lives of those to whom the nation's affairs have been entrusted at any given time. It is, of course, a not unnatural ambition to strive for position on this earth if only to win the respect of those amongst whom you live and perhaps the additional comfort which rank may bring. Only a privileged few are driven on by a wish to serve their fellow men simply for the sake of it. Most are content simply to exist and few, very few, succeed in making such a mark in life that they are long remembered beyond the small circle of their immediate family and friends, and then probably for no more than a generation. For all but a few it is as if they had never been – at all events in the eyes of those who follow. How plaintive then is Purcell's lament to 'Remember Me'. Yet a few naval officers at this critical time, perhaps driven on by naked ambition, but undoubtedly coupled with a strong sense of patriotism, succeeded in writing themselves into the pages of history. All were very different characters of vastly different achievement. At the heart of the trouble which beset Sir John lay misunderstanding in high places, a clash of strong personalities and an unfortunate combination of events. But at least he could count himself fortunate to have served in the Royal Navy through what undoubtedly were the most glorious years of its long and distinguished history.

Notes

1 *The Times*, 5 October 1799.
2 ND p. 111.
3 ND p. 112.
4 Orde Correspondence.
5 JA p. 255, and ND p. 112.
6 Orde Correspondence.
7 The *Naval Chronicle*, Vol 2, p. 440.
8 Orde Correspondence.
9 *The Times*, 8 October 1799.
10 *Spencer Papers*, Vol III, p. 25.
11 *Spencer Papers*, Vol III, pp. 25-6; *Letters of George III*, pp. 275 and 280; J Ber p. 169.
12 Orde Correspondence.
13 *Gentleman's Magazine* for 1824, p. 277.
14 *The Times*, 8 October 1799.
15 Gilbert, pp. 14-16.

CHAPTER II

JERVIS GIVEN COMMAND

The history of the British nation in the 200 years or so leading up to Waterloo could so easily be written through the eyes of the developing Royal Navy, for the two marched hand in hand. As T. Gibson Bowles MP observed in his *Sea Law and Sea Power* published in 1910, 'To gain and keep the command of the sea when at war was always for England the condition of success; to lose that command, even for a time, was always the forerunner of failure. This truth, always known to seamen, has now been perceived by the landsman, and has become an article of national faith.'[1]

For the last 100 of those 200 years, France, as the most populated and the most powerful nation in the world, had been the common enemy. With a population of more than 25 million[2] she outnumbered Great Britain by 3 to 1. Rivalry between the two for trade across the world with the emerging countries was intense. The threat posed by France to British commercial interests abroad, and indeed at home, was correspondingly great for France appreciated well enough that invasion of British territory would very quickly stifle all competition. And so, as trade routes opened up in distant parts, so did competition for them amongst the great nations of Western Europe. This stark reality dictated the basic need. If these island shores and British territory and commercial interests around the world were to be protected from predators and armies of invasion, a strong and commanding naval presence was required to guard these many highways, playing a defensive role, for Great Britain really stood alone. And, rather than concentrate British ships in home waters in immediate defence of the island, it became the central policy of the Admiralty to seek to dominate the Channel by blockading France's Atlantic ports twenty-four hours a day, principally that of Brest, and so prevent the French Fleet putting to sea, confident that if British ships were blown off station by winds of gale force, that same circumstance would prevent the French Fleet from setting sail. Likewise, exploiting the geography of France's divided coastline, a blockade would be mounted at Toulon to prevent the French Mediterranean Fleet from being able to sail to combine with any fleet which may have succeeded in breaking out into the Atlantic. The same strategy was to be applied off Cadiz should Spain rally to the support of France. Other ships, the while, would be deployed in protection of British convoys and British territories across the world, but in three main areas, North America, the West Indies and India as the British Empire proceeded to grow.

The year 1793 had found Great Britain at war with France yet again. Across the Channel a few years before, Frenchmen had become preoccupied with revolution. By fighting with the rebels in the American war against the British king, they had undermined the authority of Louis XVI and sown the seeds of revolution. The King of France had then, for the first time in more than a century, finally delegated the responsibility of government to a Parliament of the Estates General which had then turned on him, looking for its support to the Committee of Public Safety, Robespierre, Danton, the hard-pressed and overtaxed majority of ordinary Frenchmen and a starving Paris mob which had been unable to meet the exorbitant price which the sale of bread commanded. In its wake came the uprising, triggered off by the storming of the Bastille in 1789. The country was now in the grip of revolution. It was the hope of new France that the revolutionary idea and spirit could be exported, and that, encouraged by infiltrators and agitators, it would quickly and spontaneously spread across the Channel and there capture the hearts and minds of ordinary Englishmen and so overthrow all established order and peace. And there was ground enough for such hope for many a leading Englishman had expressed support and sympathy for the revolutionary idea, amongst them William Wordsworth. But the mood of the average Englishman had been badly misread. As the Terror, ordered by the National Assembly and later by the Convention, gathered momentum, so it rapidly escalated like a Frankenstinian monster grown beyond the control of its creator. And as it did so, so the ordinary decent Englishmen, sickened by the atrocities and bloodletting and butchery and the drunken thirst for more, and, finally, by the executions of Louis and Marie Antoinette in 1793, quickly lost all interest in the French solution. Prominent amongst those so converted was the same William Wordsworth. Indeed, such was the revulsion for the whole spectacle that it set back proper movement for reform in Great Britain for a generation or more. In the result the French Republican Army marched into Belgium and Holland in violation of all treaties of neutrality and now threatened to use those territories as a springboard to cross the English Channel. At the very least British commercial interests were now put at risk by the French occupation of the Flemish coast, the Scheldt Estuary and the water highways across Europe. Austria, Prussia, and then, finally, England, alarmed by the threat of invasion, found themselves at war with France which had been declared in Paris on 1 February 1793. They were to remain at war for the next twenty years or more until matters were finally resolved at the Battle of Waterloo. And yet all this was seen by the ordinary British seaman below decks as just another conflict in the long list of struggles with the old enemy, rather than as an armed resistance to the spread of the revolutionary idea.

As has so often been the case, the declaration of war found the British nation unprepared. It is true that the country had recovered its composure since the embarrassment of the American War of Independence which had petered out in 1783, leaving Britain alone and friendless. Since then she had won back Holland and Prussia as her allies, and, under William Pitt the Younger as Prime Minister, the country had enjoyed ten years of peace, prosperity and consolidation. But ships and manpower had been scaled down to a dangerously low level. The Navy had for many years operated as a mercantile fleet, ill-equipped to wage war and with little or no experience of battle conditions, and many trained officers, such as Nelson, had been languishing at home unoccupied without a command and on half pay. But now officers were rapidly brought back and all the great admirals of the day were given fleet commands. Admiral Lord Hood, First Sea Lord and much admired by Nelson and Collingwood as a forward-looking professional naval officer who owed nothing to birth or influence, was soon to be given command of the Mediterranean Fleet. He was now almost seventy years of age. And Admiral Lord Howe, brother of the General, and claimed by George III as a blood relation through his aristocratic Hanoverian mother, an illegitimate daughter of George I, was also now recalled at the age of sixty-eight at the insistence of the King.[3] A dapper, inaccessible and apparently cold man, he was in truth kindly and compassionate and much loved by the ordinary sailor for the concern he showed for the welfare of those who served under him, without ever wishing to advertise the fact or claim the credit for doing so. Although he was very much the product of a highly privileged background with an awesome reputation in the service as a professional sailor who had gone to sea at the age of fourteen, he was at the same time entirely without ambition and very much the darling of the service. Despite his Tory sympathies, Pitt the Younger had replaced him as First Lord of the Admiralty in favour of his own brother, Lord Chatham, in 1788, but now, with Pitt Prime Minister once again, Howe, that most accomplished of Admirals, was brought back as Commander-in-Chief of the Channel Fleet. Such was the need for battle experience. Henry Dundas, the Edinburgh lawyer, was made Secretary of State for War. At a count there were probably about 300 ships available, 120 of them ships of the line, but less than half were then in commission and ready for sea and less than 50,000 officers and men were on hand to sail them,[4] 64 of whom were Admirals, 400 by then Post Captains and

Admiral Richard Howe

up to 1,500 in the rank of Lieutenant. It seemed that Great Britain now lay at the mercy of the French invader. The Pitt Administration, which had been in office for almost ten years of uneasy peace, was unused to war. And, like so many British governments before and since, it had been lamentably slow to recognize the danger and just as slow to respond to it when it appeared. As a war leader Pitt was as yet untried. Now, the previous ten years of consolidation and stability were to be rapidly dissipated to meet the war effort and the initial demands of war, not least the cost of subsidizing the support of other European nations. Yet ships were rapidly brought into commission, shipbuilding in the dockyards was stepped up, volunteer forces were hurriedly put together and an amateur attempt was made at coastal defence. Officers were recalled to the colours, amongst them Captain Horatio Nelson and Captain Sir John Orde. It now remained to be seen whether the patriotic and revolutionary fervour of the recently emancipated Frenchman, which was to be the winning ingredient for so many victories on land when harnessed and directed by the military genius of the Corsican Bonaparte, would be sufficient to produce a like result at sea where the trained and experienced pre-Revolution officer class had been all but decimated or dispersed in the Revolution. Discipline had all but collapsed in the French Navy which would soon be required to face a comparatively efficient British Royal Navy staffed for the most part by highly professional officers. The French had at their disposal recently and well-built ships of some size, but the use to which they put them depended almost entirely now upon the courage and patriotic spirit of those who sailed them, for there was precious little else; lacking were seamanship and experience.

In 1794 the National Convention had dismissed the 6,000 trained seamen gunners it still had at its disposal upon the ground that 'it savoured of aristocracy that any body of men should have an exclusive right to fight at sea'. It was a suicidal sacrifice made on the altar of ideology. Lacking too were supplies and provisions. French seamen were kept on meagre rations and issued with the barest minimum of clothing. It did nothing for their morale.

In those early days of unpreparedness it is not therefore surprising that the British Government found itself unable to send reinforcements to assist the Fleet at Toulon in support of the French Royalists who had seized the town in the year 1793 and opened the harbour to Lord Hood's ships. It was not possible therefore to exploit the advantage. And so it was that it was soon recaptured by French Republican forces, thanks in no small part to the crucial intervention of Napoleon Bonaparte, then a humble Lieutenant Colonel of Artillery, courageously disobeying the written orders of the Committee of Public Safety sitting in far-off Paris. Thus was Fort L'Aigulette, which commanded the entrance to the harbour, recaptured and the British Fleet forced to withdraw, abandoning all but three of the French Fleet which had previously been captured behind them together with those local Royalist supporters whom it had not been possible to evacuate. They were left to their fate as the incoming Jacobins and their guillotine moved closer. Nelson had played his part dancing attendance on the King of Naples at Hood's instruction which had produced military assistance for Toulon with the help of Sir William and Lady Hamilton. Alas, the Neapolitan contingent dispatched took fright under attack and could do nothing to save the town or to stop the wholesale slaughter of its citizens, a massacre which left an indelible mark on the mind of the young Napoleon who witnessed it.

However, in the year following, 1794, the British tasted some success. Admiral Howe had put to sea with a fleet of ships with orders to blockade the port of Brest when he found, to both his astonishment and delight, that the French had already broken out in order to provide escort for a large convoy of ships carrying vital supplies of grain from America to the blockaded French nation.

Ship for ship they were evenly matched and the French were confident. 'Never before did there exist in Brest a fleet so formidable,' wrote the Moniteur before the battle. After two days of searching followed by peripheral skirmishing in poor visibility and fog, Howe managed to bring the French Fleet to battle off Ushant and there he scored a decisive victory on what came to be known as 'The Glorious First of June' from the date of the encounter, for it was fought so far out into the ocean that no geographical point was available to identify the exact location.[5] Six French ships were captured, one was sunk and no less than 7,000 Frenchmen were killed, wounded or taken prisoner. Eight of Howe's ships suffered severe damage and there were 1,500 British casualties. The cost in human life had therefore been great. A commemorative panel was afterwards designed around the simple message, 'England expects every man to do his duty',[6] advice later employed by Nelson in his Trafalgar signal. It is sure that every man had done his duty on this occasion and those many who died had given much more! Indeed victory could to some extent be attributed to good fortune which had favoured the British for the battle had not gone according to Howe's plan which had been to pass through the French line from leeward. Despite the advantage by this time of the signalling system which had been devised by Admiral Kempenfelt and later codified by Howe for the use of Home Fleets,[7] some of Howe's captains found themselves unable to comply. Very few ships had followed Howe through the enemy line as planned, the rest had hauled up to windward and fired at a distance. In the result, the attack went in from all sides which threw the French into confusion, disarray, and, ultimately, defeat. The British had eleven vessels dismasted, the French twelve, and six French ships were captured.

For all that Howe's plan for the destruction of the French merchantmen under escort had failed and the French achieved their aim which had been to land their vast cargo of grain on the shores of France for consumption by a starved and very desperate population. There was therefore much rejoicing in that quarter for it had been a matter of life or death. But King George saw it as victory enough to persuade him, contrary to all previous custom, to visit Lord Howe on board his flagship. When the victorious Fleet docked at Spithead on 17 June, Lord Howe stepped on shore in the presence of a great crowd to the music of 'See the Conquering Hero Comes', 'Rule Britannia' and 'God Save the King' and that night he and Lady Howe were dined by the Port Admiral, Sir Peter Parker, in great splendour. And then, on 26 June, King George and Queen Charlotte descended on Portsmouth and there went on board Lord Howe's flagship, where the King presented the Admiral with a diamond-hilted sword. It was a royal occasion without precedent. Although the victory had not been as decisive as it was at that time thought to be, it had nonetheless restored confidence in the mind of the British sailor who ever afterwards believed that he could always defeat a Frenchman at sea, which the enemy too seemed to accept, for the French Navy ever afterwards demonstrated a marked reluctance to join battle with the British Navy.

Yet there followed a lean period lasting many years during which the British had little cause to rejoice, whilst the threat posed by a France torn by revolution daily grew more menacing now that she had the military genius of the fast-emerging Napoleon Bonaparte at her disposal. Once the Terror had abated and the Directory had taken control of France, his contribution at Toulon was remembered, when, two years later, Barrass gave him command of the forces of Paris. And there, with the skillful and determined use of cannonade, he quickly scattered and repulsed an attempt on the legislature. It was but the beginning of a meteoric rise to the very summit of power. A year or so later, given command of the Army of Italy, he force-marched his army across the Alps and down to the plains of Lombardy with the promise of riches and glory plundered from the conquered lands. And there, despite overwhelming odds stacked against him, he routed the Austrian Army and became, overnight, the sword and hero of the Revolution. One by one the armies of Western Europe were defeated in battle. Belgium was annexed to France, Italy became a vassal state, Venice an Austrian province, Milan, Piedmont and the principalities of northern Italy were welded into a new Cisalpine Republic, and the whole of Europe now lay at the feet of France. On every front she was triumphant, and yet, with Bonaparte's territorial ambitions no more than whetted and an insatiable appetite for conquest in battle still unsatisfied, France looked for fresh fields to conquer. Accordingly, in 1797, Bonaparte was ordered by the Directory to the shores of northern France to review the progress of plans for the invasion of Britain, possibly through the back door of Ireland where there was great unrest. Britain now feared the worst. It was in the climate of this emergency that Sir John Jervis, later to become Earl St Vincent, was given command of the Mediterranean Fleet, then lying off the island of Corsica, in the year 1795 with the rank of full Admiral. He was then sixty-one years of age.

Notes

[1] Bowles, p. 1.
[2] Clarke, p. 29.
[3] OCSS.
[4] Gardiner, p. 183.
[5] Preston, p. 79.
[6] Warner FS, p. 121.
[7] Spencer Papers, p. 208.

CHAPTER III

OF JERVIS AND NELSON

St Vincent was by this time a very formidable and highly complex character, totally dedicated to the efficiency of the Royal Navy. Most of his adult life and much of his youth had been spent at sea, and it had left its mark. Until he married his cousin in the year 1781 when forty-seven, he had turned his back on life outside the Service. The ordinary pleasures of life had been subordinated to duty so that he could devote all of his waking hours and the whole of his energy to his chosen profession. Born many miles from the sea at Melford Hall in the county of Staffordshire in January 1734, there had been nothing in his background to arouse an interest in ships or the sea. Indeed his father, Swynfen Jervis, had been called to the Bar, and was, in the year of his son's birth, struggling to support his family on what little he was able to earn from a modest court practice. Nonetheless, John Jervis, his second son, was sent to grammar school at Burton-on-Trent with the hope that he may, in due time, follow his father into the law. But then Swynfen Jervis had decided to seek security for both himself and his growing family by moving into paid employment at Greenwich on Thames as solicitor and Treasurer of Greenwich Hospital, which he did in 1747. The records there show that he was a spasmodic attender at meetings and an inefficient officer when he did attend, but the job gave him security.[1]

Jervis the boy was then still in his formative years and at a very impressionable age, and, not unnaturally, his imagination was soon fired by the naval presence all around him which so dominated Greenwich village. Even at that age, although but thirteen years, his determination was great and not many months of his life in Greenwich had gone by before he expressed to his father a strong wish to seek a career at sea. He found himself pushing at an open door for his father, who was still operating on a very tight budget, and saw here an opportunity to reduce the dependency. He was quick enough to encourage the boy in the wish he had expressed. And so, at the tender age of fourteen, and whilst still on the very nursery slopes of life, John Jervis was entered for the Navy. A place was quickly found for him on the ship *Gloucester* with the rating of Able Seaman, and a donation of £20 was made by Swynfen Jervis to launch him in his career. According to Brenton, long a devotee and ardent follower of St Vincent, in the *Life of Earl St Vincent* which he wrote, albeit long recognized as a thoroughly sycophantic and largely unreliable work, St Vincent would often claim in his old age that this was the last donation which his father ever made. Feeling that he had sufficiently discharged his duty as a parent and that his son was now well enough established, he left the boy, at the age of fourteen, to make his own way in life. It was a salutary experience which Jervis never forgot. That he should cling to such a memory indicates that it clouded his whole outlook on life and bred in him a complete independence of others which prevented much in the way of friendships in the future. That he had indeed been signed off by his father was made all too clear to him a year or two later when he referred an account for £20 which he had incurred, to his father, which his father promptly dishonoured. St Vincent's claim in later life was that he had then, at that moment of penury, been obliged to detach himself from his colleagues on the lower deck and live a life of frugality so that he could pay off the debt and support himself on what little pay his rank brought him. It involved great sacrifices in his way of living.

Many of his formative years were thus spent amongst warrant officers and seamen on the lower deck. Yet this was the making of him for he was able to learn first-hand from men of practical skill and experience how to handle a ship at sea. It was to give him an advantage over his contemporaries and a sturdy independence and ability to survive on his own resources for the rest of his career. His claim was that, such was his poverty, he even had to sacrifice his own bedding on one occasion to run up a pair of trousers he needed for duty. Of course these were the claims of a man when in old age, but, however accurate or inaccurate they may have been, there can be no doubt but that Jervis had been largely abandoned by his father to make his own way in life at a very early age. But, for all that, by sure application to duty, St Vincent became complete master of his profession, and advancement and promotion followed inexorably in its wake throughout his life and without interruption. In the ordinary way, a boy joining as a Midshipman at the age of thirteen or fourteen could expect to be commissioned Lieutenant when he reached the age of twenty, always provided that he passed the necessary exams for promotion. But if he failed, and stayed in the service, he would probably remain a Midshipman for the rest of his life. So too, specialist officers such as the chaplain and the surgeon usually remained at one level ranked in seniority below Lieutenant,[2] whilst pursers, boatswains, navigation masters, gunners and masters-at-arms ranked as warrant officers.[3] But the major promotion in an officer's life was to Post Captain, for, once achieved, he was then eligible, not only for prize money, but also for promotion simply by seniority. For the same reason it was important to reach that rank as quickly as possible and get on the conveyor belt when young for otherwise the seniority of others could block promotion for many a year. A further relic which had survived from the days of Pepys was the distinction made between flag officers of the same rank. They were arranged in order of seniority as of the Red, White or Blue and flew the appropriate flag accordingly, a Red squadron taking a position of control in the centre of the fleet, the White squadron leading from the front and the Blue squadron bringing up the rear. There were therefore nine separate ranks of Admiral above the rank of Post Captain, with, at the top of the pyramid, an Admiral of the Fleet of whom there was but one at any given time. And because of the custom of promotion by seniority, that ultimate rank was never won by any officer before extreme old age had set in. His duties were therefore largely ceremonial. Lord Howe held the rank from 1796 to 1799, to be succeeded by the aged Sir Peter Parker.[4] Jervis moved easily and steadily through each of these ranks, from the moment he passed his examination for the rank of Lieutenant in January 1755 when twenty years of age.

From the very start of his very long naval career Jervis had sought perfection and he became in time the supreme professional, a master of his craft, for he well understood that a lazy or incompetent officer can be both a liability and a danger to those ordered to serve under him. Jervis proceeded in the firm and very correct belief that there should be no place in the Navy for such an officer who could otherwise place the lives of men who were in his care and custody, at risk. With that eye for detail which so often marks off the professional, he sought to correct and improve whatever system he inherited. He seldom spent his leaves on shore. Where many another officer lost no time returning home for relaxation and comfort, Jervis preferred to take a busman's holiday at sea so that he could add to his knowledge and experience and store away what he had acquired for future use. The tale is told that he chose to spend his leave in 1774 on board a merchantmen bound for distant parts. To the irritation of the ship's Captain he then devoted the whole voyage to redrawing most of the ship's private pilotage charts which he judged to be 'all incorrect'. And then, whilst visiting St Petersburg, Germany and Scandinavia, his entire time was occupied in compiling notes as to the location of arsenals and other matters of naval utility in case these should have relevance or use to him in future warfare. The following year a yachting cruise off the west coast of France was turned over to an examination of port facilities and approaches which he noted down for future reference.

His reputation as a naval officer stood high after his service in the Seven Years War. Clearly General Wolffe had recognized in his old schoolfellow a man of integrity whom he could trust for, as he approached an absurdly premature death in that campaign, it was upon Jervis that he relied to deliver his fiancée back in England the miniature which hung about his neck. Jervis had promised that he would, and it is believed that he was as good as his word.[5] But the public first became aware of him during the American War of Independence. By then a well-respected officer, recognized as an honest man, he put forward a spirited defence on behalf of Admiral Keppel at the unedifying court martial which Sir Hugh Palliser had demanded in January 1779 following the abortive action off Ushant. Jervis's allegation that Palliser, as Keppel's Rear Admiral, had disregarded signals and had failed to support or help his commander to chase the enemy, played no small part in Keppel's acquittal. His star was now in the ascendant and three years later he was rewarded with a KB when wounded slightly in the action off Brest involving his ship the *Foudroyant* which had captured the *Pegase*, a French first rater, with no loss of British life, although, in truth, newly commissioned as the *Pegase* was with untried officers and untrained men, it had been an uneven contest from the outset. After a brief spell in Parliament as the Whig member for Launceston and then for Yarmouth, he had been promoted Rear Admiral in 1787 and then Vice Admiral in 1793 with command of an expedition to the West Indies.

When, on 1 July 1795, Jervis had been given command of the Mediterranean Fleet, his arrival was greeted by some with consternation, those who were fearful of the fierce and rigid discipline which would, inevitably, be imposed. But the Admiralty saw this new regime as necessary, faced as they were with the growing danger presented by a Europe increasingly dominated by the French invader. The need was for a firm and well-ordered blockade of Toulon where the French Fleet lay in harbour. Alarm bells were ringing at home for Pitt's Government was now fully alert to the possibility that the invasion which had for so long been promised, could soon become a reality if the French were ever allowed to break out of Toulon and link up with the Fleet at Brest, and then gain command of the English Channel long enough to cover a crossing by an invasion force. Jervis found himself in command of a fleet which had deteriorated badly whilst under the more lax discipline of Hood, and, later, Hotham, and, for a short spell after Hotham had struck his flag, by Sir Hyde Parker.[6] But he nonetheless applied himself to the matter of blockade with resolve and determination, and, in the two years which followed, he stamped his firm character upon the ships and men under his command by imposing a regime of iron discipline and by demanding a devotion to duty twenty-four hours a day. He required near perfection and largely succeeded in producing seamanship and gunnery of a high professional standard which has seldom been equalled. It was to serve both Nelson and the British nation well in the decade which followed. Without doubt this was the greatest contribution Jervis was to make in his long and distinguished career in the Royal Navy. His habit was to keep a close and watchful eye on every movement of every ship under his command and even on the smallest detail of its administration until the stage was reached when every one of his officers came to assume that his own performance was being daily scrutinized and monitored. He insisted that strict hygiene be observed on board ship, and that sick bays be provided. A hospital ship was established where the sick and wounded could be ministered to in a modicum of privacy and comfort. But any insubordination, however trivial, would be met with condign punishment. Gunnery and sail practice became a primary and regular routine and he impressed upon his captains the paramount importance of a ship of the line keeping in formation when in battle, at all times. And, although he lost no opportunity to obtain increased supplies of stores for his men, the need for the utmost economy and frugality was daily impressed upon his captains for he would not tolerate any degree of waste. A routine of frequent inspection was kept up in order to make sure that every ship under his command was up to his standards. In this way Jervis in effect stamped on the Fleet an impression of his own stern character. Occasionally, just occasionally, he demonstrated that there was another and more human side to him, but when he did so, he took care to make sure that every act of kindness or generosity was very well advertised and made public,[7] thus suggesting an ulterior motive, for his real and central purpose was to ensure a strict obedience to his every command.

It was here therefore that he made the first of his two great contributions to the defence of the nation, and indeed to naval history, for, within months of taking up his command, by imposing such an iron discipline and by insisting on seamanship of the very highest standard he had, in that short period of time, transformed an ill-disciplined and largely mercantile marine into a well-ordered fighting machine which was ever afterwards able to maintain the round-the-clock vigil and blockade of French ports required of it and to so dominate the French in battle when placed under the command of Horatio Nelson. Indeed, in the twenty-two years of warfare between 1793 and 1815 the British Navy lost but 6 ships, all captured, whilst the French, Spanish, Dutch and Danish fleets lost in total 156 ships, 127 of them by capture, half of them French. However, great though Jervis's contribution undoubtedly was, it was won at a price for there were many defectors and there was much discontent. The second and more obvious of his two achievements was to ensure that Nelson was appointed to the Mediterranean Command in 1798, thus unleashing the brilliance of that Admiral against the French to the eternal advantage of the British nation.

Jervis therefore was a man of considerable stature before either Nelson or Sir John Orde had really ever crossed his path. And it is true also that before

Sir John Orde sailed out to join Jervis and the Mediterranean Fleet, Nelson had by then won a place of special favour in Jervis's affections which was to explain much that followed. It was on 19 January 1796 that Nelson, in the battle-worn *Agamemnon*, sailed into St Fiorenza to join the Mediterranean Fleet. There had been a brief encounter many years before when Captain Locker had introduced them,[8] but this was his first real meeting with Jervis. Here were two very different characters, yet they took to each other immediately. So much so that Jervis started by offering Nelson the choice of another ship, and then, in almost the same breath, promised him promotion to the rank of Commodore. Although this was not a rank in itself at that time it gave an officer authority to perform the duties of a flag officer as occasion demanded.[9] Not surprisingly Nelson immediately warmed to the man.

Of medium height, thickset and strong, Jervis was heavy jowled and loose-skinned, and, with head sunk into shoulders and eyes sitting low in their sockets, he resembled nothing so much as an ageing Bassett hound. Although very different in character there were, however, some similarities between these two men. Each had made himself master of his profession in both seamanship and gunnery and both were supremely meticulous, efficient and dedicated in the discharge of their duties. These were intensely patriotic men of great integrity, giving simple but absolute loyalty to their King, Country and the Almighty, strong of character and extremely courageous. They were both by now experienced officers, used to command. The word 'Duty' was their guide. Both were determined, enthusiastic and energetic and not a little egocentric, qualities which are so often present in those who succeed in life. And they each had that great sureness of touch and the ability to make decisions which are the hallmark of the great leader confident of his own ability. But there the similarity ended, for whereas Nelson was the romantic extrovert, susceptible, sentimental, slightly effeminate, petulant, temperamental, passionate, insufferably vain, undignified, continually looking for attention and flattery and at times openly boastful to the point of vulgarity and absurdity which occasionally made him an object of ridicule and derision, Jervis was formal, almost grim, reserved, secretive, monosyllabic, gruff, off-hand, and, at times gratuitously offensive in what he said. However, although Nelson's un-English flamboyance, theatricality and determination to make a spectacle of himself were eventually to cost him his life as he paraded the deck of HMS *Victory* at Trafalgar, medalled up like a Christmas tree, an easy target for a bullet from a sniper sitting in the tops, unlike Jervis he was without doubt an inspirational commander with a magical touch about him, a born leader of men with a magnetism and charm which he constantly used to win over and bring out the best in the most hard-bitten of officers and men, both by encouragement and example. Where Nelson won the complete support, respect and indeed love of those officers and men who served under him by showing a generosity, humanity, warmth, tender-heartedness and nobility of spirit coupled with a genuine and lasting concern for their everyday welfare, Jervis never obtained more than a grudging and mechanical obedience to his orders from his subordinates, and that only wrung from them by the imposition of an iron discipline which was at times both harsh and unnecessary. He was a stern judge of those who served under him, some of whom saw him as cold, austere, puritanical, stubborn, cheese-paring, dictatorial and thoroughly autocratic. Occasionally, like Wellington, he was heard to describe his men as 'criminals' and 'animals', as though he despised them, which he did not. 'We're carrying on the most active desultory war against the post and town of Cadiz to divert the animal,' he reported.[10] His reputation was as a hanger and flogger of men. In contrast, such was their adoration for Nelson that his men were ready to follow him to the ends of the earth, and, if necessary, lay down their lives for him. Indeed, it is not difficult to credit the report, oft claimed as true, that, as they brought him home from Trafalgar after his final battle, so much did they worship the memory of Nelson, seamen on *Victory* drank the brandy which had preserved his body as far as Gibraltar, almost as an act of communion. But perhaps the greatest contrast lay in their respective intellectual abilities. The supposedly delicate and diminutive Nelson, who stood but 5'1" in height, and who was ever prone to seasickness and hypochondria, was a ball of nervous energy driven on by a thirst for fame and glory at almost any price – 'a Peerage or Westminster Abbey' – never still, impatient, highly strung, tense, innovative, extraordinarily gifted, indeed something of a genius as a tactical commander. In his campaigns he was always on the attack, unlike Wellington who was at his best in a rearguard action. Jervis, on the other hand, was unimaginative, conventional, cautious and calculating to a degree, the product of a rather pedestrian intellect, although a prodigious worker.

And yet, from the first moment of their meeting, there was a mutual respect and admiration. Nelson saw in Jervis the dedicated professional and was flattered to have his support. Jervis recognized in Nelson a man of talent and daring who could be relied upon to take on the enemy if and whenever the opportunity arose, and so to serve the purpose of both Jervis and the British nation. And so Nelson was one of the few officers ever to receive Jervis's wholehearted confidence and support. It is as well that this was so for both men were much needed by their country at that time.

It was to be the tragedy of Jervis's distinguished career at sea that it was followed by a disastrous term of office as First Lord of the Admiralty which seriously undermined the Royal Navy as a fighting arm at a critical time and generated so much discontent that it brought about the downfall of Addington's

Administration and the return of Pitt in the year before Trafalgar. By then he had fallen out with pretty well everyone, Nelson included. As one author has put it, 'There was scarcely an officer who had not a complaint of one kind or another against the Earl.'[11] However, although a very autocratic and difficult man, his severity was at times tempered with acts of humanity, and it is undoubtedly the case that he did much to improve service conditions for the ordinary sailor, ordering an efficient postal service that they might keep in touch with home, agitating for an improved supply of fresh food, devising regulations to ensure better hygiene on board ship, later establishing a Royal Naval asylum at Paddington,[12] and introducing many other reforms which stood the test of time, many of them introduced in harness with his ship's surgeon, Dr Andrew Baird.[13] And there is no denying that the supreme fighting efficiency of the Royal Navy in the closing years of the eighteenth century was very much his work. Not entirely coincidentally it was to achieve a position of pre-eminence in the waters of the world in the ten years which followed his assumption of command in the Mediterranean, and those ten years were to be the most glorious in the long history of the Royal Navy, crowned as they were by Nelson's three great victories at the Nile, Copenhagen and off Cape Trafalgar, all won in the last seven years of Nelson's life. It was to be the age not only of Nelson and Howe, but of Cornwallis, Collingwood and St Vincent, all men in their different ways of magisterial greatness in naval command. And each of them, along with lesser admirals such as Sir John Orde, had this in common. Throughout their service, and, indeed, throughout their lives, to them the common enemy was France. Not all may have shared Nelson's pathological hatred of the French, but, throughout their lives, France was the enemy.

Notes

1   OCSS, p. 431.
2   Clarke, p. 15.
3   Gardiner, p. 182.
4   Gardiner, p. 183.
5   J Sher, p. 38.
6   J Bren, p. 135.
7   Park, pp. 24-25.
8   J Bren, p. 134.
9   N Brad, p. 124.
10 *Who's Who in History* by Treasure.
11 NJR, p. 213.
12 Gardiner, p. 197.
13 OCSS, p. 431.

CHAPTER IV

1797

The contrasting merits of these two very different characters were to be paraded and put at the service of the nation in the year 1797, before Sir John Orde ever sailed out to join the Mediterranean Fleet. The events of that year serve to demonstrate the character of the man with whom Sir John Orde was to become entangled. It had been some years since Britain had tasted the fruits of victory and the Government were now desperate for a battle won in order to revive flagging spirits at home. This Jervis and Nelson were to provide on St Valentine's Day of that year. During 1796 the menace from abroad greatly increased. Austria had been decisively beaten by Napoleon in a series of lightning and brilliant military strikes and now Spain entered the war and placed her ships at the disposal of France. The Mediterranean Command at this time extended out of the Mediterranean beyond Gibraltar and up the Atlantic coast of Spain as far as Cape Finisterre, and so Jervis was now required to include the Spanish ports in his blockade with his fleet based at Lisbon, since Portugal had remained loyal to the British flag. No port of call or refuge was left to him in the Mediterranean itself since he had been ordered to withdraw from Corsica on 25 September of that year, 1796. The reason given was French domination of Italy coupled with the entry of Spain into the war, and so it had been thought prudent to evacuate the British shore presence in the Mediterranean, much to the dismay, disgust and astonishment of both Jervis and Nelson.[1] Dundas had written to Lord Spencer, who was First Lord of the Admiralty from 1794 until 1801, to protest at the foolishness and humiliation of such a withdrawal which would leave the enemy free to roam the Mediterranean at will, simply because Britain was now faced with a Spanish fleet as well as the French. But in a lame reply Spencer had pleaded that the decision had been unavoidable for there were but twenty-one sail of the line available, not enough to contain a combined Franco-Spanish armada. It was impossible, he contended, to supplement or reinforce this from the Channel Fleet which was already overstretched with only thirty-six ships at its disposal for the defence of Great Britain, whilst Corsica was so far distant that it was proving impossible and expensive in resources to maintain a fleet in those seas since Gibraltar provided no more than an anchorage. And so Jervis had to be withdrawn to Lisbon to perform a defensive role, for there were no other resources which could be appointed for the task. There was, Spencer submitted, no other way.[2] Not surprisingly Bonaparte rejoiced at the decision which left him master of the Italian mainland and probably free from molestation.

Nelson's first assignment in that year was to continue the blockade of Toulon, keeping watch on the French Fleet. Lord Hood had, in previous years, found this a near-impossible task without a base nearer than Gibraltar. Indeed, that was why the decision had been taken to occupy Corsica, as the nearest island to France, and it was whilst assisting in that task at the siege of Calvi that Nelson sustained such damage to his right eye that all useful sight had been lost. But now the decision to withdraw from the island added to the burden of blockade which was Nelson's.

The blockade was dull, tedious, monotonous work which taxed the patience of the most long-suffering officers and men who were more concerned to have either shore leave or action. But it worked. For two long years this defensive policy succeeded in containing the French and Spanish fleets, and, for much of the time, kept them in harbour. Promotion for Nelson did indeed follow under Jervis in due time, as did transfer to another ship, namely the *Captain* of 74 guns.

BATTLE OF ST VINCENT

But then, on 13 February 1797, to the astonishment and delight of Sir John Jervis, then stationed off the Tagus, he spotted the Spanish Fleet, with twenty-seven sail of the line, at sea standing fifty miles off Cape St Vincent and drifting hopelessly.[3] In fact they were making their way from Cartegena to Brest in the hope of raising the blockade, gingerly hugging the coast as they went. Cape St Vincent lies at the south-western extremity of Portugal, a stern, sheer, precipitous, forbidding, awesome, imposing mass of rock and the scene of many great events at sea. Jervis's good fortune could be put down to the wind and the weather which had blown the Spaniards out into the Atlantic as they struggled in an easterly direction for the shelter of the harbour of Cadiz and the prospect of watering and provisioning.[4] Jervis was outnumbered two to one and in unfriendly waters but he knew that he was opposed by an untried fleet consisting, for the most part, of newly commissioned and well constructed ships but which were top heavy in their design and manned by crews which lacked both training and experience. Certainly these were men of Spanish courage but by occupation they were infantrymen, fishermen, and men who had been pressed into service for only a short and temporary tour of duty led by officers many of whom had been born of noble families and were little more than novices at sea, totally lacking operational service. Jervis, on the other hand, had command of fifteen well-ordered ships of the line staffed by well-disciplined and highly trained officers and men who had been taught to obey. To his squadron had been added a further five ships of the line under the command of Rear Admiral Sir William Parker. The result was an efficient fighting force for which the Spaniards would be no match. They were not, after all, Frenchmen spurred on by a revolutionary spirit. They were Spaniards who had recently been dragged into the war. Any ship under canvass was to a large extent dependent for its manoeuvrability upon the wind and the weather and the ability of its crew to tack about quickly and efficiently with the vast amount of rigging to be handled. These were large structures, for the most part constructed of oak to provide a platform for an arsenal of guns, alongside which many of the crew lived, slept and sometimes died. The only other wood used in construction was elm for the keel in case of grounding and fir tree wood from which the masts were built.[5] But the British ships were lighter and this gave them greater manoeuvrability, especially since most were now copper-bottomed following the disastrous loss of the ship *Royal George* at Spithead in 1782 which had gone to the bottom taking Admiral Kempenfelt with it, trapped in his cabin – but fortunately, not before he had devised the first effective system of signal communication between ships incorporated in 'A Primer of Speech for Fighting Ships'. Honeycomb decay in the bottom timbers caused by the dreaded Teredo Worm had gone undetected until it was too late. It was this event which had persuaded the Admiralty to require that thenceforth the hulls of all ships be bottomed with copper sheathing. Not only did this resist the Teredo Worm, it provided also effective resistance to accumulations of weeds and barnacles and thus improved speed and manoeuvrability.[6]

Confident therefore of both his ships and his crews, on the following day, which was St Valentine's Day, with that determination and courage and sense of duty which had been so much the mark of his service throughout his years with the Royal Navy, Jervis, in his flagship *Victory*, ordered that decks be cleared for action, magazines be opened ready for fire and that tars and their understudies all stripped to the waist, be ready for loading, and then heroically and without a moment's hesitation, set course for the Spanish line. Poor seamanship in the difficult weather conditions had caused the Spanish ships, which were moving easterly towards Cadiz on a westerly wind, to separate into two groups. They were now, on the face of it, easy prey for Jervis's squadron. Yet Jervis, predictably, steered a conventional course, and, on the principle of divide and conquer, sailed in single line of battle in a southerly direction between the two divisions, and so drove a wedge between them. Then, as the Spaniards altered course, Jervis rather belatedly ordered his ships to tack about in succession in order to engage the division standing to the windward. The tactic of breaking the enemy line was now recognized and adopted by most commanders – 'divide and conquer' – although it had on this occasion come about almost by chance for it was not part of St Vincent's philosophy to fall on one portion only.

For many years conventional naval strategy had dictated that ships of the line should stay in line when in battle so that each individual vessel could then engage the corresponding vessel which lay alongside it in a war of attrition. Indeed the French tactic of dismasting British ships with fire directed at the rigging had often disabled the British from contemplating much else. In fact such trials of strength often saw the British emerge the victors nevertheless, but now the wisdom of using the most heavily gunned vessels to break the enemy line, usually at the rear, and then of mounting a concentrated attack upon the ships so detached until they lay crippled and of no further use, was becoming apparent to many, for, if successful, it could produce a clear numerical advantage over an enemy's main fleet before the real engagement had ever begun. To a limited extent this is what occurred at the Battle of St Vincent, but it was quite by accident. However it became more acceptable thenceforth and it was a tactic which Nelson was to use deliberately and with such devastating effect at the battles of the Nile and off Cape Trafalgar. It was to transform the method of sea warfare in the age of sail.

It was a few minutes before midday when fire broke out on both sides as the British ships passed through the Spanish lines. There followed an hour or more of hard pounding until it became apparent that the British manoeuvre of each ship tacking in succession rather than all together had provided the Spanish with an obvious avenue of escape by themselves tacking north around the rear of the British ships in the hope of engaging the rearmost in battle before hauling to the wind east to rejoin the other detached division which Jervis's tactics had allowed to get away unmolested with no order to chase. Nelson, now a Commodore sailing in the *Captain* of 74 guns which was positioned third from the rear of the line of ships which were still steering a course through the two divisions, read the situation in a flash and quickly came to the rescue. Blatantly disregarding the express, and indeed the standing orders which Jervis had so recently issued to stay in formation and tack in succession, and with an ingenuity, imagination, resourcefulness and daring so sadly lacking in Jervis himself, Nelson, not waiting his turn, now broke from the line, wearing his ship round since this was a quicker manoeuvre than tacking about, and with all press of sail swung away back towards the leading Spanish ships as they circled round towards the leeward division. There he confronted all the might of the Spanish galleons which heavily outgunned him. The Spanish ship *Santissima Trinidad*, the most heavily gunned warship afloat, carried 132 guns, whilst two others which faced him, the *San Josef* and the *Salvador del Mundo*, each packed 112 guns.

British ships of the line for use in line of battle, each commanded by a Post Captain, ordinarily carried between 64 and 100 guns, for the most part manufactured in the north of England where coal and iron deposits were to be found lying side by side. Jervis's flagship, *Victory*, ran to 186 feet in length. It had been laid down in 1759 and later launched at Chatham in 1765 and was later to carry Nelson into the battle of Trafalgar. To assist in the calculation of pay for officers and warrant officers, which was determined by the number in a ship's crew, which could be as great as 800 or more men on a ship the size of *Victory*, Lord Anson in the year 1740 had devised a formula categorizing ships according to the guns carried. Those carrying 100 to 110, such as *Victory*, were classed as first rates and were usually three-deckers, those carrying between 84 and 100 were classed as second rates and were also usually three-deckers, and those with 70 to 84 guns were known as third rates, although these two-decker ships were much easier to handle and became the backbone of the fleet.[7] They were far from third rate in their usefulness. Fourth rates of between 50 and 70 guns were known as 'below the line' ships, although still ships of the line.[8] Frigates carrying between 30 and 50 guns were not ships which sailed in the line of battle. These fifth and sixth raters were the 'eyes of the fleet', used for scouting the seas and gathering intelligence.

Nelson was therefore very much outgunned by the Spanish ships, but, nothing daunted and throwing caution to the wind, he now placed the *Captain* of 74 guns across the path of the leading enemy ships and so cut off their retreat. It was an act of insubordination at once audacious and daring by which he risked not only loss of his ship and the wrath and indignation of his commander, but also the loss of his entire career at sea. Admiral Byng had been shot for less. Not only had he disobeyed the battle orders of Sir John Jervis, in breaking from the sacred line, he had also run counter to 'Fighting Instructions' to keep in formation or line of battle unless a signal was received which ordered otherwise. The wisdom of maintaining a line of battle was that it reduced the chances of ships of the Royal Navy firing into each other. In the year 1790 the Signal book which had first been issued by Lord Howe back in 1776 and later improved by Admiral Kempenfelt, had superseded the 'Permanent Fighting Instructions' which had previously required Captains of ships of the line to stay in formation unless and until they had received one of a limited number of signals. Now Captains were simply required to obey signals emanating from the flagship interpreted by reference to 'Fighting Instructions' and those signals were nine in number numbered one to nine. This made for greater flexibility and speed.[9] Nelson had received no such signal which could possibly be taken to have authorized his move.

After an hour of skirmishing, as Jervis watched in wonderment, Nelson then laid his heavily damaged ship alongside the *San Nicholas* which had by then drifted hopelessly into collision with the *San Josef*. He fastened to her as much to keep the *Captain* afloat as for any other reason and the two ships became entangled. British sailors armed with cutlasses and soldiers with bayonets drawn boarded the *San Nicholas* by forcing a quarter gallery window and then entering the cabin which lay beyond, followed closely by Nelson himself. This act too flouted all convention which was that Captains should remain with their ships, come what may.[10] But now, despite a battering received from Collingwood in the *Excellent* as he passed through, the *San Josef* opened up a heavy fire on the British. The choice which Nelson therefore faced at this moment was whether to retrace his steps back to his own ship or to carry on. Needless to say he chose the latter. After a brief struggle with the crew of the *San Nicholas*, Nelson, with the cry 'Westminster Abbey or Victory' then crossed over with his followers to the *San Josef* which lay alongside. On bended knee the Captain offered up his sword to Nelson and surrendered almost without protest. His subordinates followed suit handing up their swords, which, if Southey is to be believed, were gathered up by one William Fearney like faggots one by one. By half past three in the afternoon the *del Mundo* and the *San Isidro* had also been captured and the battle won. The remainder of the Spanish Fleet ran for the shelter and safety of Cadiz but also the opprobrium of the outraged Spanish public, which was followed by courts martials for the Commander-in-Chief and several of his officers.[11]

This had not been as bloody a battle as most in that only seventy-three British lives had been lost and the departure from Jervis's original plan had prevented a round-up of the smaller group of Spanish ships. Indeed the failure to organize and order a chase had allowed all but the four captured ships to find the safety of Cadiz, albeit they lay there blockaded for many months to come. But it had been a modest victory of sorts, thanks largely to the initiative of Horatio Nelson. And because it had succeeded, Jervis forgave him his disobedience. Had he failed Jervis would probably have court-martialled him. As it was he greeted him with open arms and undisguised joy. Such are the fortunes of war. The British public, desperate for news of a victory, were in no mood to examine the minutiae. In their eyes the threat of invasion had been averted and when the news reached London on 3 March, Jervis was hailed as a national hero. As for Nelson, Jervis had witnessed his potential at first-hand and now also stood in his debt. It was to stand him in good stead when command of the Mediterranean Squadron came up for consideration.

Defeat or victory at this time was to be counted more in terms of ships captured than ships sunk given the limited gun capability then available. Indeed, comparatively few ships were in fact sunk. Those conversant with the fairly rapid breech-loading of the modern 25-pounder field gun will appreciate how cumbersome muzzle-loading must have been in those days before a breach capable of withstanding a gunpowder propellant explosion had been devised. And so the bag of powder, the shot and the wadding had all to be rammed home down the muzzle each time before a shot was fired. And, although the ball was of comparable weight, thus giving the gun which fired it its classification, as, for instance, a 32-pounder which was the standard weight of shot, unlike the modern gun discharging high-explosive shells, solid round shot had very little penetrative capability and certainly not enough to sink a ship of the line, especially a Frenchman which was on average bigger and better designed than its English counterpart. And although ranges of up to a mile and a half could be achieved with the gunpowder then in use, a ship's gun was really only accurate at fairly short range, crudely aimed as it was by its gunner using a basic sight on the muzzle aligned with a notch on the breach whilst at the same time trying to compensate for the movement of the vessel. It had no more precision than a shotgun which is traversed, elevated or depressed. But there the British had an advantage for the saltpetre used as the main ingredient of gunpowder was of a superior quality, imported from Bengal after its conquest by the British. This produced a higher muzzle velocity. They also had by now the cannonade produced by the Cannon Ironworks in Stirlingshire and first used by the Navy in 1779, and this gave them quicker firepower and a decided advantage over the enemy.[12] However, because of the limited range of these weapons, the technique adopted in battle was to endeavour to sail alongside and then attempt to cripple the sides of the ship and dismast her by prolonged and hard pounding until she drifted helplessly on the sea and into captivity. In fact as much devastation was caused by decimating her crew with cannonballs and grapeshot and flying debris in the form of splinters, as by attempts on the structure of the ship itself.

But the real value of the victory off Cape St Vincent was that it destroyed for evermore the morale and confidence of the Spanish Navy and gave a corresponding boost to the officers and men of the Royal Navy. And it brought Horatio Nelson to the national stage as an officer of consequence. After the battle the true character of these two remarkable men was again to show itself. At daybreak on the day following the battle, Nelson, anxious that his version of events should be made known at home, hastened to join his friend Gilbert Elliot who was then on board the frigate *Lively*, on his way to England.[13] When Viceroy of Corsica, Elliot had come to know Nelson well and now admired him greatly. But, as chance would have it, Nelson's first encounter when he stepped on board was with a Colonel who was also travelling home with Elliot. This was Colonel John Drinkwater, who was later to take the name Bethune when his wife inherited her brother's estate in Fife. Drinkwater was already a firm supporter of Horatio Nelson and all that he now witnessed in the battle simply served to confirm him in that regard. Born near Manchester, the son of a medical practitioner, he had served in the Manchester Regiment at the siege of Gibraltar and later produced a history of that event which became something of a military classic. Promotion followed until, after the British occupation of Corsica, he became secretary for the military department and Deputy Judge Advocate during the Viceroyalty of Sir Gilbert Elliot. This had brought him into contact with Nelson and he, Elliot and Nelson had become firm friends. Not surprisingly therefore, when it was ordered that Corsica be evacuated, it was on the *Minerve* which came under the command of Nelson as Commodore that they travelled home, later transferring to the frigate *Lively*.[14] Drinkwater was to be the first to bring home news of the battle, as Nelson had supposed he would be, hence his anxiety to place his version of events on the record with Elliot or Drinkwater before any other was put in circulation. He was not content to allow events to speak for themselves. His confidence was well placed, for, soon afterwards, Drinkwater published, anonymously, a pamphlet entitled 'A Narrative of the Battle of St Vincent', which did not understate Nelson's contribution in the battle.[15]

And so, to that Colonel he reported his account of the course which events had taken. The Colonel's first reaction was that for Nelson's distinguished service he should be made a baronet. To his surprise Nelson was appalled at the suggestion, claiming that he would prefer a Knighthood of the Bath so that his services could be noticed and recognized by the general public. The Colonel afterwards said that he understood this to mean that Nelson wanted an honour which he could wear about his person so that the public would be able to see it. Later, in his official despatch to Sir William Locker, Nelson gave an account of his exploits not unflattering to himself and ending with the note that, 'There is a saying in the fleet, too flattering for me to omit telling, viz, "Nelson's Patent Bridge for Boarding First Rates," alluding to my passing over an enemy's 80 gun ship. If you approve . . . you are at perfect liberty to insert the account in the newspapers, inserting the name of the Commodore instead of "I".'

For his part, John Jervis, in his official report, made no mention of the name 'Nelson', and so Nelson's contribution to the victory would have gone unrecognized but for other reports which other officers made to the Admiralty. A charitable view is that Jervis omitted mention of Nelson's name to avoid drawing attention to his act of insubordination, for, in a private letter Jervis wrote to Lord Spencer, he did report that Nelson had 'contributed very much to the fortune of the day'.[16] Again, perhaps Jervis took the course he did in order to avoid naming some Captains whilst omitting mention of others, for, reporting in that way had caused a great deal of ill-feeling amongst many, including Collingwood, only three years before after the battle of the 'Glorious First of June'.[17]

Jervis was granted a pension by a grateful nation and raised to the peerage in one step to an earldom, taking his title from the scene of the battle at the suggestion of King George III. It was to be the highest honour bestowed on any naval officer during the whole of the war.[18] He had narrowly escaped death in the battle, for a marine standing next to him had been felled by a shot.[19] Soon afterwards Nelson was promoted from Commodore to Rear Admiral of the Blue, although this had in fact occurred as a matter of seniority and been gazetted a few days before the battle had ever begun.[20] But he received the Knighthood of the Bath he so coveted. It was an honour well earned for the fighting efficiency of his ship had been his own work for the most part and the decision to engage the enemy in spite of the odds against him had been his also. And as a flag officer he was entitled also to his share, which was appreciable, of whatever money the Spanish prizes would fetch. But his fragile body had been damaged yet again, although not, on this occasion, seriously. A flying splinter caught him and may have caused a rupture, although not diagnosed until after his death.[21]

Rear Admiral Sir William Parker, who was to feature prominently in the trouble concerning Nelson's appointment to the Mediterranean Command in the following year, now raised a note of dissent. As commander of the *Prince George* and as third in command in the action off St Vincent, he questioned indignantly Nelson's version of the battle once he learned of it which was not until July of that year.[22] He then made his protest public the moment he later returned to Spithead. According to him the *San Josef* had already surrendered to the fire of his ship, the *Prince George*, long before Nelson ever boarded her. He maintained that the *San Josef* had been crippled by fire from his ship, had then fallen against the *San Nicholas* and so had conceded long before Nelson climbed over. However, by now, Nelson was too firmly established as a hero in the eyes of the British public to be dislodged from that position so that Parker's protestations fell on deaf ears. Although many others were to confirm Parker's version of events as correct, it is conceivable that both accounts were broadly accurate, and certain it is that each in his own mind believed his own recollection

John Jervis, 1st Earl of St Vincent

to be the true one. There is even room for the claim made that it had been heavy fire from the *Excellent* under the command of Collingwood as it passed through that had been more than instrumental in the demise of the *San Nicholas*, for it is of note that after the battle Nelson wrote his thanks to Collingwood for help received. But there is no denying the contribution which Nelson's daring intervention had made to the victory, and, in any event, his position as the nation's hero was to be confirmed the following year for the undoubted role he played as Commander of the Mediterranean Squadron at the Battle of the Nile. As third in command Parker was made a baronet, as was the other Admiral, Vice Admiral Thompson. Parker was also given the freedom of the City of London and afterwards became second in command when Thompson was invalided home by St Vincent. He was to become a contender for command of the Mediterranean Squadron the following year along with Sir Roger Curtis and Rear Admiral Sir John Orde, and was to be the first of the disgruntled candidates to protest at Nelson's appointment. Waldegrave, a man whom St Vincent disliked intensely, was granted an Irish peerage for his part in the battle.[23]

Thus had Horatio Nelson come to the rescue of not only John Jervis, but also the British nation and both now stood firmly in his debt. So much so that a firm bond between Nelson and his commanding officer had been cemented long before Sir John Orde ever joined the Mediterranean Fleet and that bond and that debt were still operative when command of the Mediterranean Squadron came up for consideration in the following year. This then was the commanding officer who later summarily despatched Sir John Orde home in seeming disgrace.

Notes

[1] N Hol, p. 47.
[2] Park, p. 21.
[3] NE, p. 113.
[4] N Brad, p. 134.
[5] N Brad, p. 21.
[6] Clark, p. 27.
[7] Warner, p. 80.
[8] N Brad, p. 22.
[9] Park, p. 12.
[10] Park, p. 37.
[11] N Brad, p. 141.
[12] Park, p. 10 and Gardiner, p. 186.
[13] NE, p. 116.
[14] N Brad, pp. 113 and 141.

[15] DNB.
[16] N Brad, p. 143.
[17] Park, p. 38.
[18] Ralfe, vol I, p. 309.
[19] N Brad, p. 142.
[20] N Mar, p. 22.
[21] N Brad, p. 142.
[22] NE, pp. 116-7.
[23] Park, p. 38.

CHAPTER V

MUTINY

St Vincent's place in the Service was now unassailable. It made him even more autocratic and tyrannical than before. The Admiralty was to put this to good use that same year, and this next chapter in his life demonstrates yet more clearly the man he had by now become and the man Sir John Orde found when he sailed out to join the Fleet. Taxes on income were first introduced by William Pitt in 1797. In April of that year, despite the emergency which faced Great Britain abroad, a potentially even more dangerous situation had arisen at home where the morale of the Channel Fleet, then lying at Spithead, was at an all-time low. Unlike sailors in the Mediterranean Fleet, many were not employed in any service activity and had time to brood and complain and this bred in some a discontent which was fuelled by contacts on shore, to which they had access. The men were now refusing to put to sea until certain grievances had been addressed. The only circumstance in which they were prepared to do so was if the French came out. It was in part due to a failure of command, not of the now elderly Lord Howe, the Commander-in-Chief who was at that time occupied elsewhere, nursing his health in Bath, but of his second in command, Lord Bridport, the younger brother of Samuel Hood. Bridport was a courageous but ineffective officer much despised by those who served under him. But low pay, poor food, little shore leave, primitive care for the sick and the wounded, hardship and cruelty and other such legitimate concerns were the real problem.

The quality of food was poor even allowing for the difficulty of storage and the lack of refrigeration. The daily diet consisted of cheese, tough beef preserved in salt, pork, biscuits and half a pint of 'grog'. This was rum diluted with water in order to reduce its potency, as dictated by Admiral Vernon back in 1740. Nicknamed 'Old Grogram' because of the grogram waterproof he so often wore, the rum ration took his nickname also. It helped a man digest the ship's biscuit which was usually alive with maggots which hatched out into weevil insects.[1] Living quarters too were cramped and congested and confined and lacked all privacy, whereas the ship's Captain and flag officers dined around polished mahogany in something approaching the Georgian splendour of a

London home. The contrast was marked and obvious and at times exacerbated when a ship had the misfortune to be officered by lazy, sadistic or capricious men who lacked humanity when on the high seas, with no thought for the welfare of those for whom they alone had responsibility, demanding servile obedience and punishing harshly, brutally and fiercely any insubordination, however trivial. A ship's Captain had it in his power to make the life of his crew tolerable when at sea, or a floating nightmare. And if he chose the latter this had to be endured sometimes for months on end without respite until the return to home waters.

One major scare had been scurvy due to lack of Vitamin C. So much so that a fleet commander in distant parts would often face a dilemma – whether to remain at sea to avoid contracting malaria whilst running the risk of scurvy, or whether to allow shore leave and so access to fresh fruit which would combat scurvy but at the same time expose a man to the risk of contracting malaria on shore. However, by this time scurvy had been much reduced if not altogether eliminated thanks to the reports of Captain Cook and the studies of Dr Lind and then Dr Blane, and, on their advice, the issue of lemon juice.[2] And, for all the lack of comfort and hardship, sailors did at least have a regular meal and a roof of sorts over their heads unlike so many of their brethren on shore in those far-off days before the advent of proper housing, sewerage, hygiene or much in the way of medication. For the poor and disadvantaged on shore the prospect must have been one of squalor. At least on board there was usually a sort of camaraderie which made life a little more bearable.

Nevertheless, judged by the standards of today, the complaints at Spithead were real and fully justified. And even in 1797 the Admiralty quickly recognized them as reasonable and they gained force by the courteous and responsible way in which they were presented. At the heart of it was the matter of pay which had not been reviewed, still less raised, in more than 200 years. It had fallen far behind the inflation of prices, and, indeed, that received by the military which had, in 1795, been awarded an increase by William Pitt. A rise of a modest one shilling a day granted to the military had caused great ill-feeling in naval ranks. Those of comparable rank in the Merchant Navy and those of similar status outside the Service had also fared better on the whole. Added to that, wages were paid intermittently and sometimes only after a long period of time and then often in the form of pay notes or Admiralty vouchers cashable in London which could only be cashed at a distance immediately if a discount was accepted. And many of the crews, who were aged between twenty and thirty years for the most part, had been pressed into service against their wishes by the press gang. Some were quota men posted with the Royal Navy by local areas which lay close to the sea and so were required because of this to provide a quota of men under the Act of 1795. Not surprisingly the more astute local authorities tended to recruit from the local prison, workhouse or asylum to make up the numbers required. Others were simply taken in times of emergency from merchant ships arriving home. Impressment had first been employed in the days of Charles II when Samuel Pepys was Secretary of the Admiralty, and was now to be employed on and off until 1815 when the emergency ended and the impress service was disbanded.[3] Ports in the north-east of England, such as Newcastle-upon-Tyne, North and South Shields and Sunderland were fertile grounds for impressment, centres as they were for coastal short-distance trading with other British towns. Men of the merchant service would return home routinely to these ports, and often into the hands of a press gang who would be there waiting for them. Indeed, it is reported that in the year 1795 the ports of Newcastle and Sunderland provided more men in this way than any town in the whole of the United Kingdom outside London.[4] In theory only men in the merchant service or fishermen or watermen between the ages of eighteen and fifty-five were eligible to be pressed, but a ruthless press gang, working on commission, or in times of emergency, would apply the rule very broadly, at times even taking keelmen from the River Tyne, which they did in May of 1803 until the intervention of two local Members of Parliament, Sir Matthew Ridley and George Burdon, who argued the keelmen's case with Prime Minister Addington.[5] Only gentlemen, or those apparently so, were exempt. This then was the 1793 equivalent of conscription, supposedly only used in times of national emergency. But it succeeded in ballooning the numbers from a mere 20,000 men to something over 120,000 in fairly short time. Less than half had volunteered for service or had any wish to be there. The rest would stay only as long as the emergency required them to do so. Given the source of recruitment, drunkenness, violence, profanity and vice were rife and stern punishment followed in its wake as a necessary deterrent. For those on the lower deck there was therefore little room for relaxation and shore leave was kept to a minimum for otherwise many going onshore would never have been seen again. All of this was clearly fertile ground for dissent and mutiny and no satisfactory base on which to build the efficient and obedient fighting force of men required to fight for King and Country. In short, although the Navy was by now officered by fully trained full-time professionals, there was much scope for improvement in conditions below deck. And so, when on 16 April Bridport ordered the Fleet to sail, it refused to do so.

Fortunately, after an urgent enquiry at Portsmouth over which Lord Spencer himself presided, and after some extremely difficult negotiations with the delegates through intermediaries, the Admiralty saw all this for themselves, and Pitt eventually agreed to meet most of the demands. However, fuelled by a false rumour put into circulation by the Duke of Bedford to the effect that the Government had no intention of honouring its promises on pay,[6] four ships still held out, the mutiny revived and there were ugly scenes involving Sir John Colpoys, but then the gout-ridden Admiral Lord Howe was sent down to Portsmouth with the promise that Pitt was to announce a rise in seamen's pay together with an improvement in conditions, and with instructions to mediate a settlement, granting pardons to the mutineers. In fact the fatherly Lord Howe was already on the side of the sailors, and, with tact and patience, hauling his tired old legs up the side of every ship, he spoke to the men as a father would to his own sons and reassured them that, on his recommendation, the Government had agreed to meet most of their demands. He agreed too that one hundred or more of the supposedly more brutal of the officers should be shipped out, albeit temporarily, including Colpoys who was never in fact to go to sea again. Thanks to Howe's diplomacy and the high regard in which the sailors held him, the mutiny then quickly petered out and the King agreed to grant the general pardon upon which the men had insisted before they would accept the Admiralty's terms. Celebration then followed and Howe was cheered to the echo when he came on shore by a crowd which had assembled to greet him. Amongst them was his wife. He then took wine with the urbane and courteous leader of the delegates, one Valentine Joyce, along with other representatives of the seamen. And when the Royal Pardon arrived in more tangible form, he proceeded to every ship in order to read it aloud and then was carried on shore shoulder high to Government, now Admiralty House, by the jubilant seamen and to the music of 'God Save the King' and 'Rule Britannia', and further celebrations followed. It was to be the last of Lord Howe's naval victories! Happily this set a precedent for the future where concern for the welfare of his men was thenceforth expected of every serving officer. These were the birth throes of the modern Royal Navy and marked a turning point in its history.

The situation abroad was now critical and so, on 18 May, Bridport's fleet of twenty-one sail of the line left to assist in the blockade of Brest. However, the quick surrender by the Admiralty at Spithead had served to encourage mutinous demands at Plymouth and Torbay and then, on 12 May, at the Nore. This was a much more sinister, ugly, anarchic and politically motivated affair which erupted on ships lying in the Thames Estuary. It was led by one Richard Parker who was a professional agitator in search of revenge from a service against which he nursed a personal grievance. A one-time schoolmaster and purveyor of golf balls,[7] he had been discharged from the service many years before for immoral conduct when a Midshipman,[8] but then, at a later date, had re-entered the Navy and risen to the rank of Mate. From that rank he had been reduced to the level of Able Seaman for insubordination and later imprisoned for debt at

Edinburgh. In order to obtain his release, he had enlisted in the Navy once again under the Quota Act and had been drafted to HMS *Sandwich*.[9] And there were many excitable but articulate and well argued calls for mutiny, albeit this was a mutiny without a cause, a mutiny for the sake of mutiny. Parker had the red flag of mutiny raised on *Sandwich* and several other ships followed suit and for a time they held the mouth of the river.[10] Then the mutiny spread to Yarmouth and even to the Fleet lying off the island of Texal which was then engaged in preventing the Dutch Fleet from sailing to join the French and the Spanish for an invasion through Ireland. It was crucial work, yet the spread of mutiny was such that it left the flag officer commanding, Admiral Duncan, a bluff 64-year-old Scot of immense courage, size, strength and character, with but two ships which remained loyal, the *Venerable* and the *Adamant*, thus effectively crippling the blockade. Some of his ships had even sailed to join the mutineers at the Nore, flying the red flag of mutiny.[11] However, with great ingenuity Duncan saved the day by positioning one of the two ships left to him within sight of the Dutch, frantically making fictitious signals to non-existent ships out of sight over the horizon. The Dutch swallowed the bluff, assumed that the entire fleet was present and stayed in harbour for five months or more until twenty-nine of the mutineers at the Nore had been hanged at the yardarm, the mutiny quelled and the disaffected ships had come back under Duncan's orders.

There followed the Battle of Camperdown, on 11 October which provided the British with another much-needed victory, this time over the Netherlands which had been forced to become an ally of Napoleon Bonaparte in 1795. For over two years Duncan had kept watch on the Dutch Fleet. Now news was brought to him as he lay at Yarmouth harbour that the Dutch were out of the Texel. Duncan quickly made sail with his North Sea Squadron. As the fleets closed on each other, the story told is that one of his officers, unable to see the enemy fleet well enough to be able to count and report its number to Duncan as was required, asked Duncan how many there were. 'Really, Sir,' came the reply, 'I cannot exactly ascertain,' but he reassured the young officer that 'when we've taken them then we'll count them.' Now he positioned himself between those ships and the mainland shore, broke their line, and then, after three and a half hours of firing at close range and at the great expense of 1,000 men lost on each side, the Dutch retreated with the loss of seven ships of the line and were no longer a force to be reckoned with in the naval war. It was the bloodiest battle of the war, and it was fought in front of thousands of Dutch spectators who had lined the coast to watch the spectacle.

But the mutiny had lasted until 12 June during which Great Britain had lain at the mercy of the French and Dutch fleets, which, fortunately, had not taken advantage of the situation. Lord Spencer and the Admiralty, fearful now of the revolutionary idea, had held out against the mutineers for several weeks until shortages of food and water, ordered by a determined Parliament,[12] together with the threat of foreign invasion and a growing suspicion of Parker who had given himself the rank of Admiral and demanded all the privileges which went with it, had caused the mutineers to relax the blockade in the Thames and the mutiny to collapse. The leaders were then brought to book. Parker was hanged, going to his death 'very penitent and with great composure',[13] but an amnesty was granted to several of the remainder and further concessions were made as to rates of pay, the division of prize money and the use of punishment which the Admiralty agreed to curtail. In the end, 412 men were tried, 59 of them were condemned to death, 29 of those were executed, 3 were imprisoned in the Marshalsea, some were flogged around the Fleet and the remainder were either pardoned or acquitted altogether. President of the Court which tried many of the mutineers at Portsmouth, was Sir John Orde, then a Rear Admiral of the White.[14]

There were still, however, many potential revolutionaries at the Nore expressing mutinous ideas. The Admiralty decided to deal with these others by posting them to active service with the Mediterranean Fleet, thus subjecting them to the stern discipline of Lord St Vincent. He already had potential mutineers in the Fleet, not least on Nelson's own ship, the *Captain*.[15] His technique was to transfer a Captain who was already in post, and so familiar with St Vincent's ways, to a disaffected ship newly sent out from England so that his regime of discipline could be brought to bear immediately. He then imposed a ban on communication between ships' crews to prevent the cross-fertilization of mutinous sentiments. St Vincent was concerned for the efficiency of the blockade lest it be undermined and so he let it be known that any act of insubordination in his command, however trivial, would be stamped on without mercy. And it is fair to note that his strong hand was welcomed, not only by the Admiralty, but also by the ordinary loyal and law-abiding sailor, provided always that punishment meted out was fair. But as a policy it was at times enforced with ferocity.

One Saturday in July of that year, four mutineers from the ship *St George* were condemned to death at a court martial held on St Vincent's flagship. By then darkness had fallen so that St Vincent, anxious that the Fleet should witness the execution, ordered that they be hanged at dawn the following day and not, as was the custom, by crews from other ships but by fellow sailors from the *St George*. This led to protest all round, save from Nelson who approved St Vincent's decision.[16] The condemned men themselves had asked for five days' grace to compose and prepare themselves, the crew of the *St*

George were loathe to be involved in hanging messmates and friends, and a flag officer of the Fleet, Vice Admiral Thompson, objected to such a profanation of the Sabbath. But the will of St Vincent prevailed. The men were hanged at the yardarm that Sunday morning, and they were hanged by the crew of the *St George*. Then, to the order of St Vincent, every ship hoisted a pendant to signal the onset of Divine Service as the unfortunate dead hung suspended from the yardarm. It was a solemn moment and the incongruity of it all does not seem to have struck St Vincent. And yet, as soon as it was done and the pendants for prayers had been hauled down, every man sprang into action to repulse an attack by the Spaniards coming out of Cadiz, confident that they had caught the British off guard and in mutinous turmoil. Brenton was to write that: 'The prompt and energetic sacrifice of four men saved the lives of thousands and perhaps averted the most terrible calamities. His firmness and determination were under the Almighty's direction, the means of saving his country!'[17]

St Vincent wrote to Lady Spencer complaining of insubordination amongst the Admirals and Captains in his Fleet[18] and then promptly wrote to the Admiralty demanding the recall of Thompson, adding, 'I do entreat that no more Admirals are sent hither.'[19] Not surprisingly Thompson then became yet another enemy of the many made by St Vincent in the course of his career, and this example of St Vincent's way whenever an officer stepped out of line or questioned his authority or crossed him, to some extent serves to explain the course of events in the squabble between St Vincent and Sir John Orde which was to follow.

As an example it was but one of many. One of the final acts of mutiny came in May of the following year when the ship *Marlborough*, which had been in Irish waters, came out from England with Sir Roger Curtis's squadron to join the Fleet, seething with discontent. However the leading dissenter had only raised his voice in protest in an attempt to save the life of a fellow seaman who had been condemned to death. He was himself tried, found guilty and condemned by St Vincent to death. Again he ordered that the man be hanged at dawn by members of his own crew. *Marlborough*'s Captain, one Ellison, more in hope than expectation, went in protest to St Vincent on board his flagship, the *Ville de Paris*, suggesting that his crew had indicated that they would refuse to carry out the order. Surrounded by his officers on the quarter deck, St Vincent heard him out in silence, hat held above his head as was his custom when addressed on matters of business. But then came a response which the Captain could have predicted. 'Do you mean to tell me that you cannot command His Majesty's ship HMS *Marlborough*? For if that be the case, Sir, I will immediately send on board an officer who can. Not a hand from any other ship in the fleet shall touch the rope.' And to ensure that his order was obeyed, launches ready to fire, and, if necessary sink the *Marlborough*, were ordered to surround the ship at the appointed hour. Within seconds of the signal being fired by the *Ville de Paris* the offender was hanging from the yardarm and St Vincent's reputation for discipline and ferocity was preserved undiminished. Mutiny he regarded as more dangerous than the enemy. Ten years later he was able to retire, in the words of Richard Brinsley Sheridan, 'with his triple laurel over the enemy, the mutineer and the corrupt, intact'.

Notes

[1] Clark, p. 27.
[2] Clark, p. 28.
[3] Clark, p. 14.
[4] McCord, p. 163.
[5] McCord, p. 168.
[6] N Bry, p. 235.
[7] OCSS.
[8] JA, p. 185.
[9] OCSS.
[10] Marshall (Chapter of the Nore Mutiny), p. 160.
[11] JA, p. 189.
[12] N Bry, p. 12.
[13] Marshall (Chapter on Sir John Knight), p. 164.
[14] Letters of George III 1584 and 1591.
[15] J Sher, p. 121.
[16] NE, p. 121.
[17] J Bren, p. 368.
[18] J Bren, p. 369.
[19] J Sher, p. 121.

CHAPTER VI

JOHN ORDE

Sir John Orde was a handsome man – tall, spare and distinguished. He cut a good and superior figure on the quarter deck, and he was, by all contemporary accounts, a very efficient and courageous officer and a man of integrity with a passion for fairness and justice. Although a strict disciplinarian, he was undoubtedly a humane commander of men by the standards of that somewhat harsh and brutal age. As one author has written, he was:

> not only a very nice man but a very fine one, who possessed in great degree that candour of soul called uprightness. Taking the rather advanced view for an eighteenth century Admiral, he hated the routine flogging of naval discipline, and if on assuming command of a ship he found it practised, with a man regularly appointed to lay on the punishment, he put a stop to it. He liked his ship's company happy and comfortable and therefore inclined to obey cheerfully . . . Far ahead of his day in notions of cleanliness, he hated dirt in any form and living dirt like weevils was no joke . . .[1]

Elsewhere he has been described as a 'proud and sensitive man [who] had nevertheless been a successful officer and one who had treated his crews with humanity in a period when many Captains still relied upon the cat-o-nine tails to maintain discipline on board'.[2]

Ralfe's Naval Biography described him, perhaps a little charitably, as possessing every manly virtue . . . as an

> officer, firm, strict, cool, decided, zealous, considerate, kind, indulgent. In commanding, he had a dignity and clearness which always ensured that respect and prompt obedience so essential to the naval service . . . a high and manly spirit, ever ready to defend his honour . . . he possessed the strictest honour, integrity, punctuality, and liberality; and though he had a dignity of manner and deportment, which, to a stranger or casual observer,

savoured of hauteur, he was warm . . . and kindly familiar to his friends
and followers . . . His purse was always open to relieve distress, and no
man ever performed acts of liberality with more pleasure or less ostentation.
He was endowed by nature with a noble prepossessing appearance,
finished by high good breeding, and whether afloat or ashore, he was a
thorough gentleman. If however he possessed any quality more to be
admired than another, it was the consideration he ever entertained for the
feelings of those below him, and which was fully exemplified in his
conduct to those officers who fell under his censure. Whenever he had
occasion to reprimand anyone, instead of doing it on the deck in the
presence of the men . . . he would retire to his cabin, and sending for the
officer, would there express his disapprobation in terms commensurate
with the offence . . .[3]

Generous words, but then it has to be remembered that they were written soon
after his death, in, no doubt, a spirit of charity. But his faults were many for
there can be no doubt that he was insufferably proud, and very sensitive in his
pride. It presented as consciousness of rank, pomposity, and, at times, arrogance.
At one moment he would stand aloof, at another he would be foolishly outspoken.
At times his petulant and almost childish behaviour caused, understandably, a
great deal of irritation to the Earl St Vincent, which, in turn brought injustice to
himself and cost him dear. Like St Vincent he was not a little egocentric, and,
almost inevitably, this was to result in a clash of personalities. With others he
was remote, which was at times resented by such as Nelson.

A revealing portrait of the man is to be found in a narrative written in 1795
by a wholly independent observer, one William Dillon, later to become Vice
Admiral Sir William Dillon. Then fifteen years of age and a Midshipman, he
had come under Sir John Orde's command on the *Prince George* that year.

'About the 20th of this month rumours were in circulation that our Captain
was to be superseded by Sir John Orde . . . He was not a popular officer, and
we had in consequence our misgivings.' But then, soon after, when Sir John
adjudicated a complaint made against Dillon over his attempt to retrieve a
ship's lamp which he believed belonged to one of his messmates, Dillon was
clearly impressed with the fairness and justice of the adjudication – perhaps
because he was absolved of all blame! 'If I failed in recovering the lamp,' he
wrote, 'one satisfaction remained. I had made a favourable impression on Sir
John Orde, to whom I was a perfect stranger.' He later, in the same narrative,
portrays Sir John as:

a tall, thin, well limbed man . . . fond of walking the Quarter Deck in a

Sir John Orde, Bart

gold laced cocked hat, with a long spy-glass which he generally poised over his shoulder; giving his orders with great precision, and rather pompously. He appeared to be much pleased with his command of such a fine ship. He took great interest in the fitting of her, making such improvements for those days . . . Sir John was fond of repeating, when in familiar conversation with some of his officers, that he was tall enough to be an Admiral.

This was somewhat prophetic for it was on 1 June of that same year, 1795, that Orde was promoted to Rear Admiral of the White and prepared to take his leave of the ship. But Dillon knew nothing of the promotion when he wrote in his narrative that,

I was astounded to learn that Sir John Orde had applied for leave of absence, and that he was to be relieved by an acting Captain. On the 3rd of the month, Captain Edge, only a Commander in rank and rather aged, came on board to take command of the *Prince George*. All the officers were much annoyed at the circumstance. Sir John had taken a great deal of pains to fit the ship, had made several very useful improvements, and appeared to be much satisfied with her. Therefore there was no accounting for his absenting himself on leave at a time when there was a chance of our bringing the French to action. But such was the case. The next day being the King's birthday, the usual salutes were fired. The officers of the Ward Room gave a dinner to several visitors. However, in the evening, we all assembled on the Quarter Deck out of respect for Sir John, who bid all his officers a friendly goodbye. But previous to quitting the ship, he came over to the side of the deck where I was walking. There were at least 20 Mids, and, to my surprise, he took me by the hand in a most cordial manner, saying, 'Farewell to you', then left the ship. This was a mark of attention totally unexpected by me. I was the only Mid whom he noticed in that way, and it proved that I stood well in his opinion. The surrounding Mids did not fail to make their observations on the occurrence. As Sir John was of a haughty disposition, his condescension to me made the greater impression on them.[4]

That account efficiently captures the character of the man. No doubt it was the product of his upbringing, for whereas St Vincent had been left by his father at an early age to make his own way in life, Sir John Orde had been born with few disadvantages, save that he had been born the youngest of three sons.

When Sir John joined St Vincent off the Tagus in 1797, that was not his first visit to the Mediterranean for he had served his apprenticeship as a Midshipman in the Mediterranean some thirty years before. Born three days before Christmas in 1751, he was the third son of a Northumberland landowner and member of an old county family. Although therefore he was not, like Nelson, the fifth child of an impoverished clergyman in a family of eleven, or like St Vincent, the son of a young barrister struggling to make ends meet, Sir John had nonetheless to endure exactly the same hardships and privation as any other Midshipman when he enlisted in the Royal Navy at the tender age of fourteen, and thus separated himself from his home and from his family. And, unlike Nelson, he did not have the advantage of a seagoing Post Captain uncle, well placed in naval command to take him under his wing and guide him on his way, especially when that officer later became the influential Comptroller of the Navy responsible for the supply of ships until removed by Charles Middleton for incompetence.[5] Nor was he as well placed as Collingwood who entered the Navy at the even more tender age of eleven, but into the care of an uncle who was married to his mother's sister, Captain (later Admiral) Braithwaite, with whom he remained for the first eleven years of his service until transferred to the *Lennox*, commanded at that time by Captain (later Admiral) Robert Roddam, of Roddam Hall, Glendale in the County of Northumberland, whose granddaughter, Sarah Blackett, daughter of the Mayor of Newcastle, he was later to marry when he was forty-three years of age.[6] That is not, however, to understate the security which his background undoubtedly gave Sir John.

He was descended from the Ordes of Tweedmouth who, according to the historian Welford, 'were established at Orde on the southern bank of the Tweed as early as the twelfth century. The whole township of that name, including East, Middle and West Orde with Murton and Unthank constitutes their patrimonial estate . . . They owned property in almost every hamlet of that wide-spreading district which . . . was known as Norhamshire and Islandshire . . . Descended from this old and honourable family came Admiral Sir John Orde'.[7] Although therefore the *Naval Chronicle* was right when it reported that the 'family Orde appears to be of great antiquity', and although Welford noted that 'their descendants married into all the great families of the County,' in fact, until the arrival of this particular descendant, few, if any, of that name appear to have made any mark outside the boundaries of Northumberland County. One bearer of the name had represented the Morpeth Constituency in Parliament and another rose to become Chief Baron of the Exchequer in Scotland. However, spelling their names without the 'e', John Orde would not have claimed them as relations. 'The Ords of Fenham have, I believe, no connection with this ancient stock or name; an aged lady of the true family designated them, with great indignation, as the usurpers of the name and arms'.[8] But then no doubt those without an 'e' would have responded in like terms.

Before John Orde was born, his father John, of Tweedside, succeeded his cousin William, of Sandy Bank House, Northumberland, one-time Member of Parliament for the Northumbrian constituency of Berwick-upon-Tweed, as heir to a considerable part of the family estates in Norham, East Orde and Grindon. However, in the year 1734 he had travelled south in the county, where he married Mary, daughter of one Edward Ward of Morpeth who had shortly before purchased the Nunnykirk house and estate. This now passed to his son-in-law John Orde and so was this branch of the family established at Morpeth in the south of the county where, through the great nephew of Sir John's elder half brother William, it remains to this day. It was here, within twenty miles of the Scottish border at its nearest point, that John Orde, his third son, was born anonymously enough, far from the great run of events. Thirty-nine years later, when granted a baronetcy, it was Sir John Orde of Morpeth that was chosen. His mother was Anne, his father's second wife, daughter of Ralph Marr of Morpeth and widow of the Reverend Pye. By her his father had two sons, Thomas and John, and two daughters.[9]

There was nothing in his birth to suggest that he was destined for a career at sea. Indeed, Nunnykirk lies some nine miles west of Morpeth, far removed from the coast. Unlike Collingwood, who, according to the baptismal register at the Cathedral Church of St Nicholas in Newcastle-upon-Tyne,[10] had been born some three years before, some twenty miles further south, but a stone's throw from the ships of the Tyne, or St Vincent who had been plunged into a naval environment at Greenwich at an impressionable age, or Nelson who had spent his childhood days by the sea at Overy Staithe two miles across the fields from his father's vicarage at Burnham Thorpe, there was nothing about Nunnykirk to encourage an interest in a seagoing career and no member of his family had ever set the precedent. Nunnykirk had been a staging post and house of rest for monks of the Cistercian Order colonized at Newminster Abbey, Morpeth (under the patronage of Ranulph de Merley) in the early twelfth century. 'Of all the religious orders, the Cistercians were the most distinguished for their taste in selecting grand situations for their houses.'[11] Set in parkland in the wooded and sparsely populated valley of the River Font, it was a convenient stopping place on the road from Newminster in the east of the county, to the Abbey of Hexham in the rich, gentle, lush and beautiful rolling pastures of the upper Tyne and north Tyne valleys some thirty miles distant to the west. The chapel and tower built at Nunnykirk by the Abbot of Newminster, gave way to a house which was built in the early 1700s for the Greys of Chillingham. Faced with mounting debts, they had sold it soon afterwards to Edward Ward. At a later time, in 1829, five years after Sir John Orde's death, John Dobson, most celebrated of Georgian architects in the north-east of England, was employed to set the 45-roomed house in the larger Greek classical style fronted with Ionic columns and with a pillared porch which survive to this day. The author's own smaller Dobson-built Georgian house in the valley of the north Tyne, noted as 1830 and 1847 by Pevsner, bears witness to the beauty and soundness of his architecture.

And so it was at Nunnykirk, far from the sea, that John Orde was born. Perhaps the order of his birth provides the clue to his choice of career for he was the third of three sons with no hope of inheriting the estate to which William, the eldest son who had been born to his father's first wife, and therefore John Orde's half-brother, was certain to succeed. It may be that some encounter whilst at the grammar school at Morpeth had turned his thoughts to the sea. It is unlikely that his more frail and sickly older brother Thomas, the second of John Orde's three sons, had influenced him, for he had, by the year 1766 when John Orde entered the Navy, left Eton College for the cloistered magnificence of King's College, Cambridge and the promise of a glittering and more comfortable career in public life. The contrast in the education of these two younger brothers could not have been more marked for whilst the second son grappled with the pleasures of Gaius and Justinian in the calm and civilized atmosphere of academic life, so the youngest son strove to endure the hardships of life below deck on board His Majesty's ship *Jersey* of 60 guns, then commanded by Captain William Dickson and bearing the broad pendant of Commodore (as he then was) Richard Sprye, officer commanding the Mediterranean Station. Potential officers were drawn at this time from a wide social background and in the three years which followed in that service, John Orde, still a boy, learned the tough disciplines of duty and practical seamanship in a hard school which were to serve him well throughout his years with the Royal Navy, whilst his talented brother Thomas moved easily into a fellowship at King's College, Cambridge, followed by a call to the Bar at Lincoln's Inn. Life on board ship was life in a wooden floating world all of its own. Thrown together with several hundred others, it taught a man to live in close proximity to his fellow men. After further service on the Newfoundland and Jamaica Stations, Orde was promoted Lieutenant in the year 1773 by the celebrated Sir George (later Lord) Rodney before taking a well-earned leave. This he put to good use by travelling through France in the hope of learning the language of the common enemy before he was recalled to the colours at the outbreak of the American War of Independence. He then sailed into American waters and a baptism of fire.

Notes

1. J Ber, p. 156.
2. OCSS, p. 617.
3. Ralfe, pp. 80-81.
4. Dillon's Narrative, pp. 185-9.
5. Gardiner, p. 72.
6. *Bell's Pedigrees.*
7. Welford, Vol III, p. 239.
8. Raine, p. 312.
9. *Bell's Pedigrees.*
10. Warner, p. 92.
11. Hodgson, p. 43.

CHAPTER VII

AMERICAN WAR OF INDEPENDENCE

In the year 1775, John Orde, then twenty-three years of age, sailed into the American War of Independence on board Her Majesty's ship the *Roebuck* of 44 guns under the command of Captain (later Sir) Andrew Snape Hamond. He was then a junior Lieutenant. The war had a profound effect on his career. He was to emerge in the year 1781 a Post Captain and a married man with experience of warfare at sea. He had been blooded in battle and had come of age. It is a popular belief, widely held by Americans in modern times, that the war was the result of a spontaneous protest against punitive and extortionate taxation levied by the home country, and the blind obstinacy of King George III. Conversely, some British commentators are prone to regard it as a war which was fought unnecessarily by an ungrateful colonial population in search of riches and prepared to elicit the help of the old enemy, France, to achieve its mercenary goal. But the simple truth is that the settlers had simply by this time begun to regard themselves as Americans living in a country which was separated by several thousand miles from the home Government. The reality was that it had become a nation in its own right. This was a war which few on either side of the Atlantic wanted, and, such were the ties of blood and kinship and the use of a common language, that those appointed to prosecute it had little stomach for the fight. John Orde was no exception. But, as a junior officer, he was prepared, and indeed, required to do his duty, and certain it is that he gained by the experience and at the same time earned the high commendation of those set in authority over him. And promotion followed in its wake.

SEVEN YEARS WAR

France at this time was all too ready to support almost any revolutionary movement which aimed at striking a blow at the British nation, which, at times during the eighteenth century, almost dominated the world. In the nature of

54

things, as a dominant power, she had few friends and many enemies who coveted her trade and Empire. France, with the intermittent support of Spain, was to challenge the supremacy of Britain as a world power for a century or more until their differences were finally resolved at the Battle of Waterloo.

After the war of the Spanish Succession, the Treaty of Utrecht of 1713 had left Britain with a presence in the New World which covered the eastern seaboard from Newfoundland and Nova Scotia in the north, both of which had been ceded in the Treaty, down through the British New England colonies lying east of the Allegheny mountains, to Georgia in the south and extending also to the islands of the West Indies. But to the west of this line lay the threat of France, well established in control of the St Lawrence river and the Great Lakes in the north, and in control too of the Mississipi Basin and Louisiana in the south. In the years which followed she steadily consolidated this barrier to British territorial expansion westwards, by fortifying her territories along the Mississipi and by cementing the link to her northern territories. Almost inevitably war between the two nations came in the year 1756, and again almost inevitably it caught Great Britain unprepared. Throughout history declarations of war have found Great Britain unprepared and this war was no exception.

At the instance of George II, still then Elector of Hanover, valuable resources had been dissipated in a futile attempt at protecting those Hanoverian interests which were of advantage to the British nation. Only Pitt the Elder had appreciated the much greater threat to British interests in the New World. Providentially, with the support of the people and in the teeth of opposition from the King, he was returned to office that same year and almost immediately succeeded in diverting the war effort to the New World. To enable this to be done he enlisted the help of Frederick the Great. The Prussian Army was mobilized and successfully held down the French on the continent of Europe in a succession of campaigns. Pitt further organized commando raids on the coast of France which were carried out with military precision by British troops. Together, these and other initiatives pinned down France's military resource near to home. At the same time he deployed the British Navy in blockade of Toulon and Brest and when eventually the French Fleet broke out and put to sea with plans for the invasion of Britain, Admirals Boscowan and Hawke were able to scatter them. It was thus possible to concentrate the major effort in the gateway to the St Lawrence river and Canada. Here the British Navy, with no little skill and a great deal of determination, kept the French in harbour until the talents of the ailing Major General Wolfe, then thirty-one years of age but with only a short time to live, could be unleashed. With the support of Admiral Sanders and the British Fleet they were able to navigate the Hudson river running north to Canada, and, in a brilliant action, seize Quebec. The war was then all but over. The following year the French surrendered. Yet, strangely, Pitt was intent on annihilation in order to remove for evermore the French threat in the New World. Fortunately, however, the year 1760 had brought George III to the throne and with him he brought commonsense and this prevailed. And so the Peace of Amiens was signed in 1763. The war had lasted seven long years and if left Great Britain unchallenged in the civilized world. Under the terms agreed she gained the whole of Canada together with Nova Scotia and Cape Breton Island. But at the same time she lost the friendship of her only ally, Prussia, for Frederick the Great was granted nothing. She lost too the services of her greatest statesman, for Pitt the Elder now saw no point in remaining if the advice he gave was to be rejected. And in turn, the loss of Pitt led indirectly to the loss of the American colonies twenty years on.

1763-1775

Clearly it was now necessary to maintain a standing army of occupation in the New World to protect American as well as British interests. George III, an honest, well-meaning, conscientious and straightforward man with British interests at heart, for he was the first of the Hanoverians to be raised wholly in England, now sought a contribution from the colonists both for the cost of the war and for the cost of quartering a peacetime army. It was met with protest and proclamation. After all, before the demands of the British Government had ever been made they had felt that there were far too many restraints placed upon American trade by the home Government. For a century or more it had been the policy of the British Government to legislate for reciprocity between the two economies for the advantage of both, although undoubtedly for the greater advantage of Great Britain. Accordingly, the colonists were obliged to purchase those commodities they were unable to produce for themselves, from the mother country at prices fixed in London to be paid for by the export to Britain of surplus produce, again on terms fixed in London at prices favourable to the merchants of London, all of this to be transported for reward by the British mercantile fleet or other colonial transports. Trade on any scale by the colonists with any other country was discouraged, if not outlawed altogether and here again it was ordained that any foreign commodity which was imported by the colonists had to be channelled through a British port, thus attracting levies and business for the home country. And a total embargo was placed both on the manufacture of any goods which might be sold in competition with any British product, and on the export of goods to foreign countries of which the British economy may have need. The instruments of such policy were the

Navigation Acts, the first of which had been passed one hundred years before, in 1651. It was a policy of advantage to both countries, and of immense advantage to Great Britain, but it amounted to a distortion of the terms of trade and a restriction on the New England merchant which he came to resent. The population of the thirteen colonies had swollen to over two million residents by this time, yet it was saddled with a running trade debt to the home country and prevented from competing openly in the markets of the world. Although they enjoyed the advantage of a guaranteed market for their produce in Great Britain, it was not on their own terms and they felt that their enterprise was stifled. In the outcome many sought to compensate for this by engaging in the illicit export of goods to foreign countries despite the embargo. These were smuggled through and carried by pirate ships. Allegiance to the home Government in matters of trade became even more lukewarm once the threat of French invasion abated and the colonies were now less ready to pay for a British presence in their country or to accept the terms of trade which had been imposed on them when they had faced a common enemy.

But the greater truth was quite simply that an independent and exciting new nation had begun to emerge, anxious to conduct its own affairs in a way more appropriate to its own situation, some 3,000 miles or more distant from the Westminster Government. The New Englanders were after all for the most part descended from the Pilgrim Fathers who had been men and women of tough resolution, independence and enterprise who had left their native shores in Great Britain, prepared to risk all in their search for a new life. Colonies are the fruit which drops from the tree when ripe (said a French statesman at the time). At the same time there had been no clamour for independence or even so much as a request for a formal break with the home country. Strong bonds of friendship remained, united as the two countries were by the ties of blood and kinship and a common language. Perhaps no more than a quarter of the population were bent on a formal break, and as many again were hotly opposed to it. The majority were simply content to leave matters as they were. It was therefore particularly unfortunate that King George III and his chosen Government should have misread all this as ingratitude and rebellion. George III was a well-meaning, homely but obstinate man who was determined to have his own way, and, despite the advice of Pitt the Elder from outside the Government which cautioned it to be temperate and conciliatory, the King and a Government which was both subservient to his wishes and sycophantic to his person, were determined to impose their will on the colonists with measure after revenue-raising measure to pay for the recent war which had been fought on behalf of both nations and to pay for a continued military presence. But these imposts simply generated discontent and provided ammunition for the revolutionary minority to whip up more widespread support for their cause, and so the two nations drifted into a war which was wholly unnecessary and which few wanted. Whilst Pitt's sympathies lay with the colonists, once war was declared, ever the patriot, he placed himself in support of the home country.

A handful of extremists and agitators, as ever, exploited the situation to the full, led and orchestrated as they were by the Bostonian Samuel Adams who had waited long for the opportunity. In 1763 came the Proclamation which sought to prevent colonists settling further west, in the hope of saving the expense of conflict with the Indian population. This the colonists, who had been victors in the recent war, refused to accept. In 1764 came the Sugar Act, quickly followed by the Stamp Act of 1765 under which stamp duty was to be paid on all legal documents, newspapers, licences and so on. Now it is a measure accepted on both sides of the Atlantic as a legitimate way of raising revenue. Then it was bitterly resented since it fell substantially on the powerful newspaper lobby and the influential brewers. And so were born the 'Sons of Liberty', dedicated to bringing the power to tax into its own hands, with the battle cry, 'No taxation without representation'. A more organized rebellion by the mob had begun to emerge and a campaign was formed to boycott the purchase of goods from England which threatened the pockets of the powerful merchants in London. Less than a year later the Stamp Act was repealed, to be replaced, in 1768, by the Declaration Act, by which Charles Townshend, then Chancellor of the Exchequer, sought to recover and retain the home Government's authority to raise revenue in the colony by way of taxation, if and when the need should arise and to pay for the salaries of the colonial governors. Customs duties were levied on glass, lead, paint and tea where it was imported from America. But again the protest was such that the Government relented and all was abandoned save the duty on tea. The radicals now sensed that the agreement was no longer a commercial one, the power lay with them and the death of five Americans who had been shot when throwing snowballs at British soldiers, was dressed up as a massacre. Even so the majority of citizens remained calm and refused to be drawn into condoning the activities of the radical minority.

The change was to come in the year 1773. In a moment of supreme foolishness, Lord North's Government gave the East India Company a concession which allowed them to send tea direct to the colonies. American merchants had until then been making a fat living smuggling in tea from Holland. Now, with the East India Company tea taxed at a low level coming in, the price of American imported tea was no longer as competitive. The measure had given the company an unfair advantage. And so, to prevent it being brought on shore,

$75,000-worth of imported tea was tipped into the water in Boston harbour on 16 December 1773. The British response to the Boston tea party was to close the port to further business until full compensation had been paid. At the same time they extended the French-speaking Catholic province of Quebec as far south as Ohio so that those puritan lands could be developed by the French papists. It was a response the radical minority had been waiting for. They now called a conference at Philadelphia to challenge the authority of King George III and the British Government. Anticipating trouble the British then sent in troops to seize an armoury of weapons and ammunition which had been assembled by the colonists at Lexington. They met with opposition, shots were fired, and the war had begun.

And yet the majority on both sides of the Atlantic were still reluctant to support it. It was a war they did not want, or need. The thirteen colonies, after all, had little in common with each other. There was no common allegiance and many who remained loyal to the King continued to trade with both sides. At the same time there were many at home who voiced sympathy for the radical cause. There followed Thomas Paine's book *Common Sense* which presented a powerful argument for independence, and led to the Declaration of Independence. The work of Thomas Jefferson, it was a propagandist appeal to liberals the world over, although targeted in the main at France in the hope of enlisting French support for the radical cause. 'We hold these truths to be self evident that all men are created equal . . . Life, Liberty and the Pursuit of happiness'. Thus did they justify the revolt. They had few resources and no standing army. Part-time soldiers came and went as the mood took them. But their good fortune was that they were opposed by a weak and indecisive home Government which was led by the sycophantic Lord North and which included the competent, likeable but possibly corrupt Lord Sandwich as First Lord of the Admiralty, and, as Colonial Secretary, Lord Germain who had been dismissed from the Army twenty years before at Minden. Their policy was to engage a large contingent of German mercenaries to fight for the cause, but there was no clear direction in the war and even less enthusiasm for it. Many Americans fought with the British. But it was to provide Lieutenant Orde with his first experience of battle conditions.

LIEUTENANT ORDE

Orde's service in this theatre of war demonstrates the character and efficiency of the man at an early stage of his career, and it was much the same man who was later to become involved with Lord St Vincent. Captain Snape Hamond was an old friend of his who had been given post rank on 7 December 1770 with command of the *Barfleur* of 98 guns, then being fitted out for the reception of Lord Howe's flag. Orde had joined him in that same year as a nineteen-year-old Midshipman, and, despite a difference of rank and twelve years in their ages the two had become firm friends. This was to be renewed five years on, in the year 1775 when Orde served again with Hamond, now commander of the *Roebuck* of 44 guns with a crew of 280. Although still a junior Lieutenant he was soon entrusted with a great deal of responsibility, and the trust reposed in him was to be fully justified. This was well illustrated in May of the following year, 1776, in the evacuation of Norfolk. In the year 1770 John Murray, fourth Earl of Dunmore then aged forty, had been appointed Governor of the colony of New York, to which was added, subsequently, Virginia. He survived as Governor for six years. It was six years of trouble. From the first moment of embarkation at New York in October 1770 he was met by a hostile Assembly intent on orchestrating opposition to the colonial tie. So much so that Dunmore prorogued the Assembly in the spring of 1772, and then, in March 1773, dissolved it. It met again and a further dissolution followed in May 1774. Thus provoked, opposition to Dunmore's Governorship mounted and a convention was appointed to meet in May 1775, which Dunmore banned by proclamation. Then, in June of that year, matters came to a head on the first day of that month. Dunmore summoned the Assembly to meet to consider Lord North's proposals for compromise with the home Government. But matters had by then gone too far. On 5 June a riot broke out, and, alarmed by this turn of events Dunmore and his entourage took refuge on the ship *Fowey* then lying off Yorktown, and, from there, he steadfastly refused to give his assent to any bill presented to him by the burgesses, unless they came before him in person. The response was immediate. The Assembly treated this as abdication and decided to govern without him. Dunmore, for his part, declared his own war on the Assembly with a series of abortive naval attacks in the Chesapeake, principally at Hampton on 25 October and at Great Bridge on 9 December. Then on 1 January 1776 he directed a heavy bombardment on the town of Norfolk and raised it to the ground before beating a hasty retreat with his small fleet of ships and 500 soldiers to Gwynn Island in the Chesapeake, an island of 2,000 acres which lies some 500 yards from the mainland.[1] Here he set up a base just south of the Rappahannock.

The *Roebuck* was the ship detailed to evacuate the Governor and his staff, preceded by a sloop tender under the command of one Lieutenant Whitworth, which contained Lieutenant Orde who had been instructed to go on shore under a flag of truce and negotiate a ceasefire whilst the British fleet of ships regrouped and procured/took water and provisions. It was something of a tall order and a great responsibility to place on the shoulders of one so junior. And it did not end there for the Governor had also ordered him to try to persuade the enemy to lay down their arms and come over to the British standard in surrender. But then Orde had all the confidence of youth, and not a little courage, and he accepted the challenge with enthusiasm. The Governor optimistically equipped him with copies of a written proclamation addressed in general terms to the American people which he left Orde to distribute as he saw fit. And with this somewhat inflammatory and incriminating material on his person, Lieutenant Orde set forth.

His first encounter with the enemy was not at all promising. When he got within sight of shore and an American fortified position, Orde transferred to a row boat, and then, flying a white flag of truce supported by a drummer beating a parley and two unarmed men at the oars, they rowed for the shore with Orde at the rudder. Not surprisingly their approach was being observed by a contingent of American troops and the moment they came within range the Americans opened fire. It was not a warning shot fired across the bows, but a round carefully aimed at the boat and its occupants. Mercifully – unless it was the result of deadly accuracy – it struck the side of the boat and then passed between Orde and the drummer within an inch of their bodies, the ball of the shot lodging itself in the far side of the boat. Either it had been aimed to miss with marksmanship of the highest order, or it had been a deliberate attempt on their lives. Either way it was an ominous warning for they were unarmed and very much at the mercy of the Americans. Many another would have turned tail and run for safety but Orde did not lack courage. Calmly he told his men to rest on their oars as a gesture of peace and await developments. This served to persuade the Americans that this was not so much a raiding party as a mission of peace and they beckoned the party to come ashore, where, nothing daunted, Orde complained bitterly and in the strongest terms about the reception they had received when their flag of truce had been so conspicuously displayed. Not surprisingly the officer commanding the post responded in like terms by apologizing for the inaccuracy of his shot. He regretted that it had not hit its target, which was unusual for him! He then took them prisoner. The deputation was marched off under escort to a headquarters ten miles inland. It is an indication of the sort of war that this was that, on the way, they were offered both sustenance and horses by passers-by who were sympathetic to their plight, and such was the spirit of the man that when they were put before the commanding officer, one Colonel Dangerfield, Orde promptly renewed his complaint and laid before the Colonel the message he brought from Lord Dunmore. Colonel Dangerfield considered it for no more than a moment before rejecting it but did then apologize for the conduct of his Lieutenant and promised the deputation safe passage back to their boat. Fortunately the mutinous proclamation documents which he carried in his waistcoat remained hidden from the eyes of his captors until they got back to the shore, where, under cover of darkness, he was able to dispose of them. He would not otherwise have survived. It had been a close-run thing for it was proposed at one stage that Orde be searched by a woman there present, but, with great presence of mind and with no trace of fear, he had replied, 'Then I hope, Madam, you will be the person appointed to perform the duty!' It produced a smile and no more was heard of the suggestion.

But then, before they were freed, news arrived by messenger that British ships standing off Gwynne's Island were firing on American boats. The deputation were threatened with incarceration. However, so loud was Orde's protest at this that he was allowed to go on his way, only then to discover that the boat they had left had been stolen. But such was the confusion of this war that an American loyalist who happened to be on shore, one Patten, led him to a small boat which was hidden in the bushes which Orde and his men then paddled across the water to the *Roebuck* using their hats and caps in place of oars. The party's safe return was greeted by his Captain with not a little relief.[2]

That last vestige of Royalist authority was later taken by the American Army on 8 July after an artillery bombardment of the island which met with little or no resistance for Dunmore's camp had before then been decimated by smallpox which had taken a heavy toll leaving few survivors. Dunmore had survived, but, wounded in the attack, he managed to escape the army of invasion, as did John Orde who had left long since.[3]

It is the tragedy of war that promotion often comes only when there are dead men's shoes to be filled. Such was the case with Lieutenant Orde. In March Britain had emerged victorious from the opening skirmish at Bunker Hill above the town of Boston. But it had been won at a great cost in human life. The frontal attack launched by General Sir William Howe under Gage's command had meant a casualty list out of all proportion to the victory obtained, and, like the many British victories that were to follow, it really had very little influence on the outcome of the war. Just as one trouble was put down, so another would break out as the conflict spread like a forest fire. After the battle at Bunker Hill the bombardment of Boston continued until Howe decided to move his base north to Halifax in Nova Scotia. And then, in the summer of 1776, New York became his target. The Declaration of Independence on 4 July found the British Army poised on Staten Island ready to launch an attack on General Washington and his army then stationed on Long Island and in New York. Vice Admiral Lord Howe, the General's illustrious brother now joined him, bringing with him the British Fleet. Against this fearsome combination the result was a foregone conclusion.

A combined offensive was launched in the following month. A flotilla of ships, including the *Roebuck*, was deployed in a supporting role and advanced on New York using the Hudson river. Not surprisingly they were met with a heavy bombardment from batteries of artillery strategically placed onshore. In running the gauntlet of this sustained barrage of fire, nine men and one officer lost their lives on the *Roebuck* and eighteen more were wounded. That one officer was the first lieutenant, one H.S. Leake. Orde was now promoted to take his place before the vessel reached New York, and those who had perished were buried with all the decency available in the circumstances. New York fell with little opposition as Washington withdrew, largely unmolested. It was to some extent a tactical withdrawal for it enabled his army to fall back to Lake Champlain, regroup and live to fight another day whilst the British Army was forced to endure the rigours of a winter in New York. The British Navy now occupied New York harbour which was to remain its centre of operations for the rest of the war.

Only a matter of months later Lord Howe appointed Orde first lieutenant of his flagship, the *Eagle* of 64 guns, and then, soon after, promoted him to be Master of the sloop *Zebra*, with the rank of Commander, all in the year 1777. All for him was now set fair.

With their navy the colonists had thus far presented little opposition to the activities of the British at sea, relying, as they did, on guerilla warfare operated by privateers. But now came the turning point of the war which persuaded the French to come to the aid of the Americans. And it surprised all informed opinion across the civilized world. The British strategy had been to isolate the colonists east of the valley of the Hudson river. General 'Gentleman Johnnie' Burgoyne was now given command of an expeditionary force with orders from Germain to march on New York from the Canadian border using the Hudson valley to link up at Albany with General Howe who was to bring his troops up the valley from New York. But it was a plan ill-prepared for Burgoyne was supplied with less than half the number of troops which had been promised whilst Howe was left in the dark as to what the detailed plan was, being left by Government officials with the negligently general instruction simply that he was to cooperate with Burgoyne. The result was misunderstanding, and, in the confusion that followed, instead of marching north, Howe conducted a diversionary campaign by attacking Philadelphia as the home of the Revolutionary Congress, approaching it by a slow and indirect route on land and by sea. In 1777 Commander Orde assisted in the reduction of Philadelphia and the forts of Delaware whilst commanding the *Zebra*.[4] Washington was defeated and the British took the city. But further north Burgoyne's troops had ground to a halt in the valley of the Hudson, isolated, stranded, outnumbered and surrounded without either supplies or communications. Five weeks later in October 1777, to the astonishment of the whole world, they laid down their arms and surrendered to a larger force under the command of Horatio Gates at Saratoga. Even so Gates's Army lay at the mercy of the British, trapped as they were in the valley. Yet Howe allowed the opportunity to pass, preferring instead to winter in the comparative comfort of Philadelphia. It was an opportunity lost and he was to pay for it for he was recalled to England in the new year. But for his part in the campaign, in May 1778, Commander Orde was advanced to the rank of Post Captain and given command of the frigate *Virginia*, of 32 guns, which had been captured from the Americans.[5] He was but twenty-six years of age and had made the important transition to a rank which gave him the prospect of a flag in the fullness of time. Ralfe's *Naval Biography*, written a few years later, was to report his service at that time in this way: 'The ardour, activity and undaunted firmness manifested by Captain Orde when the French Fleet appeared off the Bar of New York, were not exceeded by that of any individual in the fleet, great as were the exertions made on that occasion.'[6]

News of such an American success brought France into the war. She was persuaded at last that there could be profit in lending her support to what no longer seemed a hopeless cause. Despite the opposition of Louis XVI France recognized the rebel flag and signed a treaty with the Americans in the hope of both causing damage to her old enemy, and of regaining Canadian territory previously ceded to the British. The efforts of Lafayette now had the support of the French Government. Shortly after the battle of Ushant, the French Fleet under the command of the Comte d'Estaing, a soldier turned sailor, crossed the Atlantic unmolested. He brought with him a formidable force, since the French Navy had been transformed since the days of the Seven Years War by a vigorous programme of shipbuilding promoted by an energetic Navy Minister, the Duc de Choiseul, and by the arrival of a new breed of officer, the product of the Marine Academy at Brest, albeit they were largely unblooded.

The British Navy, by contrast, had lain dormant through many years of peace, resting on its laurels, untried and untested. They looked no match for the French armada. For all that, for reasons best known to himself, d'Estaing chose to ignore Howe's small fleet of ships which had gathered in the Harbour at New York for coastal escort duties, and sailed on to Rhode Island to support the American attack on the beleaguered British garrison. Although Howe had a much smaller force under his command at New York, nonetheless he set off in pursuit intending to draw d'Estaing off and occupy him at sea until reinforcements under the command of Vice Admiral 'Foul Weather Jack'

Byron arrived from England to help defend the garrison. Unfortunately for Captain Orde, his command, the *Virginia*, was in dry dock at this moment, undergoing repairs. But the chance of active service was not to be missed so he offered his services to Lord Howe in whatever capacity was needed. Howe promptly transferred Orde with most of his officers and crew to the *Raisonable* of 64 guns, with a pocket order appointing him to take command of the ship in the event of Captain Fitzherbert's death.

Howe caught up with the French Fleet in August that year, 1778, as it lay dispersed and at anchor off Rhode Island. But the moment the French spotted the British ships they weighed anchor and emerged in concentrated line of battle. All day long the two formations shadowed and skirted each other without opening fire, until, as evening came, a violent storm blew up which scattered the ships on both sides and disabled some, thus frustrating Howe's endeavours. Howe had shown great resourcefulness keeping the French at bay, but then, again for reasons best known to himself, d'Estaing suddenly abandoned his American allies and turned tail for Boston and refitting. On 26 September, Howe left the American station altogether and sailed for home, followed by d'Estaing, who, after a brief foray in the Caribbean, returned to France. Howe no longer had the stomach to wage war on members of the same family, for he so regarded the Americans and the British.

It was in December that Rear Admiral Samuel Barrington, in command of a small squadron of ships standing off the sugar island of St Lucia, had repulsed all d'Estaing's attempts to dislodge him until the French learned that Byron was on his way with the expected reinforcements. It was this which persuaded d'Estaing to quit the Caribbean altogether.

The following summer produced a more promising opportunity for action in the Bay of Penobscot which lies between Boston and the St Lawrence gateway in the north. Here the British had established a settlement of 650 men and sent out three ships of war under the overall command of General Francis Maclean, to prevent incursions by the enemy into Nova Scotia where much needed resources of ship timber lay. In July of that year, 1779, the executive Government of Massachusetts Bay, sitting at Boston, assembled an expeditionary force of nineteen armed ships and lingantines, twenty-seven transports and 3,000 men to lay siege to Fort Maclean to remove that obstacle to the north. Although outnumbered and ill-prepared, Maclean demonstrated considerable ingenuity and determination in holding the enemy at bay, repelling all attacks for twenty-one days until information came from a deserter that a final and more determined onslaught was planned for 14 August. There was little hope of holding out much longer, until, mercifully, news of their plight reached the ears of Commodore Sir George Collier, now Commander-in-Chief of the British naval

Destruction of American Shipping at Penobscot Bay

force, and he quickly came to the rescue. On 3 August he sailed from Sandy Hook at the entrance to New York harbour with six ships of the line and one sloop, although this was subsequently lost on the voyage. Captain Orde in the *Virginia* was appointed by Collier to lead the squadron up the narrow and shoal-ridden river Penobscot in pursuit of the American Fleet, then under the command of Commodore Saltonstall. After a difficult navigation the Americans came into view at 11 o'clock on the day appointed for the attack, drawn across the river in battle formation. But yet again the opportunity for a skirmish eluded Orde for the American Fleet, on sight of the British, lost its nerve, turned tail and ran for the shore hotly pursued by Collier's ships. There the Americans burned all but one of their boats, deserted their positions and escaped into the undergrowth. They would otherwise have been easy prey for the British. And so, with hardly a shot fired, one ship was captured and the rest destroyed. It is not possible to know how many of the Americans survived the tramp through the thick woodland and desert wastes which bordered the river, but Collier's decisive action had saved the fort.[7] The British had lost 14 men, the Americans 474. Saltonstall took the blame and was duly dismissed the service at his court martial.

That same year Spain entered the war on the side of the Americans, followed, in 1780, by Holland, whilst Russia, Denmark and Sweden formed the 'Armed Neutrality of the North' league to protect the trade of neutrals threatened by the efforts of the British Navy to cut off the transport of supplies to the enemies of Britain. England now stood alone against three European nations as well as their own colonists in America.

In the year 1780, Orde was to earn the commendation of Admiral Arbuthnot who had succeeded Lord Howe and Sir George Collier on the American station. The capture of Charleston in South Carolina in the spring of 1780 was seen by many as the largest of many defeats suffered by the American Army during the eight years of conflict.

Nine thousand men under the command of Sir Henry Clinton, an able but diffident officer, who had become Commander-in-Chief of the British Army in North America, set sail for Charleston from New York on 26 December 1779 in a convoy commanded by Admiral Arbuthnot. It was to be a combined naval and military offensive. After a turbulent voyage in heavy seas during which one vessel was lost and most of the Army's horses died, Clinton eventually landed his troops on 11 February on Simond's Island which lies down the coast from Charleston by some thirty miles. Arbuthnot then lay outside the bar of the estuary in which the town itself lies, sited as it is on a peninsular bounded by the river Ashley to the west and by the river Cooper to the east. It was not until 7 March that Clinton, taking John and James Islands on the way and ever careful to preserve his line of communication to the British-held Savannah in the south, crossed the Ashley at Wappoo Cut with the assistance of a small naval brigade and took up a position on the neck of the peninsula behind the town. There he waited before taking the town, for reinforcements to be brought up under naval protection and for his line of communication to be secured across the Ashley once Arbuthnot had cleared the estuary. They would otherwise have been stranded.

Because of the shallowness of the river at its mouth Arbuthnot was able to bring no more than his frigates across the bar and then only after the heaviest of them had shed their provisions and guns. His ships of the line were obliged to remain outside. This advance force therefore effectively lay at the mercy of an American naval squadron stationed in the estuary under the command of Commodore Whipple. They could have been easy prey. But the Commodore chose instead to retire upriver towards Charleston where he proceeded to block the Cooper by sinking several frigates and merchantmen in the channel in order to secure a line of communication north from the town for the American. In the result this precipitate and ill-conceived act both surrendered control of the Ashley which the British reinforcement then crossed in total safety to join Clinton in an advance to within a mile and a half of the town, and at the same time released Arbuthnot's flotilla of ships to secure the estuary. However, in the path of the British upriver guarding the approach to the town lay the heavily fortified Fort Moultrie on Sullivan Island, an obstacle which had successfully thwarted a British attempt on Charleston four years earlier. As Arbuthnot was to report, it was 'the chief defence of the harbour'.[8] Nothing daunted Arbuthnot decided to force a passage through the gut. It was a bold and dangerous resolution. And so, shortly after midday on 8 April he weighed anchor, and, taking his flagship the *Roebuck* under the command of Hamond, together with the *Virginia* commanded by Orde, the *Richmond*, the *Romulus*, the *Blonde*, the *Raleigh*, the *Sandwich* and the *Renown* with him, for two hours or more he bravely ran the gauntlet of a punishing heavy artillery bombardment from the batteries onshore with every ship nobly maintaining its position in line, until they emerged battered and bruised but more or less intact on the Charleston side of Sullivan's Island. They had suffered the loss of but one transport and twenty-seven men killed or wounded but every ship had sustained terrible damage. It had been an act of remarkable daring and courage. There he anchored off James Island at Fort Johnson, a mile and a half or so from the town and from there called upon the officer commanding to surrender. But Major General Lincoln stood firm, confident in his line of communication to the north.

Arbuthnot's response was to detach a military unit from Fort Johnson to secure the route for the British and this enabled Clinton to bring in further reinforcements. He then took steps to occupy Mount Pleasant on the far side of the estuary by sending in a force of 500 seamen at daybreak on 29 March under the command of Captains Orde, Hudson and Gambier. There was little resistance and in the face of the advancing British the opposition ran for the safety of Charleston abandoning their weaponry as they took to the oars. Less than a hundred were taken prisoner. From Mount Pleasant on 4 May he then directed an attack on Fort Moultrie by both land and sea. As Captain Orde waited to carry over a force of 200 men the moment the tide turned, a unit of similar number under the command of Captains Hudson, Gambier and Knowles, which had embarked earlier, succeeded in landing on the island and capturing a redoubt. The fort then quickly capitulated. Thus finally cut off and surrounded by the British expeditionary force, but only after some hesitation, Lincoln finally surrendered the town on 12 May. No less than 1,000 seamen and 5,618 other men were taken prisoner and about 400 guns and as many horses were captured. It had been a substantial victory.

In his despatch Arbuthnot singled out Captains Hamond, Hudson, Orde, Gambier, Elphinstone and Evans as officers who had distinguished themselves in this naval operation. Sadly he himself was to be much criticized by certain commentators in later years as a commander but if contemporary report be at all accurate there can be no doubt that he acquitted himself well in the siege of Charleston.

At the close of the campaign, Arbuthnot detailed Orde to carry official despatches back to London. But then, his mission accomplished, he was given command of the *Chatham* of 50 guns and promptly returned to the American Station at the urgent request of Arbuthnot, who clearly valued his determination and spirit. This is well illustrated by an entry in the diary of Rear Admiral James.

We were detached ahead of the Squadron to look into Delaware for the French fleet, which, not finding it there, we proceeded again to sea in quest of the Admiral. On the 11th we spoke the *Chatham*, which had also been dispatched in the search of the enemy, and also, having taken a prize, had been informed therefrom that she was a part of the fleet from St Domingo bound to Philadelphia under the convoy of the *Dean* and *Confederacy*, rebel frigates and which must be very near us at the period, she having only parted company with them the preceding day.

Captain Orde very prudently proposed to Captain Symonds to cruise off the capes of the Delaware for a few days, to intercept this valuable convoy of the enemy's, which, unfortunately for us, was refused by the latter, who was the senior Captain; at the same time allowing Captain Orde to act himself as he pleased, we made sail and stood to the northward. On the 13th we gave chase to a brig we pursued for 7 hours and captured, which proved the *Peggy*, rebel privateer of 14 guns and 70 men loaded with rum and indigo from Carolina bound to Philadelphia. We arrived at New York the 18th with our prize, where we learned that the Admiral had not only approved of Captain Orde's conduct, but had despatched the *Roebuck* and *Orpheus* to put themselves under the command of Captain Symonds, which we had prevented by returning into port, which lost us the share of the *Confederacy* and several of her convoy, who was taken by the above ships.[9]

Whilst Commander of the *Chatham* Orde captured the *General Washington* of 22 guns and 118 men,[10] and then, the following year, 1781, he celebrated his meteoric rise in rank whilst on the American station with marriage to Margaret Emma, the daughter and heiress of one Richard Stevens of St Helena, Charleston.[11] On 14 April of that year, Orde, now Captain of the *Roebuck*, captured the American frigate *Confederacy* with the assistance of the *Orpheus*.[12]

Later that same year Admiral Arbuthnot was recalled to London and was conveyed home in the *Roebuck*, then under the command of Captain Orde. And so John Orde sailed out of the American War of Independence. He had left England six years before an inexperienced and very junior officer and a single man. He now emerged blooded in both battle and matrimony, senior in rank and a married man.

Notes

1 Cassels.
2 Ralfe, II pp. 59-60; TNC, Vol XI, p. 185.
3 Cassels.
4 TNC, Vol XI, p. 180; ND, p. 64.
5 Ralfe, II, p. 61.
6 Ralfe, II, p. 61.
7 Ralfe and Marshall and TNC, Vol XI, p. 181.
8 Despatch of 14 May 1780 cited at p. 139 of Vol I of The Keith Papers.
9 James, p. 108.
10 GM, 1824, p. 276.
11 Bell and TNC, Vol XI, p. 171.
12 Sweetman, p. 12.

CHAPTER VIII

DOMINICA

On arrival at Spithead, Orde was posted to home waters where he remained for a further eighteen months, firstly in the North Sea under Admiral Sir Hyde Parker and his successor Commodore Keith Stewart, and then off the coast of France as senior officer in a small squadron. It was in January of the following year, 1783, that he met for the first time the man who was later to become his arch enemy, John Swinfen Jervis. Jervis had by this time taken his first step towards flag rank as Captain of the *Foudroyant* which he had licked into shape as one of the most efficient ships in the British Navy. Lying off Brest it had fallen in with the French ship *Pegase* of 77 guns. In the action which followed the British boarded and captured the vessel but Jervis lay wounded with a splinter lodged in his head. He was afterwards rewarded with a knighthood followed by a posting to serve in Lord Howe's Fleet. Orde, now commanding the *Roebuck*, was appointed to join Sir John Jervis's squadron which was then under orders to undertake a secret mission of some importance. Their meeting was professional and cordial enough but it was destined to be of short duration, for the end of the America War now caused a further twist to John Orde's career.

Throughout the American war the British Navy had operated at grave disadvantage for only a handful of ships had been kept in American waters so that the bulk of the Fleet under Admiral Viscount Keppel could be deployed in protection of the English Channel where the need was greater. The French had therefore had almost a free run off the American coast where British merchant shipping had been dangerously exposed to attack with very few frigates or ships of the line available to protect them. This weakness had been further exposed at the seaport of Yorktown in August 1781 which effectively saw the end of the American War of Independence. General Clinton had succeeded General Howe as commander of the British forces and he had left General Cornwallis with the troops under his command to subdue the southern states. In 1781 Cornwallis had retreated to the port in the face of strong American opposition in the hope and expectation that the British Fleet would be there to reinforce and supply him. But the French Fleet, commanded by De Grasse and superior in numbers, stood in their way in Chesapeake Bay. In the battle which followed the French, as always, directed their fire at the masts and rigging of the British ships with a view to crippling rather than destroying them and in this they were largely successful. This method of fighting had been the foundation of the Crown's case in the prosecution of Admiral Keppel back in 1778, brought most unjustly. In the face of this form of attack, many ships in the British Fleet were disabled and Admiral Graves, who was now in command with the assistance of Lord Hood, withdrew his force to New York for repair and refitting, leaving Cornwallis and his men to their fate, for there was no hope of escape, trapped as they were on the peninsula. After a punishing bombardment from the French guns he had no alternative but to capitulate to General Washington. The war was now over, for the British public had no appetite to pursue it further. The intervention of the French Navy had been decisive.

It had been a war in which the British had won almost every battle yet had lost the war. Had she won, Washington or New York would now be the capital of Great Britain and Britain a satellite of the United States of America. Prime Minister Lord North now retired from the fray.

The pride of the Royal Navy was restored to some extent the following spring, when, on 12 April, Admiral Lord Rodney overtook De Grasse and the French Fleet off that group of islands known as the Saintes which lie between the islands of Dominica and Guadeloupe in the West Indies. They were headed for Jamaica with orders to mount an invasion of that island. As both fleets confronted each other, Rodney took advantage of a slight change in the direction of the wind, suddenly altered course and cut through the French line, thus forcing an engagement which the French had no time on this occasion to avoid. Five ships were taken before they could escape. The breaking of the line had been unplanned, but, in the outcome, many felt that the badly damaged reputation of the Royal Navy had to some extent been restored, and it is to be remembered that throughout the war it had been opposed by the combined resources of the French, Spanish, Dutch and American navies. And, on the credit side, the experience was to cause the British Government to introduce a programme of modernization in the Navy which was to serve the nation well in the years to come. In the peace treaty negotiated by Lord Shelbourne in the following year, 1783, the terms agreed were reasonably favourable to the British, in part thanks to Rodney's victory at the battle of the Saintes, although she was required to cede some of the territories in the West Indies which had been acquired in the Seven Years War, and, of course, to recognize the independence of the American colonists. Senegal and Tobago and St Lucia were now handed over to France but the rest of the islands were recovered by Great Britain, including the island of Dominica, for which a Governor was now required.

In February of that year, after but one month in Sir John Jervis's squadron lying off the coast of France, Captain Orde was appointed to the Governorship of Dominica and set sail for the West Indies where he was to remain, on and off, for the next ten years, until he returned again to active service with the Royal Navy.

GOVERNOR OF DOMINICA

He accepted the Governorship on the clear understanding that should hostilities involving the Royal Navy ever be resumed, he would be allowed to return to active service. There followed almost ten years of peace. For almost the whole of that period he presided over a thoroughly quarrelsome and truculent people of differing and mixed ancestry and conflicting objectives who had been thrown together in an impossibly humid climate on an island barely fifteen miles wide and thirty miles long from its northern tip to its southern extremity, an island smaller than the Isle of Wight. Yet he tackled the problems which faced him with a military efficiency which initially won him the praise of the settlers, the Assembly and the Council alike, and throughout he had the support of the home Government and King George III who was, at the end of it, to grant him a baronetcy.

The indigenous population was not quite so supportive, and understandably so. The oldest inhabitants, the fierce, warlike, hard-drinking Caribs, were as violent in those times as the hostile terrain itself, far removed from the gentle, peace-loving Carib people who still occupy part of that island to this day. Intrigued by their reputation for feeding on the flesh of man, but never of woman or child, Christopher Columbus had gone in search of the Caribs, described by the Spaniards as Caribals, when he discovered the island in November 1493. Landing on a Sunday (Domingo in Latin) he named the island Dominica, pronounced 'Domineeca', not to be confused with the Dominican Republic. He soon beat a hasty retreat, never to return, leaving the island to the domination of the Caribs with their dislike of foreigners and preference for the flesh of Frenchmen which they found more appetizing than that of Spaniards whom they found less digestible even when spliced with vegetables (the priest de Rochefort, 1658).

Almost 200 years later white settlers, mainly Frenchmen, arrived with but one object in mind, to exploit the island's reserves of coffee, and, later, to grow sugar. In their wake came African black labour imported by the settlers and with them came political unrest, the more so as the black population began to exceed by far that of the rest of the population on the island put together, and yet they were condemned in those harsh and cruel days to live in cramped and often primitive conditions which they openly and understandably resented. Twenty-five years before the arrival of Governor Orde the Caribs had finally surrendered their domination of the island to the French who had not only reduced them in number but had also exiled them to an existence on a reservation on the eastward, windward coast of the island which they continue to occupy to this day, the only population of Carib people now surviving in the West Indies. When Orde took up his post they too were living in abject poverty. Add to that the constant battle between the British and the French for possession of the island which had such immense strategic importance as a naval base, and it can be appreciated that when John Orde landed in 1784 the island was a seething cauldron of discontent. It is clear from Orde's correspondence that the overriding concern of the British Government was the development and security of the fine natural harbour at Portsmouth in Prince Rupert's Bay at the northern tip of the island, as a haven for British ships in need of water and victualling. This formation was a legacy of volcanic eruption and geological subsidence. The mountain range which had at one time straddled the Caribbean in an arc from Florida on the coast of America to the island of Trinidad off the coast of Venezuela, thus enclosing the Caribbean, had subsided, conveniently, leaving mountain peaks across the waters separated by sea. The highest of these form the central backbone of the island of Dominica, which throws into relief the sure beauty of its volcanic scenery and its rain forests on either coastline, and produces a climate no less dramatic than its wild and turbulent history. The harbour of Portsmouth is well enclosed and sheltered, and, not surprisingly, it was to be fought over for more than 150 years until the matter was finally settled at the Battle of Waterloo. Originally French, it became one of the 'Ceded Islands' of the West Indies, namely one of those islands which were ceded to Great Britain in 1763 together with Granada and St Vincent, only to be recaptured by a French invasion force under the command of the Marquis de Boville which crossed over from the French island of Martinique at the start of the American War of Independence in 1778. Then, under the Treaty of Versailles in 1783 at the end of the American War, it had been returned to Great Britain, and entrusted to the care of Captain Orde. It is now, since 1940, known more appropriately as one of the Windward group of islands, lying as it does some twenty miles south of the French island of Guadeloupe and a like distance north of the French island of Martinique, all of which are formed by the same range of mountains. But in 1783 it was described as one of the Leeward islands. Orde's primary objectives in taking up office were to develop the harbour in

Prince Rupert's Bay, restore law and order amongst the population, and, above all, retain possession of the island for the British. And he was to be, in all these respects, successful for the most part. But the climate he found disagreeable and unhealthy.

It was in January of 1784 that he landed on the island, received possession from the French officer then in command and took up his Governorship, arriving in the *Adamant* of 50 guns. His ability to govern was put to the test almost immediately. After years of French rule he was faced with a declining population of white settlers and a slave population which was increasingly hostile. In 1773 those living on the island had numbered approximately 23,000 with the imported slave population outnumbering the settler by almost six to one. The loathsome slave trade flourished in the capital town of Roseau as did the coffee plantations outside. But during five years of French occupation no trade had been encouraged with Great Britain, punitive conditions had been imposed on British settlers as the price for their being allowed to retain their estates on the island, many of the cattle which had been used as labour on the plantations had been slaughtered to feed the occupying forces and black slaves had been encouraged to turn on their English masters in the hope of killing off the British interest in the island. And it worked, for British settlers had left in large numbers leaving a population of whites which numbered no more than 1,000 alongside a slave population of more than 13,000, many of them with thought of rebellion in their minds. Harsh working conditions and, at times, sure cruelty had persuaded many to take to the hills where they hid away in dense woodland with little fear of being recaptured by their owners. The runaway slaves, known as maroons, encouraged by the French, had then banded together to conduct a guerilla warfare on the white settlers, principally those of them who were English. Pillaging and formenting discontent was rife amongst the slave population as a whole and this had become a serious problem by 1783 with which the Government on the island had been quite unable to deal.

Coming fresh to the problem Orde at once devised a plan of his own using those few resources which had been laid at his disposal by the Colonial Assembly, and, the following year, a punitive expedition was mounted. By the standards of the day it proved to be surprisingly successful in that government forces succeeded in hunting down several hundred runaway slaves in the dense forests and mountains of the island and more than a third of them were either killed or captured including their leader who was put to death on the gibbet. So delighted were both the Council and the Assembly at this rather ruthless turn of events that they united in praise of Governor Orde, and, on 18 August, presented him with a unanimous vote of thanks couched in euphoric terms.

This Board and House taking into consideration the readiness with which your Excellency was pleased to engage in the service of the Colonies, under the Act for the suppression of the Runaways, the zeal and ability with which the forces raised by that Act have been put into action, and the unremitting attention Your Excellency has shewn in the whole progress of this business, cannot permit the Colony to derive those advantages without testifying our grateful thanks to your Excellency as the author of them, imputing to these services the present security of our properties, and the tranquillity of the public. We beg to offer to your Excellency this acknowledgement of our obligations; and, in presenting a pledge of our gratitude, we venture to hope your Excellency will meet the just reward of His Majesty's most gracious approbation.[1]

No doubt their joy at this turn of events was in some part generated by the knowledge that the value of their lands had risen by almost 50 per cent since Governor Orde first set foot on the island, for little thought seems to have been spared for the unfortunate and largely defenceless slaves except by Orde himself who, in a letter to the Assembly, urged that the slave laws should be made more humanitarian. Indeed those American loyalists who had supported the Crown during the recent war and had later found refuge on the island, had already passed an address in like terms which had been printed in *The Times* on 11 November 1785.

Governor Orde turned next to the fortification of the island which was to be assembled to the specification of an engineer sent out by the British Government, using slave labour. In a letter written from the Admiralty and dated 13 August 1786, Lord Howe acknowledged receiving a report from Orde as to the geography of Prince Rupert's Bay together with his plans for the development of the harbour, and then he too referred to the success of the expedition which had been mounted, adding, 'I can only express my hopes that the account I read in the daily papers that you have nearly restored internal peace in your Government by the dispersion of the fugitive negroes, is well founded.'[2]

Later that same year Prince William sailed in to witness these developments. During that visit his ship, the *Pegasus*, anchored at Roseau on 13 December and the Prince then visited Prince Rupert's Head and Bay with Governor Orde and an engineer officer, one Major Frazier. He so reported in a letter to the King dated 7 January 1787, adding:

The manner in which I was received by the inhabitants convinced me of their affection and loyalty for Your Majesty . . . The island is too mountainous ever to be well cultivated; its principal use to Great Britain is the wood and water found in Prince Rupert's Bay, and the situation between Martinique and Guadeloupe two of the most powerful islands belonging to the French. Prince Rupert's Head, which is the defence of the bay, is a most noble headland, almost as strong as Gibraltar, and if I may venture an opinion on the proposed fortifications, Major Frazier . . . has shewn great judgement in the manner he intends if approved of rendering it very strong. In the Bay there are three noble rivers, and all round the shore the wood grows in forests close to the sea side; the large fleets may lie in the greatest safety except in the hurricane months and an inferior force may under the batteries lie perfectly secured from the attacks of a superior one, as the wind constantly blows out of the Bay, so that ships are obliged to work in. Dominique is charmingly situated to rendezvous a fleet for the attack of Martinique or Guadeloupe, as in four hours it is easy to reach either of them. The 30th Regiment and a company of Royal Artillery are upon the hills above the town of Roseau; they enjoy good health, and are all well disciplined. The trade in slaves at this island is very great owing to our supplying the French with that valuable commodity.

The Prince so described those unfortunate human beings.[3]

Nelson who had been with the Prince at Dominica on the 2nd, was to write to his wife of the Prince's visit, in a letter dated 12 December 1786:

Some ladies seem very much charmed by him. He is volatile but always with great good nature. There were two balls during his stay and some of the old ladies were mortified that His Royal Highness would not dance with them, but he says he is determined to enjoy the privilege of all other men, that of asking any lady he pleases. Mrs Parry dined at table the first day at the Government House, but afterwards never appeared at dinner nor were any ladies at Governor Orde's dinner.[4]

In his fifth year on the island Orde began to tire of its climate and of its quarrelsome inhabitants. In all that he tried to do he was met with opposition from one quarter or another and he began to fear for the completion of his plans for Prince Rupert's Bay. And back in London an action in the Vice-Admiralty Court being pursued on his behalf had met with little progress. Both he and his wife now yearned for home, and so, in his correspondence with Lord Howe he hinted at resignation, claiming that he despaired of the Assembly and its failure to advance at the pace which he had set. But Howe was not sympathetic. On 16 February of 1788 he wrote to Orde, 'Having the satisfaction of knowing when I received your letter by the *Nautilus*, that the cause for the operations in which you were engaged at the time it was dated, had ceased; I was under less concern for the state of Prince Rupert's Bay. And as we may promise ourselves, no such call for quitting your present situation as you meditated, will be likely to take place for some length of time . . .!'[5]

In the light of this it was not until the following year that Orde sought permission to come home on leave on the ground that the climate was not agreeable to his health, although, in truth, his greater concern now was for the well-being of his wife who had fallen pregnant and indeed for the health of his brother Thomas back in London for this was reported to be in decline. Eventually, on 3 May 1789, Lord Sydney reported that Captain Orde had obtained the leave of His Majesty to return home on leave and *The Times* so reported on 4 July, 'Mr Orde . . . has for some time back been soliciting leave to return home on account of his ill health. The climate he has found unfavourable to his constitution. Leave has at length been granted to him, and he is expected in England towards Autumn.' In his absence the Government of Dominica was to be carried on by the new Lieutenant Governor, Lieutenant Colonel Bruce, successor to one Stuart who had fallen victim to a palsy.[6] On 14 July the Council of the island submitted a 'humble' address which was published in *The Times* in London on 13 October, in which it expressed the hope that Orde's absence would be short and that he would in the meantime enjoy both private comfort and public prosperity and happiness. It recorded the harmony with which they had worked together and the vigilant regard which he had shown for the security of the Colony, the impartial administration of justice and the commercial interests of the mother country. Perhaps fearing that Orde would not return, the Council went on to refer to the obstacles to government which had been put in his way which they then dismissed as no more than was to be expected of any administration. They reassured him that he had overcome them with such zeal and sacrifice that he had won the applause 'of the well meaning part of every community'. The Council doubted not that he would 'receive the entire approbation of our Gracious Sovereign'.[7] In this forecast at least they were proved to be correct.

Back in England the Marquis of Lansdowne confirmed that many were indeed concerned for his brother's health. His brother had served with Lansdowne, when, as the 2nd Earl of Shelbourne, Lansdowne had been at the Treasury. In a letter to Orde dated 1 September 1789 he wrote from his home in Perth that he was 'very glad to hear of yours and Mrs Orde's safe arrival', especially at this time 'on account of your brother's state of health which gives me great uneasiness, so much so that you will oblige me if you will let me know what you think of it'. He hoped to have the pleasure of seeing Orde in Perth, or, if not, when he got back to Wycombe or London.[8]

Back in 1784, during his first year out in Dominica his father had died in his eightieth year. Now, sadly, the health of his brother Thomas, always frail, had indeed begun to deteriorate and his wife's pregnancy had also reached a critical stage. And so *The Times* of 2 September reported that 'Governor Orde does not return to Dominique. Robert Browne, Esquire, his Secretary, is left in charge of the Island and from his experiences and abilities, it cannot be placed in better hands.'[9] And then, early in October, tragically, the child born to Orde's wife at their house in Queen Ann Street in Westminster, London, died shortly after birth. Orde was distraught. *The Times* reported this event on 14 October, and, with kindness, offered its condolences. 'No Gentleman ever returned from his Government abroad with a fairer reputation, or to the greater sorrow of those he left behind him, than his Excellency Governor Orde. Every action of his Government was guided by the strictest honour and showed that the welfare and happiness of the natives over whom he governed, was infinitely more valuable to him than any private consideration of his own,' it read.[10]

But then, exactly one week later, pity spent, that same newspaper reported that a correspondent had pointed out that the 14 July address which the paper had printed 'was only from the Council, who are generally nominated by, and considered the particular friends of, the respective Governors. Governor Orde perhaps can say why on this occasion, this singular mode should be adopted; and that no address should be presented from the Assembly, who properly represent and therefore must be supposed to speak the sentiments of the inhabitants.'[11]

They were to receive their answer in the new year, for, after being created baronet by the King for his services to the colony, taking his title as of Morpeth in the county of Northumberland, Orde decided to return to the island, for his wife had since died and he was now alone.

Work seemed to be the therapy now needed to distract him from his grief. This was soon available for he was met, at the end of the year 1790, by a dangerous revolt of runaway slaves which had been simmering in his absence. Once again he was able to restore law and order and once again this won him an address of thanks in like terms to that which he had received before. Dated April 1791, it expressed 'gratitude for the measures so prudently formed and promptly executed by your Excellency, for the suppression of the late alarming and dangerous revolt of the Slaves.' But this time the address had come from 229 planters, merchants and inhabitants, and not from the Assembly. He did then receive a letter dated 6 May from the merchants of the City of London who thanked him, for themselves, for the 'judicious and effectual measures' which he had taken, 'which had produced the accomplishment of the object so speedily and with so little bloodshed and inconvenience.' But, ominously, the Assembly was not signatory to the address of thanks for it had by now applied to the Privy Council in London for Sir John's dismissal. Ever since 1786 they had opposed his plans for the development of the island's harbour and fortifications for the advantage of the British, and they had resented his proposal that the island should contribute to the cost of maintaining law and order. The Assembly had been determined to retain its own control over public expenditure for this was no docile population. And so, whilst agreeing that black labour in sufficient numbers be put at the disposal of the engineer sent out to fortify the island, they had balked at Orde's proposal that the joint address which they had presented to him should be amended to include an agreement that such labour would be supplied 'when called for by his Excellency'. Orde had been forced to back down and produce a compromise by which it had been agreed that such labour would only be provided when the Committee of the Assembly voted to authorize any requisition put in by the engineer. In practice it had amounted to the same thing, but, more serious, the Assembly had then refused to make any contribution towards the cost of maintaining the armed force on the island which Sir John had raised for the suppression of slave revolt. With some justice he had pointed out that the Assembly had by resolution delegated that very task to the Governor and they could not now withdraw their financial support.

Proceedings were brought before the Privy Council in June 1790 by the Assembly which sought Orde's dismissal, but they almost ground to a halt because of the failure of the Assembly to provide the documentary evidence required. It was not therefore until April 1793 that the Privy Council delivered its judgement, dismissing all charges which had been brought against Sir John as entirely frivolous. He had before then, in 1792, returned home at the request of the Government. In a letter dated 11 June 1793, Henry Dundas, then Home Secretary, had explained that this had been 'highly necessary, not only for the more complete investigation of the charges in question, but in order that His Majesty's servants might have an opportunity to communicate with you upon the general state of the island, and particularly upon so extraordinary a circumstance as a suspension, on the part of the Assembly, of its most necessary functions.' With that letter he enclosed the report of the King in Council which he described as 'highly creditable to you'.[12]

Until he received that letter the hope of release from the Governorship had seemed remote. Indeed, Lord Howe had written as recently as 19 May that 'I conclude . . . you will be obliged to resume your Government, and am sorry for it, as you found the climate rather injurious to your health'.[13] But war with France had been declared and the need now was for every trained and experienced officer to return to the colours, which, in fact, had always been Sir John's priority. Dundas therefore ended his letter of 1 June with the message that, 'In consequence of your earnest wishes, at this moment of hostilities with France, to be enabled to offer yourself for active employment in the line of your profession, I am to signify to you, that you have His Majesty's gracious permission so to do.' It so happened that this accorded with the wish of not only Sir John Orde, but also that of the Assembly of the island of Dominica!

His Governorship of that troubled island for nine years or more had not been without difficulty. But it was the judgement of planters, inhabitants, merchants of the City of London, the home Government and his King alike, that he had discharged his duties efficiently, diligently, fairly and well. Thus far, at the age of forty-two, his career had flourished without setback and there was as yet no hint of what lay on the horizon five years ahead. Indeed the paths of Horatio Nelson and Sir John Orde had not yet crossed in any meaningful way although Nelson had, in the summer of 1784 sailed into Prince Rupert's Bay for wood and water, hoping to speak with Orde in order to assist his friend William Locker in the administration of an estate Locker owned on the island. He was confident of Orde's cooperation since he had taken delivery at Madeira of four casks of wine for Orde. He therefore wrote to Locker on 7 June, 'I take for granted Orde will be civil about it, as I have taken on board for him 4 casks of wine.'[14] Clearly no meeting was achieved, or, at any rate nothing was done, for he wrote to his friend again on 24 September of that year to report that he had obtained no information when in Prince Rupert's Bay. But he promised to write to Orde on Locker's behalf,[15] although, by letter dated 15 January 1785, he apologized again that he had not yet been able to say anything to Governor Orde 'upon the subject of your estate'.[16] In that same year, when seizing a number of foreign-built vessels off the island of Nevis for trafficking illicitly contrary to his understanding of the navigation laws which forbade traffic to the islands when under the American flag, Nelson arrested a vessel which had been registered by Orde at Dominica, after which writs had then been litigated in court.[17] But otherwise he had had no contact with Governor Orde, other than during Prince William's visit to Dominica. Now, after nine or ten years away from his profession, Sir John Orde returned to active service at sea.

Notes

1. TNC, Vol XI, pp. 188-9.
2. Orde Papers.
3. Letters of George III, p. 341 and pp. 266-7.

4 Naish, p. 38 and NN, Vol I, p. 203.
5 Orde Papers.
6 *The Times*, 4 July 1789.
7 *The Times*, 13 October 1789.
8 Orde Papers.
9 *The Times*, 2 September 1789.
10 *The Times*, 14 October 1789.
11 *The Times*, 21 October 1789.
12 TNC Vol XI, p. 191.
13 Orde Papers.
14 NN, Vol I, p. 109.
15 NN, Vol I, p. 110.
16 NN, Vol I, p. 113.
17 N Mah, p. 81.

CHAPTER IX

INTO THE MEDITERRANEAN 1797-8

As soon as Sir John Orde received the permission of the King to relinquish his Governorship and return to naval service, delivered by Henry Dundas, Secretary of State for War, in 1793, he presented that authority to Lord Chatham, Pitt's elder brother and First Lord of the Admiralty.[1] He was then nominated in 1793 to the *Victorious*, which was not, as it turned out, ready for service.

In the meanwhile, in December 1793, Sir John married again, this time Jane, eldest daughter of one John Frere of Roydon in the county of Norfolk, later to become Member of Parliament for the city of Norwich. It was to be a happy marriage which lasted thirty years until Sir John's death, despite the storms which lay ahead. They had five children in that time but only two were to survive, a daughter Anna Maria Fenn Orde who never married, and a son and heir, John Powlett Orde.[2]

By letter of 7 January 1794, Lord Howe wrote his regret that Captain Sir John Orde would not be joining his command having 'reckoned to have benefited by your assistance in the Channel Fleet, early in the present year'.[3] However, later that year he was nominated again for another ship, the 74-gun third rate *Venerable* which had been built on the Thames in 1784 and carried 600 men,[4] and ordered to join the Channel Fleet under Lord Howe with command of his advance squadron.[5]

But before he could take up his command Lord Chatham had resigned as First Lord of the Admiralty, to be succeeded by the Lord Spencer. The second Earl Spencer was then thirty-six years of age and married to the celebrated daughter of the first Lord Lucan. She was probably the most handsome lady in London society at that time and certainly a very influential one. He, on the other hand, was a studious, scholarly, urbane, courteous and mild-mannered man with little knowledge of ships or the sea. However he was to hold office as First Lord of the Admiralty for five or six of the most critical years of British history from 1794 until 1801. On the whole he was a successful minister, but, for all that his achievement was never recognized adequately. Perhaps this was because of an arrogance which contemporaries put down to his aristocratic birth and constant refusal to take the advice of others, coupled with a stubbornness which made him many enemies.[6] But as a man he was firm and fair and this extended too to his own affairs for he was ever concerned for the welfare of the tenants on his Althorp estate. A man of great literary interests, he accumulated a large number of very rare books, building on a library which had been started by his great-grandfather, the Earl of Sunderland, a collection which was later bought by a Mrs Rylands in 1892 and this was the basis for the John Rylands library in Manchester.[7] Soon after his appointment Spencer offered Sir John command, not of the *Venerable*, which he had joined at Spithead, but of the *Prince George*, a 98-gun second rater which had been launched at Chatham in 1772 and which carried 750 men.[8] When Sir John, perhaps unwisely, protested that he be allowed to remain in the *Venerable*, as promised, Spencer drily informed him that it had already been earmarked for Lord Duncan.[9]

By letter to Orde dated 29 December 1794, Howe suggested, kindly, that the 'further concern [he] . . . he may . . . have with the Channel Fleet will be rendered much less grateful if you are to be withdrawn from it'.[10] So it was that Sir John eventually took command of the *Prince George* and so it was also that Spencer, in the future, was slow to offer Sir John much else which was to please him, and this was to tell against him in his quarrel with St Vincent in the years to come.

As Dillon regretted in his narrative, to which reference has already been made, he was not to remain in the *Prince George* long, for three months later, in 1795, and before the *Prince George* had ever put to sea or sailed other than round to Spithead,[11] he was raised to the rank of Rear Admiral of the White in a general promotion of flag officers and was not then asked to hoist his new flag on the *Prince George*, hence the parade of farewell by the ship's crew to which Dillon referred. That ship then sailed in successful pursuit of the French under the command of another. Perhaps not unnaturally Sir John went hot foot to London to ask the Admiralty for some sort of explanation. In reply Spencer reassured him on more than one occasion that when the *Prince George* returned to home waters it would indeed bear his flag, so much so that he recommended that Sir John's baggage and those of his servants still on board, be left there. On the strength of this Sir John went so far as to sell his house and make arrangements for an imminent departure. He was therefore astonished to discover when the *Prince George* did eventually return home that it was flying the flag of another admiral altogether, Admiral Christian. He discovered too that his own servants, who had remained on board, had been removed to other ships. This prompted Sir John to call upon Lord Spencer for explanation once again. He was simply told in matter-of-fact terms that there had been a change of plan

George John Spencer, 2nd Earl

and that his services would not, for the moment, be required!

Why the Admiralty moved Orde out of the *Prince George* when they did remains a mystery. And it was much regretted by such as Midshipman Dillon, a member of the crew which sailed off in the *Prince George* under its new Captain, Captain Edge, 'a very different man from Sir John Orde,' he wrote. 'He was only "acting" and probably did not feel the confidence he would have done had he been in full command. This is only a conjecture of mine for, although he did his duty, he allowed a brilliant chance to escape that might have rendered his name a distinguished one in naval columns.'[12] He was here referring to an action close to the Ile de Groix off L'Orient when the squadron of which the *Prince George* was a member caught the French Fleet and brought it to action. The *Prince George* opened fire as it came up and had every chance of joining the French Admiral's ship in battle – or so Dillon reported, quoting the words of the ship's Master, 'See what a chance we have of bringing him to action. I have been trying to persuade the Captain to do so, but I cannot prevail upon him to seize the opportunity.' Dillon's report went on, 'Our ship sailed well and no doubt, if the exertion had been made, we might have closed upon and engaged the French three-decker, as at that critical moment she was upon our lee bow, not two miles distant.' If correct the opportunity was indeed lost for his Captain then allowed the *Queen* of 98 guns, flying the flag of Vice Admiral Sir Alan Gardner, to pass the *Prince George* by ordering the mizzen topsail to be laid back, and a change of wind then frustrated the whole enterprise. Happily, however, a French two-decker, *Le Tigre* of 74 guns, surrendered soon afterwards whilst under heavy gun fire from Lord Bridport's flagship, the *Royal George*, and there the action closed. But the bulk of the French Fleet, nine sail of the line, escaped into the shelter of the Ile de Groix. Dillon's final word on it was that, 'Had Sir John Orde been on board the *Prince George*, all his followers declared, he would have run alongside of the French Admiral in spite of Sir Alan Gardner or any other superior officer, unless ordered by signal to act otherwise. They all deplored his absence.'[13]

By letter dated 10 June 1795, Howe congratulated Sir John on his promotion and reassured him that his 'assistance would always be welcome', but, despairing of a command, Sir John now began to talk of returning to the north of England in retirement.[14] On 29 August Howe wrote expressing the hope that he would not do so,[15] but then, in a letter dated 16 September, Howe seemed to accept that the reality of it was that no command would be forthcoming as things stood,[16] although in a further letter dated 26 September he gave his support to Sir John in his intention to try yet again with Lord Spencer.[17]

An offer of employment in a temporary post with Rear Admiral Hervey off the coast of France did then come his way,[18] but he declined it for it was employment in an inferior capacity. A further invitation to proceed up the Mediterranean also came his way but this too he declined since he was not given the right to have a Captain or officers of his own choice. In the end he languished unemployed at home for a year or more before Spencer made another offer of active service which was acceptable, this time with the Mediterranean Fleet under St Vincent. Lord Lansdowne sent him a message of congratulations on 13 March 1797, writing that he was 'very glad that justice has been done to your pretensions',[19] and then the following day, Lord Howe wrote that he was '. . . glad you are now on a footing with Lord Spencer that promises a continuance of more satisfactory consequences than were to be inferred at the termination of the previous disruption of your pretensions to his favourable notice . . .'[20] But yet again, although Sir John accepted with alacrity, the arrangement was altered and a request made that he hoist his flag on the *Cambridge*, a ship by then assigned to harbour duty,[21] and take command at Plymouth in the absence of 65-year-old Admiral Sir Richard King who had been appointed Commander-in-Chief in December 1794 when a Rear Admiral.[22]

On arrival one of Sir John's first acts was to write to Spencer to draw his attention to the plight of the sick and wounded shipped home to Plymouth. Because of the geography of the arrangements these unfortunate men had to be landed at a distance from the naval hospital and then transported an uncomfortable journey before they could be ministered to.[23]

It was Orde's ill-luck that during his short command at Plymouth, mutinous elements there had begun to surface, taking their cue from the mutiny at Spithead. But then news of peace at Spithead was brought to him by a rider from Plymouth in the nick of time and this was then confirmed that same evening in a message transmitted from Portsmouth by the shutter telegraph. He quickly spread that fact amongst those ships lying at Plymouth, but to no avail. The men disbelieved the truth and provenance of it and resolved to hold out until some more convincing information of it was obtained. They then designated the ship *Atlas* as their 'Parliament' ship where two delegates nominated by each ship would meet and that Assembly then drew up disciplinary codes and passed a resolution resolving that permission be sought of the Commander-in-Chief for a delegation to travel to Portsmouth, all-expenses paid, so that they could judge the position for themselves with their own eyes. When the news reached Spencer, he wrote to Lord Bridport at Spithead suggesting that he sail his squadron round to Plymouth so that the men there could see for themselves that the mutiny had ended, but, becalmed in port, Bridport was unable to assist. Meanwhile, Orde refused to give his authority for the proposal that an unlawful delegation of men be authorized and financed to journey up to Portsmouth.

Matters therefore reached a stalemate with delegates threatening to take the ships *Atlas* and *Saturn* to sea. Orde then summoned a meeting of all his Captains to collect their view of the proposal. To a man they suggested that the delegates should be authorized to travel to Portsmouth. But this Sir John still refused to countenance under any circumstances, although he did indicate privately after the meeting that if the men slipped away in the direction of Portsmouth without his knowing about it, he would turn a blind eye, but there could be no question of his financing the expedition. However this impasse was finally resolved by the more liberal-minded Commissioner of the Admiralty at Plymouth, one Captain Robert Fanshawe, who agreed to pay the men wages enough to enable them to go. Orde's comment on this to the Admiralty was, 'The poor deluded men are in the hands of artful wicked advisers.'

In the meantime the Admiralty ordered Sir John to muster all ships' companies and tell them that the mutiny at Spithead was over. This order was duly obeyed but the crews still disbelieved him. Flush with money the delegates now hired a coaster and sailed into the St Helens anchorage off the coast of the Isle of Wight where they boarded the *Royal George* and then ran on to Portsmouth. In both places they were able to confirm the truth of Sir John's report for themselves, and the moment they had sent that word back to their colleagues in Plymouth, the mutiny there abated too. Preferring now to return overland by stagecoach but fearful lest the press gang ran them in, the delegates then applied to Sir Peter Parker, Commander-in-Chief Portsmouth, for overland passes for protection. His reply was, 'You have no passes from Admiral Orde to come here. Make the best of your way back!'[24]

On this occasion Orde's success there in suppressing mutinous elements early in the year 1797 was quickly recognized by Spencer, who, after a visit to Plymouth, was effusive in his praise. On 27 April, Lord Gambier, whilst writing of the discontent amongst some of the seamen, hinted that 'it is very probable that a ship will be appropriated to your flag, that next to a first rate, I should prefer to any in the Service, the *Prince* is the ship I mean. This quite in confidence as it is not settled . . . You will of course not say anything of it to Lord Spencer. He has the best disposition that can be desired towards you.'[25] And yet, strangely, in a letter written by Gambier only a matter of days later on 4 May, no further mention was made of that prospect. Rather he commiserated with Orde as 'unfortunate in being in command at Plymouth at so critical a time . . . Sir R. King is urgent to return, as he hears you have made £3,000 Prize Money since you have been at Plymouth. I wish it might be true but I fear he is much misinformed . . .'[26] The following day he wrote of 'the wretches have been much worse at Plymouth than those at Spithead, owing no doubt to there being some designing Villains to urge them to it.'[27]

By letter dated 5 May, St Vincent now wrote to Orde from his flagship, the *Ville de Paris*,

> I am very much hurt to learn from Sir Robert Calder that you have not received an answer to your obliging communication of the imperious treatment you had met with from a certain quarter [referring here to Lord Spencer]; he will bear witness that I wrote to you immediately and expressed the strongest indignation on the occasion, and I greatly lament your just indignation on the occasion deprived me of the benefit of your gallant services – I am happy however to find your flag is flying, and I hope soon to hear of your appointment to a Chief Command.[28]

In fact Spencer now appointed Orde to preside over the courts martial of the more serious Nore mutineers at Portsmouth.[29] Accordingly, Sir Peter Parker wrote him on 19 May that '. . . we shall expect you here to hoist your flag on board the *Princess Royal* soon after Sir R. King returns to his duty.'[30] His performance in that duty won further and unqualified thanks and his recommendations were accepted by both Spencer and the King.[31] In the result, in October of that year, he was ordered to proceed in the *Princess Royal* of 98 guns which carried 750 men and had been launched in Portsmouth in 1773, taking with him a Captain and officers of his own choice, and then to join the Mediterranean Fleet standing off the Tagus,[32] as third in command to the Earl St Vincent. And so, at last, Orde was able to return to active service.

He therefore joined the Fleet with the plaudits of Lord Spencer for his handling of the mutineer courts martial, ringing in his ears. He took with him also not only a promise of action in the Mediterranean, but an assurance too from Lord Hugh Seymour, one of the Lords of the Admiralty, that he would in quick time stand second in command in the Fleet. Seymour spoke there not just as one of the Lords but also as a close friend of the Prince of Wales.[33] All was therefore progressing favourably for him, and he was to prove his worth in the ensuing six months of blockade duty at Cadiz, which St Vincent was quick to recognize.

In fact St Vincent had before this urged Spencer not to send him any more flag officers for he found he could not trust most of them. Spencer had replied that his request had come too late for two more were on their way, Orde and Frederick, to which St Vincent had responded on 14 September 1797, 'I have no objection to any number of Admirals your Lordship may think fit to employ in the Fleet provided they are firm men and obedient officers. I believe Sir John Orde to be of the sort above described, although I never served with him. Both he and Frederick will be acceptable, but should the war continue over the winter I beg Admiral Nelson may be sent to me.'[34]

At this moment in time twenty Spanish sail of the line lay at Cadiz, poised to break out at any moment. Sir John was ordered to relieve Commodore Collingwood in his command of a squadron of eight sail of the line standing off the harbour in blockade. Outnumbered more than two to one and in turbulent seas with the constant danger that the French Toulon Fleet may be at any moment put to sea with no force in the Mediterranean to oppose them, Orde, with calm determination, succeeded in holding the Spaniards in port until relieved by Rear Admiral Sir William Parker more than three months later in January of the new year, 1798. And when, later, Parker was driven off the station by a superior force, Orde returned to the command and successfully mounted the blockade once more in extremely difficult circumstances until St Vincent himself resumed command off Cadiz in April of that year. One of his first acts was to reward Sir John with words of appreciation: 'You have shown uncommon ability and exertion in preserving your position during the unpleasant weather, and I very much appreciate every step you have taken.'

Indeed he appears to have won St Vincent's approval all round. This is demonstrated by a letter written by St Vincent dated 11 December 1797 in which he wrote, '. . . Your observations upon the decadence of discipline and subordination is very just. You may be assured I shall exert every means in my power to support the authority of all who are placed under my command, more especially those, who like yourself, endeavour to sustain the little remains of discipline in His Majesty's Fleet.'[35] For Sir John Orde all was seemingly set fair. Indeed, one Captain William Cathcart was to write home from his ship the *Alcmène* on Sunday, 6 May 1798, '. . . we have just left Gibraltar after a stay of about 4 days. Sir John Orde gave a grand chevaux [dance] to which he was so good as to invite me. He introduced me to General O'Hara and a Mrs Fryers . . . I never saw anything neater in my life . . .'[36]

But, alas, St Vincent's appreciation of Sir John Orde's talents was soon forgotten for stormy seas of another kind lay ahead. Orde was only forty-six years of age and still in the prime of life, yet events were now to turn against him very rapidly and quite inexplicably and really through no fault of his own, and they were to all but destroy his long and distinguished career.

In April 1798 Sir John Orde's prospects were about as good as those of any other officer in the Service, Nelson included. He now stood third in command to St Vincent in a front-line fleet which was preparing to play an active and crucial role in the war with France and he had an impeccable record of service behind him both in the Royal Navy and in colonial administration. And, as a much younger man than St Vincent, he had every hope of succeeding him as Commander-in-Chief of the Mediterranean Fleet. And yet, in the space of little

The Inshore Squadron blockading Cadiz, July 1797

more than four months he was to suffer five blows in succession which were entirely unexpected and wholly unprovoked, and which all but finished him. Four of these were not known to *The Times* when the challenge to St Vincent was reported in October 1799. The first was to hurt him greatly and the second damaged his prospects. But it was the third which crippled him as an officer in the Fleet and heralded his departure, whilst the fourth and fifth simply served to confirm his exit, as shells landing on a ship which was already sinking.

The first concerned the command of the newly formed Mediterranean Squadron to which *The Times* had referred. In the spring of 1798 matters were coming to a head for there were reports of great activity by the French. Sources of intelligence told the British Government that they had massed an expeditionary force at Toulon and at other ports in the Mediterranean, ready for embarkation. The danger of invasion therefore looked to be imminent, but its destination remained a mystery. This intelligence caused much alarm at home, for whilst the engagements on the Glorious First of June and off Cape St Vincent and at Camperdown had demonstrated the superiority of the Royal Navy, and had held the invader at bay, now Bonaparte had become all but master of Europe and the British feared the worst. The belief in Britain was that they were headed for these shores. And so alarm bells had begun to sound in the corridors of Whitehall. Clearly the need was for a squadron of ships, drawn from St Vincent's Fleet, to re-enter the Mediterranean, which they should never have left, patrol those waters, and, if possible, hunt down the expeditionary force, divine its destination and destroy it. Command of such a squadron would therefore very obviously carry with it immense responsibility and great prestige. Clearly it called for an officer possessed of outstanding skill and determination.

At the time of the appointment there were many contenders for the post, not least those then actually serving in the Mediterranean Fleet who were senior in rank, including Sir William Parker, a Rear Admiral of the Red, Sir John Orde, a Rear Admiral of the White, and, of course, Horatio Nelson, a Rear Admiral of the Blue. All were officers of distinction with a lifetime of naval service behind them. The disparity in their ages was quite marked for whereas Nelson was then but forty-one years of age, Orde was forty-seven and Parker fifty-five.

Although command of the Fleet to be sent up the Mediterranean was undoubtedly in the gift of Lord Spencer as First Lord of the Admiralty, it is very surprising that the appointment was not discussed more widely than it was for there can have been few decisions made in the long history of the British Navy of more crucial importance to the interests of the nation, and indeed, of Western Europe at this moment in time when Great Britain really stood alone against the French invader and the might of Napoleon Bonaparte's army. The country now looked to the newly formed Mediterranean Squadron for deliverance from the old enemy. Upon its command '. . . the fate of Europe may be stated to depend,' wrote Lord Spencer.[37] However, it is clear that, such was the importance of the appointment at this critical time, others most certainly brought their influence to bear, not excepting the Prime Minister himself and even George III. The probability too is that, of all the advice Spencer received from these and many other quarters, it was the opinion of St Vincent which carried the most weight.

Nelson had by then accumulated an impressive record of service on the West Indies and other stations and his reputation stood high with his brother officers. Before he was twenty-one he had been promoted Post Captain and won distinction in Nicaragua when commanding a joint expedition to capture the Spanish port of San Juan. But there had been five or more years of inactivity as he languished at home in the wilderness of the parsonage at Burnham Thorpe, unemployed and disconsolate, constantly bombarding the Lords Commissioners of the Admiralty with requests for employment and then openly denouncing them for their failure to recognize, appreciate, or use his outstanding talents. It had taken the declaration of war in 1793 and the need for every trained and experienced naval officer who could be found to be put at the disposal of the nation to bring him back to active service. There had followed three years of distinguished service as Captain of the *Agamemnon* of 64 guns with Lord Hood's, and then Hotham's Fleet in the Mediterranean, but no event which had caught the public's imagination. Indeed much had been lost for Nelson had lost nearly all useful sight in his right eye when injured at the siege of Calvi. Thereafter he was to wear an eye shade, although not the mythical black patch since the eye remained in its socket and there was little disfigurement.[38]

With the loss of Toulon at the close of 1793, the British had looked to the island of Corsica, held by the French, as a useful base in the Mediterranean for British ships. The town of Bastia in the north was captured successfully by a small invasion force under the command of Nelson but it was in June 1794 at Calvi, further to the west on the island that a shell had exploded dangerously close to Nelson as he supervised an artillery bombardment onshore. Sand and debris was thrown up, some of it entering his right eye, and it was this which later cost him all useful sight in that eye. It caused disability rather than disfigurement. There was little in the way of cosmetic blemish. There had, it is true, been his capture of the ship *Ca Ira* off the coast of Genoa in 1795 and the part he played in the later evacuation of Corsica in 1796, and he had achieved some transient fame for the dashing, indeed crucial role he had played in the action off Cape St Vincent in 1797 which had won him the enthusiastic support of his commander. But the public memory is short and that had been an isolated achievement later eclipsed to some extent by the abortive and costly attempt to capture a Spanish treasure ship at Santa Cruz, Tenerife, in the Canary Islands which had tarnished some of the image. In that incident he had been injured yet again and invalided home to England on sick leave in September 1797. There he had remained waiting impatiently for the severed stump of his amputated right arm to heal. In a supposedly more enlightened age such overall disability would have cost him his career in any active role. But then it may be that the physical demands made of an Admiral are perhaps not so great and it is said to be the case that the autopsy of Nelson's body eight years later showed a man healthier than his years would suggest.

But his advantage was, of course, that he had the firm and unwavering support of St Vincent, and had had this from the moment he had joined the Mediterranean Fleet in the previous year. And, after his exploits off Cape St Vincent, Jervis had stood firmly in his debt. And so, however much he may have denied it later, St Vincent now made it clear to Spencer which of his subordinates he favoured for the command, advising that Nelson was the officer who would best be able to deliver what was required. It is probable, to say the least, that Spencer would be more persuaded by this recommendation than by any other for St Vincent was probably in the best position to know as the commander on the spot. This Lord Fisher was to misunderstand when he wrote the letter that he did referring to this episode 116 years later. It is true that Sir John Orde had the ear of the Government for his brother Thomas was at that time close enough to William Pitt, but then his relationship with Spencer, although reasonable enough, had not been all too comfortable.

Nelson had the enthusiastic support too of his friend from Corsican days, the respected and persuasive Sir Gilbert Elliot, later to become the Lord Minto, the Scots ex-Viceroy of Corsica, who lost no opportunity to sing his praises in the drawing rooms of London.[39] And the First Lord too was bombarded with Elliot's advice, for it will be remembered that Nelson had evacuated Elliot from Corsica before the battle of St Vincent. He and Colonel John Drinkwater had then been guests of Nelson on the *Minerve* before transferring to the frigate *Lively* for the passage home. So it was that Elliot was able to witness Nelson's performance at the battle which caused him to write to Nelson in euphoric terms of congratulation as soon as the battle was over.

Born at Minto in the county of Roxburghshire, across the border from Northumberland, Elliot had been educated alongside Mirabeau at the *Pension Militare*, Fontainebleau, and afterwards at Edinburgh University and Christ Church, Oxford. He was called to the Bar at Lincoln's Inn in May 1774 and then travelled the northern circuit, pleading his cases in Northumberland, Durham and the north of England generally, whilst at the same time serving as

Whig Member of Parliament for the town of Morpeth in Northumberland from 1774 until 1784.[40] That seat he lost but two years later he was returned for the town of Berwick-upon-Tweed, also in Northumberland, and then, later again, for a constituency in Cornwall. Appointed Commissioner at Toulon in 1793 he supervised the evacuation to Florence of refugees from that town when the revolutionary forces recaptured it, and so was well placed for appointment as Viceroy of the island of Corsica when it was taken by the British in the summer of 1794. It was then that he and Nelson had become such friends.

Elliot was much in favour at this time. Indeed, in October of that year, 1798, he was to be raised to the peerage as Baron Minto of Minto, and he later served for many years as Governor-General of India until suddenly and unexpectedly replaced by the Lord Moira, friend indeed of the Prince Regent.

By letter dated 28 April 1798, Elliot wrote to Nelson,

> . . . I went to Lord Spencer and told him that I could not refrain from suggesting what had probably occurred to himself, that you were the fittest man in the world for that command . . . Lord Spencer said that . . . there was no chance of any other person being thought of for the command, and that your name would certainly have been the first to have occurred to him himself. That there would be less doubt of your being appointed as it would naturally be left to Lord St Vincent to name the officer, and that I knew his high opinion of you. He added however that, in writing to Lord St Vincent on the subject, while he left the nomination to him, he should express his own opinion that you are the proper man . . . You will at least discover two motives . . . First a sincere zeal for the public service, especially in that quarter and secondly an anxious concern for all that relates to the honours and fortunes, or wishes of one who, I hope, will let me call him friend, as long as we both live . . .[41]

There was rumour that the King himself had asked for Nelson to be appointed to the command, for his third son, the Duke of Clarence, had, twelve years before in 1786 when twenty-two years of age and as Prince William Henry, commanded the *Pegasus* in the Leeward Islands on the West Indian Station and had there served with Nelson who was the senior Captain in the Squadron in the absence of the Commander-in-Chief, Sir Richard Hughes. Although they had met before in 1782 when introduced by Lord Hood on his flagship the *Barfleur*, and although Nelson had acted as ADC to the Prince on a courtesy visit to Havana, it was on this occasion that they became good friends. This was the last visit Nelson made to the West Indies until the chase of 1805, for he found the climate did not suit him and he often complained of ill health. Prince

William was undoubtedly fond of the ladies and the high life and, for Nelson, trying to keep up with the exuberant young man's round of social engagements and late nights took its toll. Added to this, certain of the officers had rebelled against the Prince's autocratic ways and had asked for courts martial. But, despite the burden this placed on Nelson as the senior Captain, he and the Prince became good friends. Indeed the Prince insisted on giving away the bride at Nelson's wedding when he married the widowed Mrs Frances Nisbet at President Herbert's house in Montpelier on 11 March 1787. Like the equally diminutive Napoleon Bonaparte he married a widow from the West Indies. Curiously the one portrait of a British commander that Napoleon was later to keep in his study was that of Nelson, not because of that event, but because he recognized in Nelson an officer of both courage and genius, like himself.

As for the Prince, he had already on many occasions by then tried to persuade his father to grant him permission to marry the lady of the moment, but without success.[42] Indeed it was precisely because he had formed an alliance with one of the daughters of the naval commissioner at Portsmouth that, at the instigation of his father, he had been appointed Captain of the frigate *Pegasus* then bound for Halifax, Nova Scotia. And from there he had been sent on to Antigua where he had arrived in the autumn of 1786. For all his faults Nelson genuinely liked the Prince and was flattered by his presence on the station and so tended to exaggerate his better qualities. Nelson had a great respect for royalty. For his part the Prince responded in full measure, applauding the concern which Nelson showed for others and his devotion to duty. This Nelson demonstrated to effect in his rigid enforcement of the Navigation Laws which placed an embargo on the use of American shipping for commerical purposes in those waters.[43] Now that they had won their independence, the American shipper was to be treated as any other foreign trader. However the loss of profit in losing the preferential terms which had previously applied caused both sides, including Nelson's commanding officer, to turn a blind eye to the law. Not so Nelson, or indeed Cuthbert Collingwood and his younger brother Wilfred, both of whom were serving on that station until Wilfred's untimely death in the year following. In this they stirred up trouble for themselves.

The Prince was no intellect and was somewhat lacking as a professional naval officer. Conscious of his birth, he was opinionated, unreliable and volatile. But he had a healthy straightforwardness, good nature and enthusiasm for the Navy, and indeed for life in general, which, coupled with quick-wittedness and an iron constitution, enabled him to perform his duties without too much criticism – although he was at times inclined to disobey the orders of his superiors in rank if those orders did not suit him, even though he had made it clear that he wanted no royal favours or special treatment! He was a friendly and popular man and he and Nelson struck up a friendship in the year 1786 to which the Prince was ever loyal. The two corresponded on a regular basis and the friendship lasted for most of Nelson's short life, with a small hiccup when the Prince dared to pay attention to Nelson's Lady Hamilton at a later date. On the eve of war in 1793, the Prince, then a Rear Admiral, had offered himself for active service as a trained naval officer, but, to his acute disappointment, Pitt, perhaps remembering an act of insubordination in 1789 when he had sailed for home contrary to orders, felt that the Government could not employ him safely in a position which his rank would command. No doubt the friendship of Charles James Fox and his cohabitation with the actress Mrs Jordan did not help in his application. Yet, to his credit, although he continued to request naval employment whilst remaining in enforced inactivity, he continued to live the life of a naval officer vicariously through the correspondence of Horatio Nelson, Cuthbert Collingwood and others, and by pursuing his interest in all questions naval. And so Nelson was to be found visiting Prince William at Plymouth when he was exiled there by his father in 1788 following the 1787 insubordination, and, before Nelson returned to the Fleet from sick leave in 1798, he was careful first to take leave of the King.

If consulted about command of the Mediterranean Squadron in 1798, therefore, the probability is that the King too gave Nelson his support. But, apart from St Vincent's request, undoubtedly the strongest backing came from Lord Spencer who had been First Lord of the Admiralty since 1794, and was no particular friend of Sir John Orde. Thus could Nelson write home to his dear wife in August of 1797, 'Lord Spencer has expressed his sincere desire to Sir John Jervis, to give me my Flag,' adding, 'I had a letter a few days since from HRH the Duke of Clarence assuring of his unalterable friendship.'[44] And then, as Nelson rested at home nursing his amputated arm and waiting for the pain to subside, St Vincent had written to Spencer in September 1797, 'I beg that Admiral Nelson may be sent to me.'[45] Indeed, whilst at home, Nelson made several calls on Spencer during his convalescence. Lady Spencer's first impression of him had not been favourable, dismissing him as an uncouth simpleton determined to upset the seating arrangements at her dinner table by insisting that he sat next to his own wife. But she changed her opinion very quickly once the brilliance of his conversation became apparent and when it became obvious too that sitting near to his wife was not just a wish to be near her because he saw so little of her, but rather because of the need for assistance in transporting food from the plate to the mouth with but one hand at his disposal to perform the operation. Indeed, Lady Spencer was later to provide an eating utensil which she had specially designed and made for him, such was her concern, and this implement he was to use constantly.[46] On 30 March 1798, the day after Nelson hoisted his flag on the *Vanguard* at Spithead, Spencer had written to St Vincent that he was very happy to be sending him Sir Horatio Nelson, which 'I have reason to believe . . . will be agreeable to your wishes.'[47] And then, the day after Nelson had reported back to St Vincent at Cadiz, St Vincent replied to Spencer (1st May), '. . . the arrival of Admiral Nelson has given me new life: you could not have gratified me more than in sending him, his presence in the Mediterranean is so very essential.' For his part, writing to his wife on 1 May, Nelson ended on a critical note, 'Sir John Orde is here giving fêtes etc., but I have no time for such things when we had better be alongside a Spaniard.'[48]

It was on 2 May that St Vincent received the expected order from the Admiralty that a new fleet was indeed to be established for service in the Mediterranean with the appointed task of hunting down, and, if possible, destroying the enemy. In a letter to St Vincent dated 29 April which gave him that instruction, the Admiralty suggested that the armament assembled at Toulon was very probably destined for Spain from which an invasion of Portugal would be launched, or, failing that, for Ireland.[49] There they were wrong on both counts. They left the choice with St Vincent himself as to whether he should take the whole of his own fleet into the Mediterranean for that task, or more constructively, establish a new squadron for that purpose with the strength of a fleet.[50] In leaving the choice to St Vincent himself, Spencer added, 'If you determine to send a detachment into the Mediterranean, I think it almost unnecessary to suggest to you the propriety of putting it under the command of Sir H. Nelson . . .'[51] St Vincent was at this time unwell and talking of retirement,[52] but his judgement had not left him, and he chose, with great good sense, not to abandon or weaken the blockade of Cadiz, especially since the Admiralty had promised to send out reinforcements if a new squadron was formed.[53] He therefore decided to detach ten 74s together with the 50-gun *Leander* commanded by Collingwood to which would be added the three ships already under Nelson's command to form the new squadron for special duties in the Mediterranean. Thus was St Vincent to release eleven of his ablest captains, including Collingwood and including also Troubridge, described by St Vincent as the 'very best sea officer in His Majesty's service' (not excepting Nelson),[54] for service in the new high-powered Mediterranean Squadron. These Captains he then placed under the independent command of Sir Horatio Nelson. Perhaps imagining himself in the part of Shakespeare's Henry V, Nelson now labelled them his 'band of brothers'. Only one of them had been at all critical of Nelson's talents and that was Sir James Saumarez who had professed dislike of Nelson's naked ambition, and had once described him as 'our desperate Commodore'. But he too was soon to be won over by the Nelson charm.

Initially Nelson was sent on his way early in May with his three sail of the line with the promise that he would be followed later by Troubridge and the ten 74s the moment the reinforcement of eight ships of the line under the command of Sir Roger Curtis joined St Vincent from the Channel Fleet.

When the choice of Nelson as chief of the new separate Mediterranean Command was made known, if not devastated, Sir John Orde was, at the very least, bitterly disappointed and wrongly saw it as a reflection on his own talents and a setback to his hope of further advancement. Both he and Parker accepted the absolute right of the Admiralty to install whomsoever they thought fit to such an important command, but, having already and so recently selected and appointed those flag officers who were to command in the Fleet and also the chain of that command, Nelson's appointment suggested to them either that they had been lured out under false pretences, or, more probably, that there had been a change of heart in high places for they were both senior to Nelson in rank. Either way it was much resented and it was the opinion of Nicholas that this was only 'natural'.[55] Had he shown proper leadership qualities St Vincent would have taken them into his confidence and discussed the situation with them on his flagship, the *Ville de Paris*, rather than allowing them to find out for themselves. The *Ville de Paris* was a first rate of 110 guns which carried 875 men. It had been built at Chatham in 1795 and then named after the French first rate which had been captured in 1782 but was subsequently lost.[56] It was Parker who first gave vent to his feelings, as he had when criticizing Nelson after the Battle of St Vincent the year before. He now went on board the *Ville de Paris*, to lodge his complaint with St Vincent. But St Vincent, somewhat disingenuously met it with the false plea that he had had no say in the appointment of Nelson which had been entirely the work of the Admiralty. Parker so reported to Sir John Orde. Indeed, St Vincent had gone on to say that he thought the preference given to Nelson over his seniors a very hard measure and such as should induce a strong remonstrance, and when Parker showed him a letter of complaint he intended to send to the Admiralty, St Vincent said that he thought it not half strong enough.[57]

Parker now proceeded to bombard the Admiralty for three months or more with letters of complaint written in terms similar to those he had used when protesting the year before at the version of events favourable to himself which Nelson had put into circulation about the part he had played himself at the Battle of St Vincent. 'I naturally expected to be sent,' he wrote, 'but the ships separated without any notice being taken of me, to be under the command of an officer very much my junior. This must necessarily be considered a doubt of my abilities or worse and I must feel it the most injurious conduct towards me and the most serious attack upon my reputation as an officer,' suggesting in

Sir William Parker, Bart

other letters that he might be allowed to transfer to another fleet rather than that he should remain with St Vincent which 'I feel degrading to me. It oppresses me and injures my health.'[58] St Vincent later turned the knife in the wound when he wrote to Parker to tell him that he had really applied for Sir John Colpoys to be his second in command and would still wish to have him.[59]

Although records of Parker's earlier career have been lost in obscurity, his later service with the Navy had been outstanding. Born in Kent he had married the daughter of Edward Collingwood in the year 1766. Their son was destined to follow him into the Navy and died a Vice Admiral. As a Commodore William Parker had been Commander-in-Chief of the Leeward Islands Station from 1787 until 1790, and then, at the onset of the celebrated battle of 'The Glorious First of June' of 1794, as a member of Howe's Channel Fleet commanding the *Audacious* of 74 guns, he had almost single-handedly put a French 120-gun ship, the *Revolutionnaire*, out of the war in a courageous action at sea. In July of that year he was rewarded for his exploits with the presentation of a medal from the King in recognition of his valour and then promoted Rear Admiral. The following February he was made Commodore-in-Chief in Jamaica with his flag flying in the *Raisonnable*. Severe illness had interrupted that command, but then, health restored, he had joined Jervis two days before the Battle of St Vincent in February of 1797. Flying his flag in the *Prince George* with command of five sail of the line, he made a telling contribution to the victory, at one point crippling the *San Josef* with murderous broadsides before Nelson ever boarded her and accepted the surrender. Hence his fury at Nelson's one-sided account of his own part in the battle which had so underplayed the performance of Parker's squadron whilst emphasizing the brilliant role which he had himself undoubtedly played. After the battle, as a newly created baronet, he had remained in the Fleet as third in command until the recall of the unfortunate Vice Admiral Thompson, which had raised him to second in command.[60] He was then fifty-five years of age, so that if either of them had a greater claim than Nelson to the new Mediterranean Command, Parker's claim on grounds of age and seniority must have been the greater.

Two years on, in the Court of Common Pleas, Parker was to bring an action against St Vincent in which he claimed for himself and for the junior Admirals in the Fleet under St Vincent their share of the Admiral's third of freight money which St Vincent had received from Captain Mansfield of the frigate *Andromada* and then kept for himself. The claim was founded on common usage in the Navy, which St Vincent steadfastly denied ever existed, but, in the result, a verdict was given for Parker and against St Vincent by the judge and jury which did nothing to improve relations between them.[61]

With hindsight, the choice of Nelson for command of the new fleet of ships was demonstrably correct and in time it was of course shown to have been fully justified. Indeed it proved to be an inspired appointment for it unleashed for the first time the brilliance of Nelson as a fleet commander and placed it at the disposal of the British nation. 'Cometh the hour, cometh the man.' And it marked the turning point in his remarkable career and ushered in seven of the most glorious years in the long and distinguished history of the Royal Navy. But to Sir John Orde it was a blow which had hurt him more than a little.

Fifteen or so years after the event, the Poet Laureate Southey wrote his pocket life of Nelson at the Lake District home of his friend Samuel Taylor Coleridge at Greta Hall, Keswick, which he had made his own in the absence of Coleridge himself. Written in majestic prose it does not at all times have a clear eye for the true facts:

> Sir William Parker,[62] who was a very excellent officer and as gallant a man of as any in the navy, and Sir John Orde, who on all occasions of service had acquitted himself with great honour, each wrote to Lord Spencer complaining that so marked a preference should have been given to a junior of the same fleet. This resentment is what men in a like case would feel; and if the preference thus given to Nelson had not originated in a clear perception that (as his friend Collingwood said of him a little while before) 'his spirit was equal to all undertakings, and his resources fitted to all occasions', an injustice would have been done to them by his appointment. But if the services were conducted with undeviating respect to seniority, the naval and military character would soon be brought down to the dead level of mediocrity.

But a second development was to follow in quick succession which was to further damage Sir John Orde's prospects. It was on 24 May that Sir Roger Curtis arrived from the Channel Fleet with the promised reinforcements – a detached squadron which he had commanded in Irish waters, which included the ship *Marlborough* to which reference has already been made. But then, to the astonishment of both Parker and Orde, Curtis was retained and appointed to the Mediterranean Fleet as second in command, thus relegating Orde, who was junior to him in rank, to fourth. Now fifty-two years of age, Curtis had a long record of service behind him. As Captain of Lord Howe's flagship, the Queen Charlotte, he had fought at the 'Glorious First of June' in 1794 and afterwards received from the King a gift of a massive gold chain on his visit to the ship at Spithead. But then the blame for Howe's failure to pursue the French had been laid by many at his door, for he had the ear of Howe at the time, and was ever a cautious and careful man. Curtis now became second to

Sir Roger Curtis, Bart

St Vincent in the Fleet.

The irony of it was that St Vincent was to condemn the officers of replacement ships joining his fleet, and their crews, as 'useless'. He claimed that it took him months to make these ships fit for active service. For instance, Captains Aplin and Ellison he described as 'useless'. In contrast, Orde who now dropped below Curtis, was an efficient officer who had fitted well into St Vincent's disciplined command.[63]

In fact, unknown to the British Government, Bonaparte had himself decided that British interests could best be damaged by striking at British trade routes to India, or indeed, at India itself, from a base which the French should seek to establish in Egypt by invasion there. His efforts were therefore bent towards persuading the Directory to authorize and mount an invasion in the Middle East. The Directory had entrusted him with their plans for the invasion of Britain nonetheless, but when he travelled to the northern shores of France and saw the situation for himself he dismissed the idea of invasion as premature and unrealistic. The force was far from ready, and, as ever, the Royal Navy stood in its way dominating and controlling the waters of the Channel. And so, unknown to Pitt's Government, Bonaparte had turned his eyes east to Egypt, the Middle Eastern states and the passage to India. His overall plan was to sail his army across the Mediterranean untroubled by the British Fleet which had withdrawn to the Atlantic, secure Malta as a strategic base on the way, and then after conquering Egypt, sweep through Turkey, then an ally of France, in the hope of promoting enough of a christian revolt there to overthrow the Ottoman rulers. He would then return to Paris absolute master of the Mediterranean and all its surrounding territories with the riches of the Orient and British India within his grasp also. Then would be the moment to plan any invasion of Great Britain, the greatest and the most obstinate of France's enemies, but one which stood alone with only the neutral and timid Portugal now left on her side and with no base left in the Mediterranean except Gibraltar, which stood dangerously close to Spain.

On 4 May, Nelson arrived at Gibraltar in the *Vanguard* where he found Sir John Orde in his flagship, the *Princess Royal*.[64] He wrote to St Vincent on 6 May that he had ordered the ships to weigh on Tuesday morning. 'Sir John Orde will know by his eye which ships go with me, therefore I shall show him the list. I do not believe any person guessed the destination . . .'[65]

Initially Nelson was sent to keep watch on Toulon and the eastern Mediterranean with his small squadron of four frigates, a sloop and two 74s in addition to his own flagship, the *Vanguard*. These were commanded by Sir James Saumarez and Captain Ball. On 20 May severe weather dismasted Nelson's flagship and drove his squadron far off station, forcing him to put in for repairs. At this moment of time, unknown to Nelson, the French Fleet under the command of Admiral Brueys, slipped out of Toulon and put to sea with thirteen ships of the line escorting Bonaparte's military expedition of 35,000 troops bound for Egypt. Captain Ball, a baldheaded, resourceful, capable and most intelligent officer, now came to the rescue of the crippled *Vanguard* and towed her into port in southern Sardinia for repairs. This was a man Nelson had disliked intensely ever since their first encounter in France when both had taken a holiday there, but this act now earned him Nelson's undying gratitude and friendship. They were to remain good friends for the seven years of life which remained to Nelson. Indeed Nelson kept up an active correspondence with Ball after he had been appointed the first Governor of Malta after it had been taken back from the French. By now Nelson had been separated from his frigates which were making for Gibraltar under the assumption that the *Vanguard* was headed there. In the weeks to come this was to prove a severe handicap to Nelson as he scanned the Mediterranean for enemy ships without the advantage of frigate intelligence.

Unlike the elevation of Napoleon to a position of high military command in France, the appointment of Nelson, when made, was greeted in many influential quarters with a mixture of surprise, incredulity, dismay, indignation and even hostility.[66] This was, after all, the key appointment upon which the very survival of the British nation could depend and here it was going to an officer of comparatively junior rank, and untried as a fleet commander. And so, as Nelson in the *Vanguard*, leading his new squadron of ships captained by his 'Band of Brothers', sailed off up the Mediterranean in search of the French Fleet, with the enormity of the responsibility placed on his all too fatigued, battleworn and fragile shoulders, so the hopes of the Admiralty, and, indeed, all England, went with him, and not without some trepidation. And as the days slipped by, and turned into weeks and then stretched into months and the French Fleet continued to elude Nelson, its destination still unknown to the British, so the fears of the British people mounted. So too did criticism of the appointment gain momentum, not least in the British press. Even Admiral Goodall, long-time friend and admirer of Nelson, was to write that he was being asked what Nelson was about. 'The French fleet has passed under his nose . . .' he wrote.[67] The fear was that he was on something of a wild-goose chase, that perhaps the French Fleet had been put up as a decoy to draw away British ships from the Channel. And out in St Vincent's Fleet a letter from one of the puisne Lords of the Admiralty was read out publicly on board the now third in command's, Sir William Parker's ship, the *Prince George*, denouncing Lord St Vincent in round terms for having sent so young a flag officer on a mission of such crucial importance.[68] There was no clamour for Nelson's withdrawal but now the claims of others who had been passed over for the command, not least those of Sir William Parker, Sir Roger Curtis and Sir John Orde, were openly being canvassed. And no one was prepared to admit or accept responsibility for the appointment of Nelson. The belief that Lord St Vincent had been responsible was scotched by St Vincent himself. He denied it categorically, and sheltered behind the assertion that he had had his orders from the Admiralty. Yet Lord Spencer, in turn, disowned this, hinting that it had been the work of 10 Downing Street. For his part William Pitt maintained a discreet and dignified silence, making no attempt to deny the rumour then in circulation that Nelson's appointment had been a royal command.

Nicholas was to write, 'It has been doubted by whom the selection of Nelson for that important service was actually made. The instructions of the 3rd of May, to Lord St Vincent, would seem to have left the matter entirely in his hands; but Lord Spencer's private letter appears, in fact, to have allowed St Vincent little discretion as he was all but ordered to appoint Nelson.' George Rose, Treasurer of the Navy, was adamant in a letter to Orde that 'Neither Lord Spencer nor Lord St Vincent were to blame; whoever made the selection of Lord Nelson had a fair and just right to do so.' The author Russell argues that in that letter Rose was seeking to protect and shield none other than William Pitt, 'who had no wish to invite the opposition of Orde's friends.'[69]

But most despondent of all was Nelson himself. The burden of such a responsibility was beginning to tell and he had too few frigates at his disposal to be able to conduct much of a search. At first he had guessed Napoleon's destination correctly for Alexandria was the only port in that part of the world capable of harbouring the French Fleet. But when he arrived there he learned that Napoleon had captured Malta,[70] plundered and ransacked the public buildings there with no resistance from the Order of the Knights of St John and so the French now had the use of its fine harbour at Valetta. Without realizing it Nelson had outsailed him. When he received this news Nelson quickly retraced his steps and raced back to Sicily. As fate would have it he left Alexandria only hours before the French Fleet arrived and proceeded to disembark their invasion force under cover of darkness. So close did they come that Napoleon was able to hear the distant sounds of Nelson's Fleet firing in signal. It was therefore not until 1 August that Nelson's frigates spotted the French Fleet at anchor in a single crescent line of formation in Aboukir Bay, the men-of-war such as the *L'Orient* too big to be able to enter the shoal waters of the harbour of Alexandria itself. Bonaparte had by now won the Battle of the Pyramids, occupied both Alexandria and Cairo and conquered Egypt. And but for his order that De Brueys should keep the Fleet at Alexandria, Nelson's chase would have produced nothing and it is entirely possible that public opinion would have demanded his withdrawal. As it was, the Battle of the Nile was to provide him with the first of his three great victories over the French.

It was not until the news of Nelson's victory at Aboukir Bay on 1 August reached London later that year, brought home by the brig *Mutine*, that wagging tongues were stilled. All criticism then abated, save from Spencer and Dundas who were concerned that Napoleon had been allowed to make good his landing and conquer Egypt unmolested.[71] Nelson was denied the Viscountcy he so richly deserved but he was raised to the peerage as Baron Nelson of the Nile and Burnham Thorpe. And the rejoicing at home was great. A close friend of his, Alexander Davison, even commemorated the battle in a tangible and permanent way at his Swarland Hall estate north of Morpeth in the county of Northumberland which he had purchased only three years before, by putting down a large plantation of trees in carefully located groups to represent the battle formation of the two Fleets. Born at Lanton House, Kirknewton, Northumberland, it was whilst operating in Quebec as a shipowner, military agent and government inspector in partnership with his brother that he had come to know Nelson well in his early days in 1782. Indeed he had had such influence with Nelson that he was the one person who had been able to dissuade him from sacrificing his career for the sake of a marriage to the daughter of one Colonel Simpson, a Provost Marshal in the Garrison.[72] Back in London the two would often meet at Davison's rooms in Lincoln's Inn and Nelson was to retain him as his agent for prize monies due and as treasurer of his affairs.[73] After Nelson's death, such was his devotion that he erected an obelisk at Swarland privately with a dedication recording a friendship of many years, later relocated on its present site on the west of the A1 road when the hall was demolished.[74]

When, two and a half years later in 1801, the news of Nelson's second, albeit lesser, victory as second in command at Copenhagen, filtered through, claims that they had been responsible for Nelson's appointment back in 1798 then began to surface. And these gained further momentum after the glorious victory at Trafalgar four years on when there were many falling over themselves to claim the credit. Such is human nature which is one of the few unchanging factors in a very changing world. It is not uncommon for a newly appointed judge to be told by ten or a dozen solicitor clients that it was he who provided the judge with his first brief and so set him on his way at the Bar towards the Bench.

And so, as was to be expected, St Vincent wrote in a letter to Nelson dated 27 September after the news from Aboukir Bay had reached Cadiz, 'God be praised, and you and your gallant band rewarded by a grateful country for the greatest achievement the history of the world can produce.' And then, equally predictably, he referred to the allegations which had been made by Orde and Parker concerning Nelson's appointment for which St Vincent now claimed the entire credit: '. . . the original sin was appointing you to command the detached squadron, the event of which has proved that my judgement was correct . . .'[75] 'The Duke of Clarence,' says Sir Edward Berry, in a letter to Lord Nelson dated London, 30 December 1798, 'insisted I would tell you from him that it was the King that sent you with the Squadron up the Mediterranean, and formed the whole plan. I believe it seriously.'[76]

Nelson's own word on the matter of the appointment was not received until the year 1801. On 6 July of that year, Sir John wrote to Nelson that:

I yesterday called ineffectually in Lothians, to offer you personally my sincere congratulations on the many marks of distinction which your eminent services have obtained. An act of attention due from me as a member of the community you have so much benefited; as an officer in that service you have contributed so highly to distinguish; and one greatly interested in your welfare. I felt true satisfaction in acquitting myself of it by the first opportunity that presented since our meeting in Gibraltar. I wished also to offer you for your perusal a copy of the correspondence which passed between me, the Board of Admiralty, Lord Spencer, and Lord St Vincent, on a subject where your name is implicated, and to add my verbal assurances to its ample testimony, that though I complained, as I must still do, of the preference given your Lordship over me, yet that I did so, merely in consequence of my seniority, and some peculiarities in my situation, and without the slightest intention of derogating from your great sufficiency, which I shall ever feel true satisfaction in acknowledging . . . This Correspondence also indisputably shews the good ground of my subsequent difference with Lord St Vincent and the cause of my return to England were totally unconnected with your Lordship's nomination . . . I have the honour to be, with great condescension and regard . . .[77]

By letter dated 7 July, delivered by the hand of Captain Parker, Nelson thanked Orde for his 'kind and friendly letter . . . [and] congratulations,' adding, 'I never did try to supplant anyone, or ever pushed myself beyond a laudable ambition to try and get forward, and having no friends or connections to assist me, that I never thought any person would say a word against me, much less you an old and friendly acquaintance, who I never did, or would wish to do any injury to in my life . . . Hoping soon to have the pleasure of meeting you . . .'[78]

In a further letter of the 13th Sir John wrote that he had 'found difficulty in reading your letter sent by Captain Parker . . .' but he reassured Nelson that in the correspondence with St Vincent and the Admiralty, he had been very far from saying anything against Nelson.[79]

In a more legible reply, Nelson wrote, 'I return your pamphlet with many thanks for the perusal. I cannot but see clearly the cause of Lord St Vincent's differences latterly with you – they evidently took their rise from my being sent up in the Mediterranean . . .' And then this, 'I can assure you on my word of honour, that neither Earl St Vincent nor Lord Spencer were the original cause of my being sent to the Mediterranean. The arrangement was made in April 1797, a year before I was sent . . .'[80] This clearly suggests that Nelson knew with whom the responsibility lay and that it lay in high places, although it is a little difficult to accept that the decision had been made one year earlier, long before forces had begun to assemble at Toulon or the emergency had arisen. *Quite*

In yet another letter to Orde dated 25 July, Nelson advanced what he stated was his belief that it was his extensive knowledge of Italy and the Italian Coast which had prompted his appointment![81]

In 1798 the appointment of Nelson had been far from supported universally, and the claims of others, including Sir John Orde, had been real, albeit they have long been forgotten in the light of the Nile, Copenhagen and Trafalgar. On New Year's Day of the year 1802, Sir William Parker died in a fit of apoplexy.[82]

Why should Nelson know anyway?

Notes

[1] Orde Correspondence.
[2] *Bell's Pedigrees.*
[3] Orde Papers.
[4] ND, p. 91.
[5] *Letters from the Lower Deck*, p. 352.
[6] Gardiner, pp. 192-3.
[7] DNB and ND, p .68.
[8] ND, p. 91.
[9] Orde Correspondence.
[10] Orde Papers.
[11] ND, p. 107.
[12] Dillon, Vol I, p. 193.
[13] Dillon, Vol I, p. 194.
[14] Orde Papers.
[15] Orde Papers.
[16] Orde Papers.
[17] Orde Papers.
[18] ND, p. 108.
[19] Orde Papers.

20 Orde Papers.
21 ND, p. 109.
22 Spencer Papers, p. 208.
23 Spencer Papers, pp. 208-9.
24 Duggan, p. 123.
25 Orde Papers.
26 Orde Papers.
27 Orde Papers.
28 ND, p. 70.
29 Letters of George III 1584; Ralfe.
30 Orde Papers.
31 Letters of George III 1584 and 1591.
32 Ralfe, Vol II, p. 64.
33 ND, p. 91.
34 Spencer Papers, pp. 416-17.
35 ND, p. 71.
36 *The Naval Miscellany*, Vol I, p. 291.
37 JA, p. 208.
38 N Mar, p. 19.
39 N Brad, p. 169.
40 DNB.
41 JA, p. 208; JT, p. 350.
42 Fulford, p. 108.
43 N Mar, p. 18.
44 NE, p. 110.
45 N Brad, p. 169.
46 N Brad, p. 170.
47 N Brad, p. 170.
48 N Naish, p. 395; NN, III, p. 12; J Ber, p. 150.
49 Park, p. 59.
50 N Brad, p. 174; N Hol, p. 117.
51 NN, III, p. 24; Park, p. 59.
52 Park, p. 60.
53 Park, p. 59; N Hol, p. 120.
54 N Brad, p. 175.
55 NN, III, p. 25.
56 ND, p. 65.
57 Orde Correspondence; Ralfe, p. 55.
58 Spencer Papers, III, p. 27; J Ber, p. 160.
59 Orde Correspondence.
60 DNB.
61 Ralfe, Vol II, p. 55. Parker v S^r V prize money
62 NS, p. 118.
63 Park, p. 60.
64 NN, III, p. 12.
65 NN, III, p. 13.

[66] N Walder, p. 257.
[67] N Brad, p. 186.
[68] NC & M; N Hol, p. 126.
[69] NJR, p. 26.
[70] Park, p. 61.
[71] Ehrman, III, p. 147.
[72] N Mar, p. 17; NWH, p. 123.
[73] NWH, pp. 110 and 167.
[74] NWH, p. 140; DNB.
[75] NN, III, p. 84; N Kerr, p. 169.
[76] NN, III, p. 25.
[77] N Pet, p. 108; Orde Papers.
[78] Orde Papers.
[79] N Pet, p. 110; Orde Papers.
[80] N Pet, p. 112.
[81] Orde Papers.
[82] Ralfe, Vol II, p. 56.

CHAPTER X

THE CONFLICT DEVELOPS

Despite two such great disappointments, Sir John Orde had thus far uttered no word of complaint, but then events, from his point of view, took a more serious turn for the worse when a third and more damaging broadside was fired in his direction.

DESBOROUGH AND THE MARINES

Later in that month of May a most unfortunate and very childish squabble arose between Sir John and Lord St Vincent. But, trivial though it undoubtedly was, plainly it soured for evermore a relationship which had until then been cordial enough, and it was the precursor of much trouble to come. It is often thus. It came about in this unfortunate way.

One Lieutenant Colonel Desborough of Marines, then thirty-nine years of age and destined to remain in the rank of Lieutenant Colonel for the rest of his life in the Army, was ill-advised enough to write St Vincent a blunt letter in explanation of conduct by a certain marine under his command who had been sent on board the brig *Mutine* which had been captured from the French the year before.[1] For some reason never explained St Vincent wrongly assumed that that letter had been written by Sir John Orde, although it had been signed clearly enough by Desborough. Sir John was therefore surprised, to say the least, to receive a letter of reprimand from St Vincent dated 22 May in which St Vincent wrote: 'I do not look to an Admiral whose flag is flying on board any ship under my command, for the conduct and economy of her . . . nor do I think an Admiral should interfere in such matters, as the one alluded to in your letter . . . Without entering into the merits of Captain Hardy's representation respecting the marine in question, it would be the height of injustice to admit the testimony of a private marine against him in the case, and I am persuaded, after a little consideration, you will see the impropriety of the letter you addressed to me on the subject . . . I subscribe to Don Juan de Langara's creed that the whole system of discipline is comprised in one word – obedienza; . . . I assure you any jealousy or suspicion you may have harboured is totally unfounded . . .'[2] Don Juan de Langara, then sixty-eight years of age, was the Commander-in-Chief of the Spanish Fleet which crowned a long and distinguished career.[3] By letter of the same date Sir John quickly disowned even the slightest knowledge of the letter. When, after two or three days, his disclaimer had produced no response from St Vincent, Sir John took the initiative himself and went on board the *Ville de Paris* and there confronted his commander on his quarter deck. To Sir John's astonishment St Vincent at once admitted that he had not read Sir John's letter, and once again accused him of writing a letter in 'a very improper style'. Sir John very naturally protested that he had not been the author of the offending document. And yet St Vincent still insisted that he was. The matter was so easily resolvable by consulting the letter itself that Sir John then asked St Vincent to show it to him as tangible proof of his accusation. Thus, put on the spot, St Vincent went below, and then, some five minutes later reappeared much chastened and sought Sir John's forgiveness: 'I ask you ten thousand pardons, the letter is from Lieutenant Colonel Desborough of Marines.' Perhaps foolishly Sir John sought to explore the matter further for St Vincent was obviously embarrassed and, indeed, annoyed at being shown up. And so, with, 'I have begged your pardon, I can hear no more, no explanation or discussion,' St Vincent turned on his heel and went below.[4] Sir John later attempted to salvage the position by writing to St Vincent on 27 May a letter which assured him of his complete loyalty. Indeed a letter from St Vincent dated 27 May concerning a wholly unrelated matter, would suggest that they were still on perfectly amicable terms '. . . I seize the earliest moment to return you my best thanks for your masterly reports, relative to the crews of Her Majesty's ships, *London* and *Hector*; and I very much approve the consideration you had for three young gentlemen, rated Midshipmen in the *London* . . .' Orde had requested that they be kept in that rank, although incorrectly rated as such. With it he returned the letter which St Vincent had written him. St Vincent replied to Sir John's letter on 28 May, with, 'The return of my letter, written under a thorough mistake, does equal honour to your head and heart. The reply you made is returned unopened . . .' And yet, despite the obvious misunderstanding involved and the sure triviality of it all it was to poison relations between them for the rest of their very long lives, for St Vincent did not like to be questioned or doubted.

These three developments now caused Sir John, very foolishly, to put pen to paper. In a letter dated 16 June he complained to Lord Spencer of both the appointment of Nelson to the independent command, and of the installation of Curtis as second in command of the Fleet, thus 'lowering me to fourth – I must say I am not surprised at those measures,' he wrote, 'although very different from what I hoped to have experienced, but I cannot conceal from your lordship how much I feel hurt, at the former in particular . . .' although he went on to reassure Spencer of his wish to serve his country.[5]

Anxious not to go behind his commander's back, on 18 June Sir John went on board the *Ville de Paris* to show St Vincent a copy of the letter he had written to Spencer. He found there that St Vincent had lady guests in for dinner and so the opportunity did not arise. As the hour for dinner approached, therefore, and in the presence of his guests, Orde drew St Vincent to one side in his cabin and told him of the hurt he felt at the preference shown to Nelson. St Vincent responded to this by assuring Sir John that he had had no part in the appointment, that it had been the work of the Admiralty, supported by a private letter from Spencer which he had shown to Parker, and he went on to say that Parker had been writing letters about it and would therefore have to be recalled. To some extent this satisfied Sir John, relieved that he still had the confidence of his commander at any rate.[6] Indeed St Vincent wrote to Sir John two days later on 18 June to say that Sir John's letter to Spencer 'expresses precisely what I should have done in similar circumstances; for I never was blessed with prudence and forbearance; at the same time, it must be acknowledged, those who are responsible for measures, have an undoubted right to appoint the men they prefer to carry them into execution. You have a just claim to my entire approbation of your persevering services during the winter blockade of Cadiz.'[7] St Vincent's choice of words suggests that harmony still prevailed at that moment in time, but it is probable that he had by then resolved in his mind to rid his command of both Parker and Orde, for he was not a man who liked to be crossed. Certainly the storm clouds were looming.

CAPTAIN DRAPER

Further misunderstanding was now to arise. A few days later one Draper, Captain of Sir John's flagship, the *Princess Royal,* was summoned on board the *Ville de Paris* to be severely reprimanded by St Vincent for sending a sick man to hospital in Gibraltar and also for not making more sail when approaching the Fleet. When Draper then tried to explain that it had been done on the orders of Sir John, he was told that it was not the concern of a flag officer and to 'hold (his) tongue and at (his) peril say a word in reply.'[8] In fact Captain John Draper had some experience at sea. He had taken part in 'The Glorious First of June' four years earlier as a Lieutenant in Lord Howe's Squadron and had been promoted Captain in the year following.[9] When reported to Sir John, he considered the reprimand of Draper most unjust and said as much to his friends Sir Robert Calder and Captain George Grey. But they advised, perhaps wisely, that it would probably not be in Draper's best interests to take it up with St Vincent, and this Draper seemed to accept. Sir John did not therefore pursue it.[10]

Captain Grey was a Northumbrian too and a compatriot in whom he could confide. He was the third son of General Sir Charles Grey, who was, in turn, the second son of Sir Henry Grey, owner of Howick on the far north-east coast of Northumberland who had been created a baronet for services to the county as High Sheriff. His son General Grey had, however, won more national fame as a Major General in the American War of Independence, so much so that he had been appointed military commander of the British forces, although before he could take up his command the war had ended. General Grey had then come to know Sir John Jervis well when they commanded, respectively, military and naval contingents of a joint expeditionary force against the French West Indies islands then in revolt in the years 1793 and 1794, and they found they were able to work together in perfect harmony; and because of the knowledge of naval matters he gained on that mission and the high regard in which he was held by the Admiralty, when the Nore Mutiny erupted in 1797, General Sir Charles Grey was placed in command of Sheerness and held also command of the southern district which comprised the counties of Kent, Sussex and Surrey.

For his services he was raised to the peerage by Addington in 1801 as Baron Grey of Howick in the County of Northumberland, and then, in 1806, he was advanced a further step in the peerage to become Viscount Howick and Earl Grey. The following year he died at Howick at the age of seventy-eight.

Captain Grey's career was somewhat less dramatic, but perhaps because of his father's association with Jervis, he became one of St Vincent's favourite Captains, and later, as an Admiral, was appointed Superintendent of the dockyard at Portsmouth with a baronetcy.[11] His wife was the daughter of Samuel Whitbread and a close friend of William Wilberforce, but his most famous connection was of course his older brother Charles, the celebrated Grey of the Reform Bill who later succeeded to the Earldom. As a somewhat diffident, studious, almost intellectual and certainly reluctant politician who represented the Northumberland constituency in the House of Commons, Charles Grey was nevertheless a most eloquent speaker, a great orator and a powerful ally for any cause he supported. But Fox and his colleagues in the Whig Party found it extremely difficult to prise him away from his beloved Howick, the home by then of his Uncle Henry, the more so when, to his dismay, his father accepted a peerage which would inevitably, and in the not too distant future, put an end to his political career in the House of Commons. Thus did he absent himself from Parliament for many months at a time. At all events, when Sir John spoke to his brother Captain George Grey of his concerns, he knew that here was a sympathetic ear.

BRENTON'S EXPEDITION

And then, early in July, there arose a more serious quarrel which demonstrated the rift which was now opening up between these two Admirals. With his knowledge, recently obtained first-hand, of the mutiny in the Fleet, Sir John had been more than a little concerned to learn before coming out that the ship fitted out for his flag, the *Princess Royal*, had been allocated a crew which was both Irish and of bad reputation. He had made representations about this to Lord Spencer, but to no avail. Then, on joining the Fleet, St Vincent had transferred men from the *Romulus* to the *Princess Royal* who were also mutineers but of English and Scottish descent in the hope of fragmenting and disrupting any plan for mutiny. But this scheme had not worked. Reports of successes in Ireland and the arrival of Sir Roger Curtis's ships from the Irish Station had encouraged the crew to rise. Their plan had been simple – murder the officers and then take over the ship and, indeed, other ships in the Fleet, before sailing for Irish waters in aid of the Irish cause. Fortunately for Sir John the plot was discovered, although only two hours before it had been due to be put into effect. Six men were tried for conspiracy, all were found 'Guilty' and five of these were executed the following day on board the *Ville de Paris*. In his report to the Admiralty, St Vincent had commended Sir John highly for the way he handled the trouble. Central to Orde's policy when dealing with mutineers on his own ship had been the need to promote and support respect for their officers by members of the crew. But, ironically, this was to bring him into yet further conflict with his Commander-in-Chief when St Vincent published in his Public Orders of 14 July that 'It is very painful to the Commander-in-Chief to have occasion to pass public censure on many of the officers who commanded boats of the Fleet this morning, by whose misconduct, a brilliant coup has been missed, and a disgrace brought on His Majesty's arms. In future the Lieutenants of this duty are to be selected, and none but officers of approved firmness employed, who will be sure of their reward for any successful enterprise they exhibit.'

In reply Sir John sent Lieutenants Duffey and Nowell over to the *Ville de Paris* to present Sir John's compliments to St Vincent and to enquire as to whether it was being alleged that they were amongst those who had conducted themselves ill, for they were the two officers who had commanded the boats provided by Sir John's flagship, the *Princess Royal*. The reply came that none had done their duty apart from those officers who had been provided by the *Ville de Paris*, the *Coloffus* and the *Marlborough*. Not content with such a blanket and general condemnation which included those two officers from his own command, Sir John and Captain Draper proceeded to question each of them closely as to their conduct after which they could but acquit them of any blame. And then, with perhaps more courage and loyalty than tact and diplomacy, Sir John sent the result of his enquiry to St Vincent, delivered by the hand of the officers concerned, so that the Lieutenant who had been in charge of the foray of the previous night, one Brenton, could be confronted with the facts. Those facts were that St Vincent had ordered each ship to send a cannonade and a rowing boat to the mouth of the harbour at Cadiz to prevent the ship *La Vestale* from breaking out. At dawn, when Brenton had ordered the boats to return to their ships, a division of Spanish gunboats had come out and taken possession of the launch which had been sent by the *Prince George*. This they had been able to do since the crew of the boat had fallen asleep and the Midshipman of the boat lying nearest them had decided to leave them there as a practical joke whilst the others pulled back to their ships! Brenton had then ordered other boats to go to the rescue, and his later allegation was that some within earshot had failed to do so, whilst some of Brenton's own men were killed as they retreated. However Sir John's officers were quite adamant that they had responded to the call and were in fact amongst the few who had got nearest to the Spanish gunboats during the contest.

Needless to say, the two Lieutenants were not permitted to see either Brenton or St Vincent who wrote Sir John a public letter to make it clear that he stood by Brenton's original report. With it he enclosed a private note to the effect that the officer who should have been sent to wait on him was Captain Draper, and not the Lieutenants since it was Captain Draper who had chosen them for the assignment. Instead of letting the matter drop there and holding his peace, Sir John continued to back his own officers and, perhaps foolishly, replied in a public letter that he had taken the course he did rather than that the two officers concerned should have to call for a court martial to clear themselves. And in a letter marked 'Private' he wrote that

> I cannot allow my public conduct has been informal, or questionable, in the smallest degree [as St Vincent had suggested] . . . I must assert my claim, on every principle and practice of the service, to make a direct application to your Lordship, as Commander-in-Chief, on such occasions, if I judge it best; . . . justice to the . . . officers, in my opinion, seems to entitle them to be thought innocent, till proved guilty . . . I should not have

expected any officer would have been turned from your ship unheard, when sent by me, and on the most liberal errand . . . I am aware of the duty imposed by the present awful moment on every good subject, as well as soldier, to avoid all appearance of difference with a superior that might give encouragement to the disaffected; I will try a more cautious conduct (if possible) to avoid being misunderstood by your Lordship in future, either in my words or actions.[12]

It should be appreciated that Jaheel Brenton was very much a favourite of St Vincent at this time. Born in Rhode Island, he later rose in the service to become a baronet in 1812, Lieutenant-Governor of Greenwich Hospital as a Rear Admiral in 1831 and a Vice Admiral before he died in 1844.[13]

It may well be that the Lieutenants concerned would have preferred it if they had not been identified by Sir John. But matters had gone so far that, by Captain Draper, each now applied to St Vincent to order either a court of enquiry or a court martial as to their conduct. These applications they then delivered in person. St Vincent received them on this occasion, read their applications, described them as very improper, said that there was no answer and told Nowell that he would not order any court martial and advised him to 'take care of himself in future'. There the matter had to rest but it was another nail in the coffin of Sir John Orde as a flag officer in any fleet under the command of Lord St Vincent.

SIR JOHN'S COMPLAINT

It could be argued that Orde was himself responsible for now bringing matters to a head for he then wrote on 31 July a most imprudent letter to his commander, in which he reminded St Vincent that it was he who had asked for Sir John's services '. . . before your going to the West Indies, when we were at Liphook (my brother, and, I believe Mr Purvis present); and again before your sailing to the Mediterranean when we met in the Haymarket (Sir R. Calder with you)',[14] that he had in St Vincent's own judgment acquitted himself well, that despite that it had been Nelson who had been given command of the Mediterranean Squadron, that word had reached him from members of the Board of Admiralty that they had nothing to do with the appointment and were not even aware of it until it had been announced in letters from St Vincent; and that St Vincent had even disclosed in a letter to Sir William Parker that he had applied for Sir John Colpoys to come out as second in command when Parker quit the Fleet as he was now anxious to do – presumably rather than allow Sir John to move up to third or second place. Not surprisingly St Vincent replied by letter on the same date,

> The moment you communicated to me the letter you sent Lord Spencer [presumably that of 16 June], I considered it impossible, you could remain an hour longer in this fleet, than was necessary to make other arrangements, and I did not choose to leave it to the Admiralty who should be sent out to me. Sir W. Parker, to whom I communicated the letter I received from Lord Spencer, touching the employment of Sir H. Nelson, knows that I had no share in that transaction. I certainly feel myself under no sort of engagement to you under the quotation, of what I admit to have passed in presence of the persons you mention; at the same time that I shall be glad of any opportunity to hear testimony to your merits as an officer.

And, by a letter dated the following day, he added '. . . had you attended to the earnest wish I expressed, that you should not remonstrate against the measure of putting the detached squadron under the orders of Rear Admiral Sir H. Nelson, you must eventually have succeeded to the command of this fleet, for, my health will not admit of my continuing in it many months longer.'[15]

Sir John replied on 1 August that he had

> only served since His Majesty honoured me with flag, in consequence of invitation from the Admiralty, and, my own sense of duty to my country when considered in danger, and from no interested views; and I shall be most ready, when duty called upon, to relinquish the situation I hold, although from public motives I did not request to do so . . . in the letter I wrote . . . to Lord Spencer . . . which you said was precisely such an one, as you would have written had you been in my situation . . .

By letter of the same date St Vincent replied '. . . I . . . desire I may not be further interrupted in my public duty, by a correspondence which leads to no measure of service; and I have further to add, in consideration of your convenience, that I shall not wait for the decision of the Admiralty to order you to England, the moment I can spare a ship for your accommodation.' By letter dated 12 August, St Vincent informed Spencer of his intention, writing that 'Sir John Orde has conducted himself in such a manner towards me that I shall send him to England in the first ship that I can spare . . . times are critical and dangerous . . . Faction must be suppressed . . . where is the Commander-in-Chief to be found who will be responsible for the conduct of a fleet in the competent blockade of an enemy's port if one half the force which may be opposed to him by the enquiry at any hour . . .' He added for fair measure, 'The Captains Aplin and Ellison are drivellers and there are others in the squadron totally unfit to command ships of war in these times.'[16] It will be remembered that Ellison was the Captain of the *Marlborough* who had dared to question St Vincent's handling of the mutineers.

Given the turn of events over the previous three months, it can be appreciated that St Vincent would perhaps have found it difficult to continue his service with the Mediterranean Fleet with Orde as his second or third in command. They had quite simply fallen out and the memory of it could never be eradicated. The fault clearly lay in some part with Sir John himself who had foolishly, petulantly and out of pride allowed himself to protest at the appointment of Nelson at a time of national emergency, especially since the man appointed turned out to be so unusually and exceptionally qualified and suited for the difficult task which he was called upon to perform. And he was afterwards to regret his outburst bitterly. But then he was undoubtedly a proud man with a distinguished record of service behind him. Still more ill-advised had he been to put pen to paper, thus recording for posterity and in a tangible form the fact of his discontent. Especially so when it should have occurred to him that the commander under whom he had to serve and to whom he was answerable, must himself have had a large say in the appointment. And since he had also in those same letters sought to expose and make public injustices in the Fleet for which St Vincent was responsible, the correspondence as a whole could perhaps be regarded as provocation amounting almost to insubordination which should never have been written. At the same time the handwritten word was the only means of communication over a distance in those far-off days and officers at sea therefore became prolific letter-writers and Sir John's conduct had never suggested any refusal to obey orders or any impropriety on any front which could possibly have justified his summary expulsion from the Fleet – especially given his rank and status. A less autocratic, self-centred and rigid man than St Vincent would have dealt with the obvious hurt to Sir John's pride in a more diplomatic and sensitive way, for his prospects had not in truth been damaged by the appointment of Nelson. It was a terrible and a draconian step to take.

On 18 July Lord Spencer replied to Sir John Orde's letter of 16 June, in which his complaints had first been made. He wrote that he was

> . . . sorry to find any event has happened to make you feel less comfortable in the situation in which you are placed, than it is my wish every officer should feel, as far as circumstances will allow it. With regard to the . . . detachment of Sir H. Nelson, I cannot say that it strikes me in the same

light that it does you; nor can I conceive why it should not appear natural, that a younger Rear Admiral, in a two decked ship, lately come out of dock, should be sent with two sail of the line on a service of that nature; and having been sent, that it was not judged expedient when circumstances made it necessary to reinforce him, to send an officer senior to him, especially, as his seniors were all in ships less calculated for detached service. As to the arrival of Sir. R. Curtis, the very peculiar circumstances under which that Squadron was detached from home, sufficiently point out, that it was a matter of mere necessity, and not of any arrangement calculated to displace you from a station, in which your conduct has been approved by the Commander in Chief; undoubtedly, nothing but that kind of necessity would have occasioned such a measure . . . I have more satisfaction in acknowledging the handsome manner in which your sentiments respecting the service of your country, at this period, are expressed. Continuing to act on that principle, you cannot fail to deserve all the credit which is due to a zealous and active officer, and all the satisfaction that must infallibly attend on consciousness that you are performing your duty to the public. I am, with great truth, Spencer.[17]

Thus did Lord Spencer, with some diplomacy, react to Sir John's complaint. He was not of course to know that St Vincent had by then resolved to send him home.

Before departing the Fleet, Sir John, in a long letter dated 14 August in reply to Lord Spencer's, accepted that sending Curtis out to the Fleet gave no real cause for complaint. And he added, 'Nor could Admiral Nelson's being detached with three sail of the line be considered unnatural.' However, he then went on to quarrel in his letter that Nelson had later been reinforced with a further eleven or twelve such ships together with many frigates and smaller vessels which left other Admirals off Cadiz with but a few whilst he went off

on a service of the greatest national importance, I might say of the greatest eventual importance to the world . . . certain to produce comparisons in all quarters, destructive to the character and credit of the officers so passed by . . . since I have had the honour of being known to your lordship, the fates have turned against me: before they had been generally favourable . . . I had been invited to serve by your lordship, through Lord H. Seymour, and twice by Lord St Vincent to serve under his command; . . . If, . . . since leaving England I have acted unworthily, or manifested an unfitness for command, then I ought not to complain, but only seek to know in what I have failed, in order to correct my conduct, or to retire; but if (as I trust will be the case) I am found, on the contrary, to have performed the various duties allotted to me, as an officer ought . . . I have been cruelly and unkindly dealt with . . . I shall not, at present, say more respecting any situation and intentions, except, that when I arrive in England . . . I will make known the cause of discontent to which I allude, and probably I may be compelled to call on your Lordship for investigation of subjects, which delicacy now forbids my mentioning.[18]

In this latter he was to be as good as his word! Writing as he did Sir John had clearly subordinated concern for the national interest to thought only for his own private grievances.

It was on 24 August that word came from St Vincent by Captain Draper that Sir John was to transfer to a named ship for the journey home and to do so within twenty-four hours. It was the order of a man in a rage. Sir John then had it reduced to writing so that he would be able to cite it at an appropriate time, before he replied that 'Ignorant as I am of the cause and object of any intended removal, I shall only say, I will prepare to embark on board any ship your Lordship may be pleased to direct to receive my flag, at the shortest notice, and in half the time you are pleased to allow in your message, if needful. I purpose to take with me, under your Lordship's offer, my servants and band . . .'[19]

St Vincent now appointed Rear Admiral Frederick to take over Orde's flag and moved the Captain of the *Blenheim*, one Dixon, into the *Princess Royal* as its Captain.[20] Later that same year he transferred Draper to a half-manned and defective frigate, but Draper survived the ordeal for he returned to command a 64, the *Ruby*, in Gambier's Baltic Squadron and in the Tagus in 1807, and was afterwards appointed agent for prisoners before he died in 1813.[21]

Late in August, a report from a fellow Admiral reached him that St Vincent was accusing some of his officers of conspiracy in allowing certain mutineers to escape the death penalty. The account was that St Vincent, whilst pacing the quarter deck, addressed Sir William Parker and his officers thus, 'By God, Sir! I will not stay here any longer. Never were such sentences awarded as the two last sentences but one; I have read the minutes. Did not the sailor say he would beat the Sentinel as soon as he quitted his post? But I know the reason for all this; the members have entered into a conspiracy or combination against me for the orders I have given respecting the marines. By God! I will stay here no longer to be so served.'[22]

Yet again Sir John put pen to paper on 26 August thus:

An officer, high in rank and character in the fleet under your command, has acquainted me, that your Lordship, a few days ago, expressed to him, in very strong terms, your disapprobation of the sentences awarded by . . . two courts-martial . . . held here: and that . . . you believed the members, of which I was one, on each occasion, to have been influenced in their decisions by the effects of a combination, or conspiracy, you stated they had entered into against your Lordship, for the measures you had pursued respecting the marines . . . I am incapable of an unofficer like proceeding, or of being actuated by such unworthy motives as appear to have been imputed to me . . .

To this letter Sir John received no answer. However, he continued to receive further reprimands from St Vincent before the final order arrived on 29 August which commanded him to 'strike your flag in the *Princess Royal*, and . . . hoist it on board His Majesty's ship, the *Blenheim*.' The quarrel between the two was now far removed from any resentment which Sir John may have felt over the appointment of Nelson to the Mediterranean Command and St Vincent was clearly now taking every opportunity to censure and humiliate Sir John Orde.

In order to forestall a version of events unfavourable to himself, Orde now wrote without delay a letter dated 29 August to Evan Nepean, Secretary to the Admiralty. In it he asked that a court martial be convened so that the dispute between himself and St Vincent could be judged impartially and objectively, the more so in the hope that such an official inquiry might forestall or suspend the judgment of public opinion which could very well presume the case against him simply because he had been sent home. So too he was concerned that respect in the Fleet should not be lost to him. To meet with the formalities he had this letter delivered to St Vincent so that he might forward it to the Admiralty. St Vincent replied, 'I have not read the letter addressed to Mr Nepean, . . . nor shall I. If you think fit to close the seal, I will forward it in the first dispatch I send.' This Sir John then did, and then, at 7 a.m. on 31 August he set sail for home in the *Blenheim*, a very old and disintegrating ship no longer fit for active service, with instructions to escort a convoy of English, Portuguese and American merchantmen from Lisbon to the Downs. Thus did Sir John Orde quit the Fleet and crawl back to England. At Lisbon, he delivered a parting shot in a final letter to his Commander-in-Chief, setting out the circumstances of his dismissal for the record, adding,

The Ship, Captain, and several officers particularly assigned me by the Board of Admiralty, to be under my Command, are taken from me, contrary to my wish, and I am ordered to England with some of the officers that served with me in the *Princess Royal*, in a ship of the most

123

inferior quality and condition, when, with all due submission, there does not appear, in my judgement, from the orders I have received for my guidance, any material object of public service, to require a change so extraordinary in its nature, and so injurious in its immediate effects to my credit, character, and interests . . .

In fact the Blenheim, a 74-gun third-rater, had been commanded by Frederick at the battle of St Vincent the year before. However, it did not have happy associations for Thomas Lenox Frederick was to return to England that same year and he died in the year following at the age of fifty-nine. And Troubridge, when an Admiral, lost his life in her when she foundered off Rodriguez in 1807 and went down with all hands lost.[23] St Vincent's reply was that Sir John's letter was 'expressed in terms of insubordination that, even in these times, I did not conceive could have come from an officer of your mark'. It seems that the emergency of war had been forgotten for the moment as this squabble continued.

St Vincent then let the Admiralty know that 'I will make the best of my way to England the moment I receive orders upon this head as it would be highly unbecoming to continue in so important a trust as I now hold after a resolution taken to assemble a court martial . . . for alleged offences, knowing full well that those holding a pistol to the heads of the Admiralty, no court martial would be ordered which would remove me from the command so held at this crucial time.'[24]

The judgment must be that St Vincent was wrong in all the circumstances to order Sir John to strike his flag after all that had taken place. The wise commander would have tactfully found him another role in the Fleet to allow time for the hurt to his pride to subside. But then the correspondence generated by Sir John may perhaps have made this impossible, and, in defence of St Vincent's summary dismissal of him, it can be argued that St Vincent had been sorely provoked, and Sir John should have known that that was easily achieved. It is not at all surprising that, in time, St Vincent was to fall out with nearly every one of his contemporaries, not excepting Nelson himself, who could, at this time, do no wrong in his eyes. Ironically Nelson was for the moment oblivious to the storm which his appointment had created as he continued his search for Napoleon's Fleet.

As for Sir John, arriving back in England like a schoolboy sent home from school in disgrace, he immediately sought to salvage what he could of his pride and position by bombarding all and sundry with the injustice of it all. In the course of doing so he drew forth the hostility of some, including Nelson who had played no part in the affair. But at the same time he won favourable and supportive judgments from many others, including the Board of Admiralty who were to offer him another command. Thus did he remain in the promotion lists and eventually returned to sea in 1804, which, in turn, was to generate yet more correspondence, much of it by the hand of Horatio Nelson.

BACK IN ENGLAND

Waiting for Orde when he arrived home on the Downs was a letter from Nepean dated 10 October in which he reported the refusal of the Lords Commissioners of the Admiralty to grant his request that St Vincent's dismissal of him be considered by a court martial. Orde now made haste for London and an appointment with Lord Spencer in order to renew his request. Sir John's own account was that Spencer received him

> with a mortifying coldness, upbraiding him with a want of forbearance towards Lord St Vincent, who had not, he said, exhibited any charge against him; but on the contrary, in his Lordship's letter to the Admiralty announcing Sir John's return, 'because it was inexpedient they should serve together', he had expressed pleasure in bearing testimony to Sir John Orde's character as an officer, and hoped that the country would not be deprived of his able services. As to the Courts Martial, Lord Spencer declared the Admiralty could not grant it.[25]

The reality of it was that Sir John's predicament was of small account when compared with the need to keep the Commander-in-Chief at his station in this time of national emergency, undistracted by investigations as to his conduct in the Fleet. But Sir John was not to be put off. By letter dated 23 October he renewed his request for some sort of enquiry, expressing his 'extreme reluctance . . . to adopt the strong measure of requesting a court-martial on my commanding Admiral at such a moment as the present . . .', whilst at the same time emphasizing his admiration for Lord St Vincent, but also the need to relieve the disgrace and humiliation which he felt. His very long and involved letter ended with, 'The greatest part of my life has been devoted to the service of my country. I hope that I have done no discredit to it. I would die in it, free from blame or just attaint.' It was in reply to this last plea that the Admiralty recognized the injustice which had been done to him, but at the same time sought to smooth matters over without the need to detach St Vincent from his post. And so Nepean wrote on 2 November that 'I have it in Command from their Lordships to acquaint you, they do not consider the reasons his Lordship has assigned for sending you home, sufficient to justify the measure; and having already signified their opinion to him on that head, they do not think it necessary to take any further steps on the occasion.' The reprimand to St Vincent to which that letter referred, read:

> Their Lordships . . . can by no means approve of your sending home Sir John Orde, as the reasons given for doing so do not appear sufficient to justify the sending a flag-officer to England, it being at all times in your lordship's power to put a stop to any correspondence which you may think to be improper, they . . . therefore . . . direct that you do not in future send home any officers without receiving instructions from their lordships to do so unless some very strong and some very peculiar circumstances shall make it absolutely necessary . . . their lordships . . . assure you of their determination to support your lordship in the fullest manner, in every proper exercise of your authority, not doubting that you will see it necessary to show every proper degree of support to the flag officers serving under your orders.[26]

St Vincent did not receive that reprimand kindly, and wrote:

> I submit to the rebuke their lordships have thought fit to convey to me . . . but my pride of character is very much wounded by the censure . . denying positively, as I do, having ever treated him or any other officer, improperly, even when there were meetings and combinations to resist my regulations I found it absolutely necessary to make . . . I desire that you will state to their lordships . . . the extreme injury my reputation suffers by a sentence passed upon me without my defence being heard.[27]

Collingwood had on 22 July confided in his father-in-law in a private letter home, which was not therefore an act of insubordination, when he wrote:

> This appointment of Admiral Nelson for a service where so much honour was to be acquired, has given great offence to the senior Admiral of the Fleet, Sir William Parker, who is a very excellent officer, and as gallant a man as any in the navy, and Sir John Orde, who on all occasions of service has acquitted himself with great honour, both are feeling much hurt at a junior officer of the same fleet having so marked a preference over them, and have written to Lord Spencer, complaining of the neglect of them. The fleet is, in consequence, in a most unpleasant state; and now all that intercourse of friendship, which was the only thing like comfort which was left to us, is forbidden; for the Admirals and Captains are

126

desired not to entertain, even at dinner, any who do not belong to their ships. They all complain that they are appointed to many unworthy services, and I have my share with the rest. But I place myself beyond the reach of such matters; for I do them with all the exactness in my power, as if they were things of the utmost importance; though I do not conceal what I think of them. In short, I do what everybody else does – wish myself at home very much.[28]

Although very critical of St Vincent in that letter, Collingwood perhaps overlooked the fact that any dinner engagement involving officers of different ships would involve members of ships' crews on transport duty waiting alongside a ship with every opportunity to discuss mutinous ideas with their opposite members in those difficult times. And perhaps he was over-cencorious of St Vincent, when, after Nelson's return from the Battle of the Nile, Collingwood wrote to him that 'Our good chief found employment for me; and to occupy my mind, sent me to cruise off San Lucears, to intercept the market boats of the poor cabbage carriers. Oh humiliation! But for the consciousness that I did not deserve degradation from any hand, and that my good estimation would not be depreciated in the minds of honourable men, by the caprice of power, I should have died with indignation.' To accuse St Vincent of 'caprice of power' was to do him an injustice on this occasion for Collingwood had been sent to a spot, not far removed from the scene of the later Battle of Trafalgar, on perfectly legitimate business and did in fact encounter enemy shipping there which was engaged. In any event, his ship the *Excellent* was in need of overhaul and repair and not at that time up to campaign duties.[29]

Collingwood was to write home to his father-in-law on 3 December 1798, that the station of late

has not latterly been very agreeable . . . The disagreement between the Chief and other flag-officers, and his impetuous conduct towards several others on trifling occasions, shuts the door to the few comforts . . . to be found here . . . I could not help feeling disquietude at the many violences and innovations which I witnessed. The Admiralty, I find, have entirely disapproved of his sending Sir John Orde home; it seemed to everybody an unwarrantable stretch of power and . . . a hardy stroke at their authority in sending the officers of their appointment home . . . without even the slightest degree of misdemeanour . . . Sir John Orde is proud and carries himself very high . . . it needed not great sensibility to feel indignities. They were generally gross enough for the roughest minds . . . it would have been more judicious in him to have left the Board of

Admiralty to defend themselves and their appointments . . . The only great mortification I suffered was not going with Admiral Nelson. He [St Vincent] knew our friendship . . . but my going would have interfered with the aggrandisement of a favourite to whom I was senior, and so he sent me out of the way . . .[30]

These were not words of charity from a fellow Northumbrian, for Collingwood was an objectively fair-minded man, careful in the words he chose, and a close friend of Horatio Nelson. His sympathies lay with Orde, although these were never discussed openly even when St Vincent talked the whole matter over with him.[31]

In a letter to his Chirton cousin on 14 December he wrote of 'very few escaped the asperity of his temper . . . he treated Sir John Orde very ill . . . when two proud Dons meet, it is not difficult to find a cause of difference. I believe Sir John Orde is as zealous in the public service as himself, but in his manners and style of living there was a magnificence that the Chief was perhaps jealous of, and so in a very unprecedented way he sent him home.'[32]

On 16 December he wrote to Dr Carlyle '. . . The Chief . . . carried trifles with a high hand, took dislikes and prejudices most capriciously, and in the instance of Sir John Orde, and some of the Captains, carried his resentment of, I could never understand what, to such extremity as to send them home. Those who did not feel the effect of this caprice could not witness it without feeling a certain degree of disgust . . .'

But he returned to his criticism of St Vincent's ways two years later in 1800 when under his command in the Channel Fleet lying off the coast of Brest.

I see disgust growing round me very fast. Instead of softening the rigours of a service, which must, from its nature, be attended with many anxieties, painful watchings and deprivations of anything like 'comfort' . . . a contrary system is pursued . . . there is no exercise of the military part of our duties – no practice of those movements by a facility at which one fleet is made superior to another . . . whoever comes here ignorant in these points must remain so, for he will find other employment about blankets and pigsties, and tumbling provisions out of one ship into another.

And Anson, in his life of St Vincent, arrived at much the same conclusion over 100 years later, when he wrote, 'In his treatment of Sir John Orde . . . [St Vincent] was most probably in error',[33] whilst at the same time finding that it was not at all surprising that St Vincent took the course he did. Even Tucker, son of St Vincent's secretary and biographer of St Vincent was fair enough to concede that 'any attempt to uphold this as a wise exercise by Lord St Vincent of the discretionary power reposed in him would be infinitely more disparaging to the writer's candour or judgment, than the act itself derogated from his lordship's excellence as a commander.'[34]

Somewhat ironically, the later appointment from home of the young Sir Sidney Smith, immortalized in the defence of Acre, to a separate command in the Mediterranean independent of Nelson caused as much annoyance to St Vincent and Nelson as the appointment of Nelson had caused to Sir William Parker and Sir John Orde.[35]

And feeling amongst many officers continued to run against St Vincent for some time to come. Thus was it reported in 1800 that when it was known that St Vincent was to take over command of the Channel Fleet, a toast drunk by one of the Captains at Lord Bridport's table was 'May the discipline of the Mediterranean never be introduced into the Channel Fleet.'[36] It was an act of gross insubordination to the incoming commander, yet it seems that it was drunk without dissent. But then it has to be remembered that there was always a great rivalry between the Channel and the Mediterranean Fleets, and there is no doubt that St Vincent did at times show great kindness to offspring of sailors who had served under him who had fallen on hard times. In the crisis of 1798 his command had been a difficult and lonely one, faced as he was by an enemy on the move, mutinous elements in the Fleet and discontent amongst many of his officers.

With the rebuke they had administered it was hoped by the Admiralty that there the matter would rest and that peace would be restored. Indeed, soon afterwards Lord Spencer called Sir John in to tell him of his intention to employ him in the Channel Fleet with either the *Neptune* or the *Foudroyant* as his flagship, whichever he should choose. Brenton later wrote that these were two of the finest ships in the Service and that it would have given Orde a very good chance of succeeding to the chief command.[37] Foolishly and petulantly Sir John thanked him for the offer but said that if it was optional he would prefer to refuse it and wait for some employment more equivalent to the post he had vacated, for otherwise it could be seen as a rejection of his accusations, for he 'had suffered public disgrace: a whole fleet witnessed it', whereas 'censure of the Admiralty (on St Vincent) . . . was private.' What he required was some unequivocal 'mark of confidence' from the Admiralty. His reaction had been suicidal and overlooked the fact that this was a time of national emergency when personal feelings should have been subordinated to the national interest. At the same time, had he accepted, although it was not to be foreseen, he could well have found himself under the command of St Vincent once again, for St Vincent was later appointed to command of the Channel Fleet.

On 6 December St Vincent wrote to Nepean from Gibraltar, thanking him 'kindly for putting Mr Pitt in possession of the facts relating to certain transactions, which have been most basely misrepresented, for Sir Wm. P and Sir J.O. will not deny that I used every argument in my power to prevent them writing to Lord Spencer . . . I confess myself not christian enough either to forget or forgive those who have most unjustly condemned me, unheard. Much fitter would it have been to put me on trial.'[38]

Then, on 28 December in a further letter to Nepean, St Vincent resorted to abuse:

I hear Sir John Orde is endeavouring to write me down, and has not been over scrupulous and accurate in his assertions, which I shall take no public notice of unless you tell me it is necessary; nor will I mention his name to you, or argue after this date. Neither you, nor any of his nautical acquaintances, can be ignorant that he is not a practical seaman; neither has he the reach of sea understanding, ever to become a tactician. His abilities as Governor of a Colony, I have no doubt are transcendant. Of this you must be a competent judge, from the situation you hold in the Secretary of State's Office, the department which he was in . . .[39]

And on 28 January 1799, again to Nepean, he wrote, with some paranoia,

Sir John Orde has sent a copy of a printed case to General O'Hara, and artfully endeavoured to draw an opinion from him, in which he has failed. I am told (for I shall not deign to read his brochure) that he has printed private letters which passed between him and me, and I think it more than probable he is practising upon the sea officers under my command . . . if your Board suffers such proceedings to pass, without the most marked reprobation, you will give a coup mortel to subordination of which there is very little left.[40]

On 17 February he again returned to the attack in a further letter to Nepean.

Many thanks for your letters, enclosing Sir John Orde's narrative . . . The conversations related in it consist of misrepresentations, partial statements and gross falsehoods; more especially the two between Sir W.P. and me, upon the sentences of the two Courts-Martial, in which I stated to him confidentially what I had written to the Admiralty, viz., that I was convinced a majority of the members composing those Courts-Martial were determined to traverse as much as in their power lay, my carrying the system touching the Marines into execution; . . . Every other conversation is most abominally twisted and distorted for the express purpose of stabbing my character; and he has concealed his own acts of disobedience to any orders, and arrogant presumption in counteracting them . . . unless I discover that I am injured in the opinion of the King and his ministers, I shall certainly leave him to his own reflections – the greatest punishment which could possibly be inflicted on him.[41]

And then, eventually, in a letter written to Nepean the very next day he comes to what must have been the suspicion which had truly governed his thoughts and deeds.

Did you notice in Sir John Orde's Narrative an avowal of his having convened some of the senior Captains to sit in judgment upon my conduct towards him? You have no conception how far these meetings went; and with the exception of Sir Roger Curtis and perhaps Collingwood, I do not believe there was an officer of any standing who did not, in some sort, enter into cabals to pull down my authority and level all distinctions. I saw this clearly, and had no other card to play but to get rid of Sir John and . . . in the most summary way; and if your Board has half an eye . . . instead of a rebuke, my conduct merited silent approbation . . . unless the promulgaton of the narrative is stamped with some mark of high displeasure, no commander-in-chief or minister is safe, and you will see your humble servant much sooner than you are aware of . . .[42]

It is the letter of a man in temper who had begun to see enemies all around him, and, in particular, in Sir John, a man whose qualities as an officer he had earlier praised. Indeed the *Gentleman's Magazine* of 1824 was to comment after Sir John's death that his pamphlet had been written 'with temper and moderation'.[43] Even Brenton, close friend and staunch supporter of St Vincent as he was, noted in his life of St Vincent that 'I am bound to say, in favour of [Sir J.O.] that there are many passages in his Correspondence, which, as between gentlemen tell much in his favour; . . . that Sir John Orde was ill-advised was certain; and I happen to know, almost to positive proof, who his advisor was . . .' although he goes on to criticise Orde for demanding a court martial on his commanding officer, still more for calling him out and again for espousing the cause of the two officers under his command.[44] The Admiralty did not 'stamp on Sir John's narrative with some mark of high displeasure' as St Vincent had requested. In fact, in the general promotion which followed on 14 February 1799, Sir John became a Vice Admiral of the Blue, but not surprisingly, when further commands came up in foreign waters, he was passed over. And when he complained yet again, Lord Spencer told him that, having refused one, he did not choose to offer him another. Sir John's reply was to cite the case of Lord Hugh Seymour, who, after declining to serve under Lord St Vincent, had been appointed to a West Indian command, whilst Lord Keith, he reminded Lord Spencer, after striking his flag in the Channel Fleet because Sir Charles Thompson had been put in over his head, had, not long afterwards, been appointed to the Chief Command in the Mediterranean.[45]

Finally, after he had exhausted all the normal avenues of complaint, Sir John decided that only one course was now left open to him. He would await the return home of St Vincent and then obtain satisfaction for St Vincent was the author of his fall from grace. But here again he was thwarted in his endeavour, for, although, unbeknown to him as it was not to be reported in the *Morning Chronicle* until 21 August 1799, St Vincent had been '. . . obliged, from his bad state of health, to resign the command of the fleet to Lord Keith' on 23 June, '. . . returning to Mahon, leaving Lord Keith off Rosia Bay . . .', it was on the morning of 17 August that Sir John read in the *Morning Chronicle* that 'Earl St Vincent is arrived at Spithead from Gibraltar, extremely indisposed in health, owing to the long and unremitting attention he has given to the very fatiguing duties of his most important command. No officer has ever more gloriously illustrated the character of the British flag and we trust that he will soon recover in his native air the health which may yet be so useful to his country.' Sir John could then but wait but he too hoped that St Vincent's recovery would not long be delayed although not so that he might be of further use to his country! The *Morning Chronicle* of 19 August provided further detail when it reported that it was on 16 August that St Vincent had docked at Portsmouth 'in the *Argo* Man of War, and is put under quarantine', adding, 'The *Argo* captured in her passage from Gibraltar a valuable Spanish Merchant ship, which is also arrived.' He was to remain indisposed for an appreciable length of time with an illness diagnosed as dropsical,[46] answering to no one either at his house in town or at his country retreat at Brentwood in Essex. Sir John kept his distance whilst the older man recovered his health but then, eventually, report of his recovery reached Sir John as St Vincent left town for his Essex home, and Sir John quickly followed in search of revenge with the result set out at the start of this account. The *Morning Chronicle* of 5 October, after assuring its readers that it was 'unwilling to make any observation' on a matter so delicate, then gave its view that it was 'hard' to call out St Vincent as if he was a 'common midshipman . . . Nothing can more strongly demonstrate the absurdity of the barbarous practice of duelling.'[47] Two days later it was to climb down a little in its condemnation. Not so Nelson's wife however, who, then loyal to Nelson but a little ominously, wrote by letter dated 21 October,

> My dearest Husband,
> The public news you have by the papers, and truly my chit chat is hardly
> worth your reading, but such as it is you must accept . . . Lady St Vincent
> writes me her Lord recovers very fast. Sir John Orde has again made
> himself the subject of conversation. Matters are very properly set to
> rights by binding him over 'to keep the peace'. Every man who refuses a
> challenge exalts himself in my opinion. From all this you may suppose the
> Earl is a first rate favourite. I long to hear from you. My latest date was
> August 4th. I wonder Lady Hamilton never acknowledged all the prints I
> requested Mr Davison to send you . . .'[48]

In the years 1797, 1798 and 1799, Joseph Haydn had been engaged in much
creative composition inspired as he was by the 'Messiah' and other of Handel's
great choral works which he had heard performed on his recent and second visit
to London. When he returned to Vienna and his old position as *Kapellmeister*
to the Esterhazy family with new patrons in Prince Nicholas Esterhazy II and
his wife Princess Maria Hermenegild, Haydn had composed six uplifting
Masses to be performed in Church to commemorate Princess Maria's name-
days. Third of these was his 'Missa In Angustiis' or 'Mass in Time of
Anxiety'. Written as Nelson sailed into Aboukir Bay and the Battle of the Nile,
this came to be known as 'Nelson's Mass' in memory of that memorable
victory after the work was performed for Nelson at the Esterhazy Palace in the
year 1800. But even finer and more moving than these, and arguably the
greatest work Haydn ever wrote, was his Oratorio 'The Creation', an uplifting
masterpiece based upon Milton's *Paradise Lost* inspired as that work had been
by the Biblical version of seven days in which God created the world. It had
been performed in public for the first time in 1799. But for Sir John Orde,
meanwhile, these had not been years of creation. They had been years of
devastation and destruction.

Notes

[1] ND, p. 73.
[2] Orde Correspondence.
[3] ND, p. 72.
[4] Orde Correspondence.
[5] Orde Correspondence; Spencer, p. 450; J Bren, pp. 397-8.
[6] ND, p. 76.

[7] Orde Correspondence.
[8] Orde Correspondence.
[9] ND, p. 69.
[10] Orde Correspondence.
[11] ND, p. 70.
[12] Orde Correspondence.
[13] ND, p. 79.
[14] Orde Correspondence.
[15] Orde Correspondence; J Bren, pp. 402-3.
[16] Spencer, p. 452-3.
[17] Orde Correspondence; J Bren, p. 404.
[18] Orde Correspondence.
[19] Orde Correspondence.
[20] Orde Correspondence.
[21] ND, pp. 69 and 107.
[22] Orde Correspondence; ND, p. 94.
[23] ND, p. 94.
[24] Letter 185, Public Records Office, Kew.
[25] Orde Correspondence.
[26] J Tucker, p. 353.
[27] JA, p. 214.
[28] J Bren, pp. 425-6; DNB.
[29] J Bren, p. 434.
[30] J Ber, p. 163.
[31] CM, p. 125.
[32] CW, p. 88.
[33] JA, p. 212.
[34] J Tucker, p. 352.
[35] JA, p. 224.
[36] JA, p. 259.
[37] J Bren, pp. 395 and 408.
[38] J Bren, pp. 411-12.
[39] J Bren, pp. 414-15.
[40] J Bren, pp. 415-16.
[41] J Bren, pp. 418-19.
[42] J Bren, p. 421.
[43] *Gentleman's Magazine* for 1824, p. 277.
[44] J Bren, p. 422.
[45] Orde Correspondence.
[46] J Sher, p. 152.
[47] *Morning Chronicle*, 5 October 1799.
[48] N Naish, pp. 533-4.

CHAPTER XI

NAPOLEON'S PLANS FOR THE INVASION OF BRITAIN
1804–5

The following year, 1800, found William Pitt a sick and tired man, slowly dying from alcoholic poisoning. Never a strong man, port wine prescribed early in life by his doctors for medicinal reasons had given him a taste for strong drink. Although called to the Bar at Lincoln's Inn in 1780 not unnaturally it was to politics that he had turned, at first as Member of Parliament for the constituency of Appleby in the county of Westmoreland. For eighteen long years he had, as Prime Minister, occupied 10 Downing Street, the last seven of them with Great Britain at war with France. He had endeavoured to meet the emergency with a punishing schedule of his own. Little sleep, even less to eat and drinking to excess to help him get through, it was bound to take its toll on a none too robust constitution. At the turn of the year his government fell over the question of Catholic emancipation which he had promised the country following the Act of Union of 1800. He was succeeded by a political opponent but friend who almost worshipped the ground he walked on, Henry Addington, the son of the then fashionable doctor who had for so long ministered to his needs. For Sir John Orde too it marked the end for many a year of any lingering hope he may have had of reinstatement in the Fleet, for, paradoxically, with Addington, a most cautious man, came radical change. Spencer departed as First Lord of the Admiralty, and, to Sir John's dismay, he was succeeded by his old protagonist, the Lord St Vincent, now released from his command of the Channel Fleet so that he could join the Government. Clearly Orde's chance of service was now non-existent so long as St Vincent remained in office. In fact he did have a further role to play in the running war between those two implacable foes, France and Great Britain, but this lay some years ahead.

PEACE WITH NAPOLEON

Napoleon was now firmly in the saddle and had been so ever since the Coup d'Etat of 1799, when the Directory of France gave way to the Consulate of three Consuls of which of course he was First with the strength of the Army behind him. A man of colossal energy with a massive capacity for hard work, he could survive on very few hours of sleep. He now set about the reform of almost every aspect of French life and reshaped it for the future. Large programmes of public works were launched, the Banque of France was set up, a *Lycée* system of education was established so that the influential classes of the future could be educated in the spirit of Napoleon, the Code Napoleon and other legal codes were produced in order to establish a rule of law and a procedure within which commercial activity could operate. The list was endless. Since he was not a man who easily put pen to paper, he kept about him at all hours of the day and night, subordinates able and willing to match his own programme of work, recording and collating and transcribing and implementing the flow of orders and directives which poured forth from his restless and very fertile mind as he paced his study, salon or bedroom by day and by night. He was a tornado of a man.

Most favoured and most efficient of these lieutenants was Alexandre Berthier. A tall, spare, articulate, capable, honest and very hardworking man with impeccable manners and decorum, he was one of the few who remained loyal to Napoleon to the end of his life. As a military administrator and Chief of Staff he was quite outstanding. Indeed, to Napoleon he became indispensable. There can be no doubt that Napoleon's military victories in Italy and Egypt owed much to the work of Berthier who translated the General's orders into action, organizing the movement of troops, the provision of supplies, the collection and collation of intelligence, and, above all, the establishment of a network of communications which enabled Napoleon to remain in control of his Army, knowing that his divisions and battalions would receive his every order expeditiously and so respond to every turn of the battle as it developed. It was to give him a telling advantage over his opponents in the inevitable confusion in the field. Much of this he owed to Berthier who was his eyes and ears. As a Chief of Staff and administrator he was a model from whom many a staff officer and military historian has since learned. Napoleon was the first to recognize Berthier's abilities. Indeed he refused to fight any major battle without him. For his part Berthier recognized that he was in the presence of a military genius and remained loyal to Napoleon for the rest of his life. He was present at every major battle Napoleon fought until his own untimely death in 1815. It was perhaps fortunate for the British that he was not available to Napoleon at the Battle of Waterloo. Appropriately enough the day after Napoleon's coronation as Emperor of the French on 19 May 1804, Berthier was the first to be created a Marshal of the old order then resurrected by

Napoleon, becoming successively, Prince of Neuchatel with an estate in Switzerland, Vice-Constable of the Empire, Prince of Wagram and, finally, Major General of the Imperial General Staff with estates in three or four different countries. In 1801 Berthier was forty-eight years of age.

In a similar role was Rear Admiral Denis Decrés. He too burned the candle for Napoleon from early morning until late at night. He was a tough career officer with the French Navy with an impressive record of loyal service, and, like Napoleon, he achieved promotion on merit. Although a self-satisfied, somewhat conceited man, he nonetheless had a great deal of battle experience and was a man of integrity which Napoleon was quick to employ, when, in 1801, he appointed him Minister for both the Marine and the Colonies at the early age of forty. He remained in that office until Napoleon's departure for Elba in 1814. By then he had become Duke de Decrés. For more than fourteen years he had remained on call night and day.

Of those others with whom Napoleon surrounded himself, Fouché, the Minister of Police, had built up such an extensive dossier of intelligence that Napoleon found it impossible to dismiss him and judged it less dangerous to use him in his own support than to live with him on the outside. And of his Foreign Minister, the extraordinary, cunning and enigmatic Talleyrand, he forever remained a little wary. But many of the others around him, including his own family, became objects of derision in the eyes of Napoleon Bonaparte.

ADDINGTON AND THE PEACE OF AMIENS

However, diligent though he was in the pursuit of reforms to step up the efficiency of the French nation at home, his soldier's appetite and ambition for conquest, glory and territorial expansion remained unsatisfied. The seed of it had been planted in his mind as an officer cadet at Brienne and it remained with him for the rest of his life. It was this which Addington and St Vincent so dismally failed to understand when they succeeded to office at a moment in time when Napoleon happened to be making overtures for peace. As time was to show his real purpose was to win a pause and much needed breathing space long enough to enable him to recover some of France's financial indebtedness and fast depleting resources of men and equipment so that he could regroup and martial his forces once again.
Addington had really come in on a ticket of peace with the strong support of the merchants of the city of London who were more than anxious to re-establish their trade routes across the world, whilst the nation as a whole stood exhausted after eight long years of war. Addington's policy therefore was one

of peace at almost any price. The time was ripe also to renegotiate or dismantle many of the partnership agreements and coalitions which had been put in place many years before to contain French territorial expansion. Some had been established only with the help of large subsidies subscribed by Pitt's Government and many of these had served their purpose. Indeed Russia, Denmark and Sweden now signed up for neutrality in the north in defiance of the British blockade of continental Europe in order to enable their countries to trade with France, although the declared purpose was to assert the right of signatory members to trade with both sides to any conflict. Thus did Napoleon revive the concept of armed neutrality which had been so much a feature during the American War of Independence by which the member countries had been forbidden to trade with Great Britain, or to allow the power of search for contraband cargo.[1]

However, that new agreement was quickly shattered by the daring of Lord Nelson at the Battle of Copenhagen in April 1801 mounted in response to the treaty, for Britain could not be denied her trade with the Baltic. Again it involved Nelson disobeying the orders of his commander, this time Sir Hyde Parker who ordered Nelson to break off the engagement before Nelson gunned his way to victory. The entrance to the harbour was both narrow and well fortified with coastal batteries on all sides and navigation was difficult because of uncharted shoals. Nelson succeeded nonetheless in penetrating those waters at the dead of night using shallow-draught, two-decker ships and standing his squadron so that the Danish Fleet was between it and their own batteries on shore. Even so, the action which followed was protracted and seemed to be reaching a stalemate. Sensing danger the overcautious Hyde Parker then signalled Nelson to break off the engagement and withdraw, but, with the same daring he had shown off Cape Vincent, he literally turned his blind eye to the telescope and so to that order also and proceeded to destroy the resistance of the Danish Fleet as it lay in harbour and at his mercy. He then threatened to bombard Copenhagen itself unless acceptable peace terms were agreed,[2] which they eventually were several days later for all the Danes ever really wanted was to be left alone. Because of this there was very little rejoicing at home for the victory for fear of offending the Danes, and, to the great annoyance of Nelson himself, St Vincent, who was now at the Admiralty, refused to strike a commemorative campaign medal and no celebratory dinner was held at the Guildhall.[3] However, Nelson was himself advanced in the peerage, albeit but one rung to Viscount. Thus did he deliver his second great blow against France for the Danish Fleet was now of no further value to Napoleon.

Happily for Great Britain, Russia then decided to leave the 'Armed Neutrality of the Northern Powers' after the death of mad Tsar Paul by assassination.

But, thanks to the skill and guile of Talleyrand and Napoleon, France won trade and peace treaties with America, Russia and Austria, some of which provided for the cession and acquisition of territory in many bordering states and for the virtual disintegration of the Holy Roman Empire. This left Great Britain exposed and all but isolated. Accordingly, Addington sent Charles, 1st Marquis of Cornwallis and ex-Commander-in-Chief of the British Army which had surrendered at Yorktown, to Amiens with a mandate to negotiate peace with Napoleon's brother Joseph, whatever the cost.

And so, by the Treaty of Amiens signed in March 1802, Britain won a short respite from hostilities with France in the twelve-year struggle, but it was won at considerable price. Many territories previously seized were now returned, coupled with the promise to withdraw from both Malta and Egypt, whilst France agreed only to evacuate the kingdom of Naples, hand back Malta to the Knights of St John and precious little else. Nelson now set off with the Hamiltons on their celebrated tour of the Midlands and the borders of Wales about which so much has been written.[4] But it was to be a truce rather than a peace. Within a matter of months, Napoleon, by now Consul for life, made it clear by a series of hostile acts, in particular by refusing to evacuate his troops from Holland, that his territorial ambitions remained undiminished. Not twelve months after the treaty had been signed he used the failure of Great Britain to withdraw from Malta, which had been a retaliatory measure, as an excuse for the resumption of hostilities. Lord Whitworth, the British Ambassador to France, was summoned to the Tuileries in March 1803 to receive an ill-tempered lecture and upbrading in public from an out-of-control First Consul before a packed gathering of guests. Soon afterwards Addington issued an ultimatum, and then, in May 1804, Great Britain withdrew her Ambassador and declared war. Nothing had been achieved by the Addington initiative save a short breathing space.

NAPOLEON PLANS THE INVASION

Napoleon now devoted much of the next two years of his administration preparing for the invasion of Great Britain. This he planned with meticulous care and at enormous expense, driven on by his pathological hatred of the English and their code of liberty. He was confident that the outcome could not be in doubt for he had forty million Frenchmen at his disposal whereas the British had but fifteen.[5] 'The Channel is but a ditch,' he said, 'and anyone can cross it who has but the courage to try.' It became an obsession with him and many of his waking hours were spent pacing the shores of northern France around Boulogne, from which, it was eventually decided, the invasion was to be launched, his eyes fixed firmly on the coast of Kent, which, on a good day, was just visible. Napoleon's daily demands now generated feverish boat-building activity throughout all France. Yet at every turn during that year and into the next he was met and hampered by the Royal Navy's Channel Fleet under the command of Admiral Sir William Cornwallis, younger brother of the Marquis, which mounted a comprehensive 24-hour blockade of Brest and which kept a close watch on France's other ports on her Atlantic coastline at Boulogne, Flushing and Rochefort. He never relaxed his hold, whilst the Mediterranean Fleet, the while, guarded the French Mediterranean ports in a less defensive role. Together they effectively sealed the French Navy in port and prevented it from sailing. In between the two fleets stood, of course, Gibraltar and a similar watch was kept on Ferrol, Vigo and Cadiz on the Spanish and Portuguese coastline. The overall aim was to prevent any gathering of French ships large enough to provide escort duties from ever putting to sea long enough to cover a crossing by Napoleon's invasion flotilla of 2,000 or more flat-bottomed craft which had been built and assembled to carry his 'Army of England' across the waters of the English Channel. It comprised 150,000 men and was later to be renamed the '*Grand Armée*'. All the while Napoleon himself waited impatiently for his opportunity to invade with an army corps billeted at St Omer under the command of Soult, at Montreuil under Ney, at Bruges under Davout and at Utrecht under Marmont. A further 20,000 French troops had been collected at Brest under the command of Augerau ready for a landing in Ireland.[6] A junction with the Brest Fleet would have provided Napoleon with all the protection he needed for a crossing of the Channel. 'If we are Masters of the Channel for six hours we shall be Masters of the World' was his boast, although this was variously extended to twenty-four hours and then several days.

The blockade was laborious, painstaking and monotonous work which called for great fortitude and patience as the Fleet watched and waited. But it worked and it was the saviour of Great Britain. Although the French Navy, thanks to an inspired programme of shipbuilding, now outnumbered the British with ships of the line, its trained officer class had been all but decimated during the Revolution which had left crews ill-prepared and lacking in training with not enough officers of battle experience to lead them. They were no match for the skilled seamanship and gunnery of the British Navy. Of this the French naval commanders were only too well aware. What they lacked was confidence. After years of defeat at sea and a policy of avoiding confrontation if at all possible, it was not at all surprising that they hesitated long and hard before ever putting to sea in waters infested with the ships of the Royal Navy. Indeed

Pierre Villeneuve had an almost irrational fear of Horatio Nelson. In the result few French ships ever put a toe in the water during these years. Thus did the Cornwallis blockade and the threat of Nelson frustrate Napoleon's plans for an invasion of England. As a blockade from sea it was without parallel in all history. Thus was Admiral Mahan, the American naval historian, to write 100 years later, 'They were dull, weary, eventless months, those months of watching and waiting of the big ships before the French arsenals. Purposeless they surely seemed to many, but they saved England. The World has never seen a more impressive demonstration of the influence of seapower upon its history. Those far distant, storm beaten ships, upon which the Grand Army never looked, stood between it and the dominion of the World.'[7]

Centrepiece of the French invasion flotilla was the *péniche* craft which was far too flimsy to be able to withstand the waters of the English Channel save on the calmest of days. Yet Napoleon persisted with it despite what must have been a most sobering experience in the month of July 1804, when, it might have been expected, the sea should have been at its most docile. It was thus on a July day that he chose to conduct a dummy run in order to test and demonstrate the utility of his flotilla, despite almost gale conditions which blew up and despite also the long-distance pounding of British guns from the sloops *Harpy* and *Autumn* and from the brigs *Bloodhound* and *Archer*.[8] His Minister of Marine pleaded with him to postpone the experiment but Napoleon insisted that some of these flat-bottomed craft put to sea. It ended in disaster with the loss of 400 lives. Yet, nothing daunted, Napoleon pressed on with his plans for the invasion.

ST VINCENT AT THE ADMIRALTY

There can be no doubt but that the British Navy at this time was very overstretched. There was an acute shortage of available ships to enable it to respond to the dangers which confronted Great Britain, not only in the waters of the English Channel, but also in the Mediterranean and in the West Indies. This was, to an appreciable extent, the fault of St Vincent, who, from the moment he came to office in February 1801 until the day he vacated it in May 1804, emasculated the Royal Navy in the name of economy and in the hope of purging the dockyards of the corruption which undoubtedly existed and which he laid bare. In so doing he reduced its strength to a dangerously low level in the face of the mounting threat of invasion. Even Horatio Nelson, still then his friend and supporter, had to admit that this was so.[9] His cheeseparing and surgical excision had all but destroyed the Service. Sir John Orde was but an onlooker throughout St Vincent's tenure of office for he was destined to remain in the wilderness for a like period of time, but he too looked on in dismay.

Yet St Vincent chose to ignore the most urgent warnings and pleas of William Pitt from the opposition benches that the Admiralty should turn its policy about and embark on a crash building programme to match that of the French who were committed to an intensive national campaign of shipbuilding. The responsibility lay at St Vincent's door rather than at Addington's, for the Admiralty, operating from Whitehall,[10] stood independent of any other department, free of interference in its recruitment and organisation of officers and men. The Navy Board, eventually established entirely at Somerset House,[11] was charged with the responsibility of providing the ships. As First Lord of the Admiralty and its political head St Vincent was responsible for the work of the Sea Lords, namely deployment of the Fleet and promotions which occupied the time of the First Sea Lord, organizing, personnel and supervising the work of the Navy Board which was the Second Sea Lord's concern, the supply of materials which the Third Sea Lord looked after, and the provision of stores which the Fourth Sea Lord watched over. Indeed his remit covered also civil dockyard construction which the Civil Lords superintended, and he was ultimately responsible too for the work of those officers and commissioners of the Navy who sat on the Navy Board itself, the Controller, the Treasurer who looked after Navy finance and pay, and, in particular, the Surveyor who was responsible for the construction of ships. It followed of course that great power rested with the Permanent Secretary to the Admiralty, then Sir Even Nepean.

The astonishing record of St Vincent's time at the Admiralty is that whilst in office he effectively halved the numbers of those working in the dockyards, and reduced the fighting strength from 130,000 to 70,000 men.[12] After leaving office he published privately his *Memoirs of the Administration of the Board of Admiralty under the Presidency of the Earl of St Vincent.* It was written in belligerent terms seeking to justify his controversial stewardship, claiming that right had been on his side, and, indeed, that he had been the only man in the country capable of holding that office at that time. Finding corruption and theft deeply entrenched in pretty well every dockyard and amongst several suppliers, he had, he claimed, successfully eradicated it. Rebellion was quite common amongst the workers, he claimed, yet he had dealt with this too. There can be no doubt but that St Vincent did do much good work in his protracted, laborious, meticulous and thorough investigation of dockyard performance which had indeed been riddled with dishonest practice. It cried out for some sort of scrutiny. But his work at the Admiralty did little to improve the nation's capacity to withstand the threat of invasion from across the Channel. And it seems that growing allegations of neglect, spearheaded by William Pitt, together with a gathering momentum of hatred for St Vincent personally,[13] began to unbalance him and he would respond to such criticism in outspoken and even abusive terms whenever William Pitt was involved, outraged that anyone should have the temerity to question the word and wisdom of the Lord St Vincent, the greatest seaman of his generation. There were echoes here of his reaction to the complaint which Sir John Orde had made to him back in 1798. Even Nelson, his erstwhile faithful lieutenant, began to see him in a different light now, for, although he had now grown very wealthy from prize money won at sea, he was greedy for more, even to the extent of claiming prize money on vessels which had been captured by Nelson. He nonetheless felt that this was due to him and this resulted in years of costly litigation in the Admiralty Court with Nelson as the plaintiff suing St Vincent for his share of the distribution. Many another officer was also made the target of his vendettas at this unfortunate and despotic stage of his life.

PITT RETURNS WITH MELVILLE

Matters came to a head in March 1804 against a mounting and imminent threat of invasion when Pitt delivered a blistering attack on the Addington Government and St Vincent in particular, accusing him of criminal neglect. Eight weeks later, and with some reluctance for he had felt more at home with the urbane and cautious Addington, George III asked Pitt to form a government. With as much reluctance, Pitt agreed for Parliament would have none other. With him Pitt brought back Henry Dundas, Lord Melville, this time as First Lord of the Admiralty. He in turn was to become the target of a St Vincent out for revenge and was eventually hounded from office shortly before Pitt died.

In the month of Pitt's return in May 1804, Napoleon was crowned Emperor of France and Pitt immediately put the nation on a war footing. The strength of both the Army and the Navy was rapidly stepped up. Melville was able to achieve an impressive increase in the number of ships built, coastal defences were hurriedly assembled, signal beacons were built at strategic intervals along the coastline throughout the country, Martello towers were erected to act as both lookout stations and armament depots and other schemes of defence were established as a matter of urgency. There was a new spirit abroad. Taking advantage of the fact of French aggression in Europe, Pitt now organized a Third Coalition against her, this time involving Austria, Prussia and Russia.[14] As William James was to write in his *Naval History*, 'At no former or subsequent time have eighty-seven British ships of war been launched within the year . . . Nothing can better demonstrate the exertions made by the new Lord of the Admiralty . . . to recover the British navy from the low state into which it had previously fallen.'[15]

Henry Dundas had been born in 1742, the fourth son of a Scottish judge who later became Lord President of the Court of Session in Scotland. Educated at Edinburgh High School he had been a brilliant law student at Edinburgh University and a meteoric career had followed. Within three years of his admission as a member of the Faculty of Advocates he had been appointed Solicitor-General for Scotland at the tender age of twenty-four, and then, nine years on, and only twelve months after he had entered Parliament as the member for Midlothian, he had been appointed Lord Advocate in place of James Montgomery who had been raised to the bench as Chief Baron of the Exchequer in Scotland. To this was added, in 1782, treasurership of the Navy, a seat on the Privy Council, the office of Keeper of the Scotch Signet and Dean of the Faculty of Advocates. The office of Lord Advocate he held for eight long years until replaced in 1783 by Henry Erskine. But then, within twelve months, treasurership of the Navy was restored to him when Pitt became Prime Minister. Ever a devotee and close friend of William Pitt to whom he gave his lifelong support, his political fortunes rode with those of Pitt himself, and so, in 1791 he became Home Secretary in Pitt's Administration whilst Member of Parliament for the city of Edinburgh, and then, in 1794, Secretary of State for War where he remained until Pitt left office in March 1801. Utterly loyal, he chose to go with him. However, although his allegiance to Pitt remained, he gave general support to Addington's Administration and was duly rewarded with a peerage in December 1802, taking the title Viscount Melville of Edinburgh.

In his private life he had been less successful for he was no businessman and an unwise investment with the Ayr Bank early on in his career had cost him both his wife, who left him, and the dowry of £100,000 which she had brought with her on marriage.[16] Never again was he a rich man. However, a second marriage in 1793 to Lady Jane Hope, a daughter of the Earl of Hopetoun, was more successful and they remained happily married for the rest of his life.

It is clear that St Vincent saw him as an enemy. Never an elegant, inspired or attractive speaker, it seems that it was his broad Scots accent and unsophisticated and unrefined ways which so irritated St Vincent, which is surprising. He was nevertheless a prodigious worker and a lucid and forceful speaker with his facts always well researched and clearly marshalled. And very obviously William Pitt recognized in him a friend who was reliable as well as loyal and he remained so until the day Pitt died. He remained one of that circle of friends which revolved around Pitt and which included Spencer, Wilberforce and even Pitt's political opponents such as Addington. Although not a sailor by training, he was nonetheless a natural choice for the Admiralty when Pitt returned to office since it gave him a seat at any Council of War alongside the Secretary of

State for War and the Prime Minister himself. His all-important Permanent Secretary was now to be William Marsden in place of Nepean. Nepean, now fifty-three years of age, had been made a baronet in 1802 and was later to become Governor of Bombay.[17] At a lower level the return of Pitt improved the chances of a return to active service for such as Sir John Orde.

NAPOLEON'S PRECISE PLANS FOR INVASION

Unknown to Pitt his return to Downing Street coincided with the first of many plans which were to emerge from the fertile brain of Napoleon for the actual strategy of invasion. Admiral Eustace de Bruix, then aged forty-four, who had assisted Napoleon in the *coup d'état* of 1799, had, in 1803, been named the commander of the invasion flotilla. The plan was a simple one: a mass breakout of the French Fleets which would make for the West Indies and rendezvous there in the hope of drawing off a significant part of the British Channel and Mediterranean Fleets in pursuit, for Napoleon knew that the British would be quick to protect their economic interests in the West Indies, such was their importance. Thus did Napoleon calculate that he could relax British protection of the Channel to which the French Fleets would then return ahead of the British in time to cover a crossing by the invasion force. Before the end of July the Brest Squadron was to break out and head south-west, followed, it was hoped, by Cornwallis and the Channel Fleet. Admiral La Touche-Treville meanwhile, would break out of Toulon with the Fleet there of ten battleships and eleven frigates, give Nelson the slip and sail for Cherbourg, collecting the Rochefort squadron of six or so ships on the way. That combined force would then be placed at the disposal of Napoleon for escort duties in the Channel in September.

But all of this took no account of the vagaries and uncertainties of the weather or indeed of the inadequacy of the French Fleet. Unfortunately for Napoleon Admiral Latouche died before his Fleet could set sail and Vice Admiral Ganteaume, who commanded the Brest Fleet which comprised many first-class newly-built ships, reported to Decrés, the Naval Minister, that his crews were pitifully inadequate not only in number, experience and training, but also in resolution. It was clear that it would require all the Emperor's skill and drive to persuade the French Navy to put to sea. There was indeed an acute shortage of officers able to lead the crews of these many ships into battle. And, to add to his problems, the Admiral appointed to command the invasion flotilla, Eustace de Bruix, had by now fallen seriously ill. In contrast, the British ships, although also seriously undermanned, were staffed by highly trained, experienced and determined naval officers, many of whom were battle-hardened veterans of many a year's service, and they were for the most part loyal and dedicated to the service of their country. This Napoleon realized well enough for himself. As a soldier his preference was for the Army with all its successes. He treated his naval officers with disdain.

He now chose a successor for the Toulon command in place of Admiral Latouche which was to have far-reaching consequences for both the Navy of France and indeed for the entire plan for the invasion of Britain. It was to be Vice Admiral Pierre Villeneuve. No doubt he was influenced in his choice to a large extent by the advice of his loyal Navy Minister, Decrés, for Decrés and Villeneuve were old colleagues and friends. Villeneuve, now forty-one years of age, a thin-nosed aristocrat, was a Knight of Malta and a member of the provincial nobility. He was a civilized, humane, intelligent, efficient and decent man with an impressive record of service in the Navy behind him. But, ever a melancholy, mild, timid and careful man, at this stage of his life he had become introspective and cautious to a degree which resulted in inertia. In short he had lost his nerve for battle. More than that, ever since the Battle of the Nile, at which he had been present, he had developed a fear of Nelson and his Fleet which was almost pathological. That, coupled with his own lack of belief in the abilities of the men under his command, did not auger well for the French. And his pessimism was contagious. It demoralized the officers in his own command. Clearly Napoleon was blind to his faults, or the extent to which they governed the man, when he made the appointment, but, as the weeks went by they became obvious to all, not least to Villeneuve himself who begged Napoleon more than once to be relieved of his command. And yet, whilst openly despairing of Villeneuve's failure to act on his countless orders to put to sea, Napoleon kept him in post as commander of the Toulon Fleet. It is difficult to understand why but he was to live to regret it.

With any thought of defeating the British Navy now out of the question, the plan in the autumn of 1804 was much the same. It was for Villeneuve to sail for the West Indies for the invasion of St Lucia and Dominica and other British-held territories whilst other French squadrons were to harass the British in Asia and Africa and elsewhere, thus drawing off British ships from the Channel Fleet to combat these several diversions. His orders to Villeneuve were then to double back to Boulogne, take command of the Channel and escort the *Grand Armée* across to the shores of Kent, whilst the Brest Fleet was to head for Dublin in a diversionary tactic before returning to the Channel to perform escort duties also. But, even if his orders had been obeyed and the wind and the weather had been merciful, it is doubtful that Napoleon's plan would ever have succeeded for it was implicit in the standing orders issued by Admiral Cornwallis that no ship was ever to be drawn away from the Channel Fleet. His role, as he saw it, was to patrol and protect the south coast of England. And, as it turned out, Napoleon's orders were intercepted by the British on their way to Ganteaume at Brest so that this plan too had to be cancelled. But it seems obvious that the British Fleet must now have been alert to the sort of plan Napoleon had in mind, and all of the several plans he made subsequently for the invasion of Britain were but variations of the same theme.

Notes

[1] Clark, p. 33; N Hol, p. 247.
[2] Clark, p. 33; Preston, p. 93.
[3] Stokesbury; N Hol, p. 248.
[4] Stokesbury, p. 198.
[5] N Hol, p. 271.
[6] NB, p. 236.
[7] N Mah; Warner, p. 144.
[8] Park, p. 104.
[9] Schom, p. 39.
[10] Park, p. 9.
[11] Park, p. 9.
[12] *Who's Who in History* by Treasure.
[13] DNB, p. 361.
[14] Stokesbury, p. 199.
[15] James quoted by Schom, p. 143.
[16] Schom, p. 28.
[17] ND, p. 100.

CHAPTER XII

SPAIN AND SIR JOHN ORDE ENTER THE WAR – THE

GOLDEN HARVEST

In the autumn of 1804 the danger of invasion escalated. For some time Spain had remained in uneasy neutrality. The reality was that, although passive in her neutrality it was something of a fiction for she remained subservient to the wishes of France, allowing the free movement of French troops across her borders whenever requested, victualling and housing French soldiers as needed. However, despite the blandishments of Napoleon, she had as yet refused to play a more active role in support of France. Now, paradoxically, it was an order of Lord Melville which was to bring her out of neutrality and into the war on the side of France. And it was this same event which also brought Sir John Orde back into active service.

Intelligence services had told the Government that a consignment of gold and silver valued at more than £1 million was on its way from Rio de la Plata to Cadiz.[1] On 18 September Melville ordered Cornwallis to intercept the four Spanish frigates which carried the cargo lest it fall into the hands of Napoleon. Accordingly, Cornwallis promptly despatched the frigates *Indefatigable* and *Lively*, then lying off Cadiz, to intercept. Captain Moore, the officer commanding, commandeered the services of two more frigates, the *Medusa* and the *Amphion*, then under the command of Lord Nelson. Captain Gore of the *Medusa* as quickly complained to Nelson at his detachment, and Nelson replied to the effect that the neutrality of Spain was to be respected and Gore was not to violate it and was to leave the Spanish ships alone. But he later sent an 80-gun ship and four cruisers when orders from the Admiralty arrived commanding him to do so.[2] Captain Moore intercepted the Spanish flotilla on 5 October and ordered it to surrender. He was met with refusal and so opened fire. After but ten minutes of engagement three of the four Spanish ships surrendered without loss of life, but the fourth exploded with further firing and went to the bottom, drowning 240 men, women and children alike. As with the British ships, some women had been allowed on board – hence the need to 'Show a leg' on the bosun's morning round.[3] Looked at with hindsight it was an act of open hostility, indeed piracy, as unlawful as it was outrageous. Not surprisingly it brought Spain into the war on the side of France thus making reality of what had until then been something of a fiction. With her she brought a fleet of fourteen battleships harboured at Cadiz which were now put at the disposal of Napoleon.

For Horatio Nelson and for Sir John Orde this was to produce a further source of conflict for the entry of Spain into the war brought with it the prospect of rich pickings in prize money for whoever succeeded to the lucrative command of a British Squadron stationed off Cadiz. For some time now Nelson, who was never the strongest of men and who was worn out by months at sea guarding British interests in the Mediterranean, had been bombarding the Admiralty with requests for leave, hoping to be back at home at Merton in time for Christmas. Back in August (19th) he had written of it from the *Victory* to Sir Alexander John Ball, His Majesty's Commissioner for Civil Affairs at Malta and now a Rear Admiral, discussing who might take his place. He wrote, 'Sir John Orde (Lord Mark Kerr says) is gone to succeed Young at Plymouth. If so, he is either coming here, or going, instead of Pellew, to command in India; but I can only guess for none of them write me news . . .'[4] And then, by letter dated 6 September to Ball, '. . . I cannot bring myself to suppose but that one half of the Admirals on the list will perform the duty of the Mediterranean Command as well, at least, as myself; and if the other half of the Admirals list was to hear of my vanity they would think me a fool; but be that as it may, I am very far from well. At the same time if I was to get better, nothing would please me so much as returning to the Command; but I have no interest and another will come, and I think very probably Orde, or Curtis . . .'[5] In fact he had already made a formal written request for leave by letter dated 15 August 1804 and this was granted on 6 October on the basis that his second in command Bickerton would assume command in his absence,[6] although it was not until Christmas Day that that information from the Admiralty was actually delivered.[7] By then he had changed his mind about wanting to come home.[8]

On a general promotion Orde had become a Vice Admiral of the Red and Nelson had become a Vice Admiral of the White and so flew the White Ensign. His now very stale action against St Vincent for his share of the prize money which St Vincent had refused to disgorge had resolved on appeal in favour of Nelson on the ground that St Vincent had been absent when the prizes, the concern of the action, had been taken. The Judge of the Admiralty Court at this time was the much respected Sir William Scott, later Lord Stowell of Stowell Park, Stow-on-the-Wold, elder brother of Lord Chancellor Eldon, good Northumbrians both, like Sir John Orde. The principle remained that the Flag Office commanding the Squadron which took the prize was entitled to the 1/8th lion's share of the prize money obtained.[9] As T. Gibson Bowles was to state in

The Right Honourable Sir William Scott

his *Sea Law and Sea Power*, 'The Prize Courts . . . were trustworthy. They constantly decided against the wishes of their own Governments, or the interests of their fellow-subjects; they were on the whole more just and impartial than any municipal courts administering municipal law.'[10] The Admiralty, somewhat unjustly, was to use the decision in Nelson's own case to deprive him of any share of the prize money raised from the seizure of the ships and cargo taken by Captain Moore upon the ground that Nelson had by then been granted leave and so had been absent at the time, supposedly on his way home, although in fact such had not been the case. Nelson had even appointed a Prize Agent at Gibraltar to determine the question whether the ships had been taken on his station.[11]

The moment Spain entered the war with her fleet of ships, the Admiralty judged it necessary to strengthen the British presence off Cadiz if the blockade was to remain effective, for, in advance of the formal declaration of war which was to follow in December, the Spanish were feverishly making preparations, assembling crews and victuals, equipping their ships and installing shore batteries. Melville prepared to meet this increased activity and threat by forming a new Cadiz Squadron of half-a-dozen ships, most of which had been detached from the Channel Fleet off Ushant. William Marsden, who had by now taken over as Permanent Secretary to the Admiralty from Nepean who had retired through ill health, with a baronetcy, wrote to inform Nelson that two of the ships which were to join the new Cadiz Squadron, would be taken from his Mediterranean Fleet. These were to be the *Amphion* and the *Medusa* which had been involved in the capture of the Spanish merchantmen.

Nelson was a man of so many fine and outstanding qualities that it is sometimes thought to be heresy to point to a less attractive side of his character, but there can be no doubt but that these two events caused in his mind something of an insubordinate and petulant explosion. The thought that his Mediterranean Command, which had before then extended as far as Cape Finisterre beyond which it gave way to the Western Squadron, should be thus reduced with the possibility that the officer placed in command of the new Cadiz Squadron would, for all he knew, succeed in his absence on leave to command of the Mediterranean Fleet, was altogether too much for him. This development occurred to him as a distinct possibility since there was bound to be much overlapping in the administration and revictualling of the two squadrons at Gibraltar, which remained in Nelson's command. Added to this would be the responsibility, divided, of escorting shipping through that dangerous Strait. Accordingly Nelson wrote from the *Victory* to Ball by letter dated 22 October, 'Hallowell thinks the Ministers will not name another Commander-in-Chief, but see if I am able to return. I do not think so, for they are so beset by

Admirals. Sir John Orde, I am told, is likely. Lord Radstock is trying; so is Sir Roger Curtis; and if a Spanish War comes, Lord Keith loves a little money and a great deal much better . . .'[12] Nelson's outside hope was of course that the Admiralty, which so valued his services, would leave the Mediterranean Squadron in the able hands of his second in command, Sir Richard Bickerton, until his return from leave, but he realized that such a hope was forlorn given the national emergency.[13] The obvious probability was that if Nelson returned home on leave for a protracted period of time, Sir John Orde would be given command of the Mediterranean Station. What he had failed to appreciate was that when they sent out Sir John Orde, the Admiralty were under the impression that Nelson was on his way home, as requested and granted, and so would no longer be in those waters when the change took place.

The later realization that Spain had entered the war and that there was now the prospect of much prize money off Cadiz which was not to be available to him, but to another, was the thought which now caused so many of Nelson's outbursts, for he was not a rich man. The author C.S. Forester judged that '. . . his share might have amounted to quarter of million sterling – but actually, in view of his application for leave, he had no reason to complain. Complain he did, at first unreasonably . . .'[14] For Nelson had not foreseen, of course, when applying for leave, that Spain would enter the war so soon and so present such a prospect of prize money. Now that it had happened he was furious to have lost the westerly and now most lucrative part of his command.

The flag officer chosen for this new command who was thus to receive, albeit indirectly, the brunt of Nelson's displeasure, was none other than Vice Admiral Sir John Orde. In truth Melville had hesitated before appointing Sir John, not because he suspected difficulty with Nelson, but rather because of his past quarrel with St Vincent. And so he had written to Cornwallis privately some time before,

> You are no stranger to the terms on which Sir John Orde was with Lord St Vincent. He is naturally very anxious to get in employment now that Lord St Vincent is not in his way, and either himself or his brother, Lord Bolton, has made to me various propositions for that purpose. Among others he urges being put on Service in the Channel Fleet, and states that such an arrangement, from the habits you are upon, he is convinced, would be extremely agreeable to you; under such circumstances people are apt to deceive themselves! I am not sure that at any rate it would be in my power to gratify him in this wish, but before I take this proposition even under consideration it is necessary as a preliminary with me to know how you feel about it. You need not be under any uneasiness in giving me

your feelings without any reserve, for although I may act upon them, he nor anybody shall know the authority on which I proceed. If I decline his request it shall be entirely an act of my own.[15]

It seems probable that Cornwallis found the prospect acceptable enough, for otherwise, if Melville was true to his word, Sir John would not have been appointed. Although an intrigue was later mounted to remove Cornwallis from his command and substitute the now ageing St Vincent in his place, this post-dated the departure of Melville, and, indeed, Trafalgar, when it was then largely successful.[16] Sir John Orde was now, in the general promotion, a Vice Admiral of the Red and so still senior in rank to Nelson. It is probable that Melville removed the western extremity from Nelson's command in order to avoid the clash which would otherwise have been caused by the difference in seniority.[17] Nelson's outburst may be understandable but it was unjust to blame Sir John who bore him no animosity personally at all and he had not himself been responsible for the formation of the Cadiz Squadron, still less for the selection of himself as its commander. This had been the work of the First Lord who obviously did not suspect that Nelson may have thought that Sir John still resented him. In fact Sir John Orde was now everywhere singing Nelson's praises[18] and the Admiralty, in any event, supposed that Nelson was coming home on leave. Thus did the King reply from Weymouth on 26 October that he 'entirely agrees with Lord Melville that it is much safer and more prudent as Captains White and Gore differ in their states of the forwardness of the Spanish Navy at Cadiz, to send without delay a squadron off that port under the command of Vice Admiral Sir John Orde,' which, Melville had written to him, would 'watch the operations of the Spanish Fleet in that harbour, and to protect the trade of Your Majesty's subjects in that quarter.' Accordingly, on 27 October 1804, Melville wrote to Sir John Orde[19] that he should

proceed as expeditiously as possible off Cadiz, where you may expect to find the *Medusa*, and taking her also under your command, cruise off that port for the purpose of watching the movements of the French and Spanish ships of war which may be lying there; and in the event of any of the latter, either separately or in conjunction with French ships, attempting to put to sea, you are to appraise their Commanders that you have received instructions to insist upon their immediate return to port; and in case they should refuse to comply therewith you are then to use your utmost endeavours to compel them to do so, and if necessary to take possession of the said ships and proceed with them to Gibraltar, where they are to remain for our further directions. If you or any of the vessels under your command should, either on your passage or when cruising off Cadiz, fall in with any ships laden with treasure coming from the Spanish colonies and bound to Spain, you are to take possession of the said ships and send them forthwith to a British port for our further directions respecting them, taking every possible precaution to secure the treasure which may be on board them from plunder and embezzlement . . . It being our intention to place His Majesty's ship *Glory* under your command, you are upon being joined by her to shift your flag to that ship, and direct the commander of the *Swiftsure* to proceed in her off Toulon, where he may expect to find Vice Admiral Lord Nelson, and upon joining him to follow his Lordship's orders for his further proceedings . . .[20]

It was in these circumstances that Nelson shelved his plan to come home on leave, partly because his second in command, Rear Admiral Campbell, had suffered a nervous breakdown and had gone home, but more so because he was fearful lest in his absence his command was taken from him and given to another, probably Sir John Orde.[21] He therefore sent Este back to London on 6 November with that news, using the illness of Rear Admiral Campbell as the reason for his change of plan, writing to the Admiralty on 30 December that he thought it right to wait until a replacement for Campbell had been appointed.[22] It was not to be a happy tour of duty for Sir John who was not unaware of Nelson's growing animosity which was all the more surprising for they had corresponded with each other in 1801 on perfectly amicable terms concerning Sir John's pamphlet. For instance, by the letter dated 7 July 1801, Nelson had written, 'My dear Sir John, last night I received your kind and friendly letter and feel much obliged by your congratulations . . . I am free to own, that conscious to myself, I never did try to supplant anyone or ever pushed myself beyond a laudable ambition to try to get forward . . .'[23] Again, by the letter dated 25 July 1801, he had explained his belief that he had been chosen for the Mediterranean Command in 1798 because of his knowledge of the Italian coast after five years of service there, 'I beg you to believe that I never could have a wish to sow dissension between any two officers and also believe that I am with real respect my dear Sir John . . . Hoping soon to have the pleasure of meeting you . . .'[24] Indeed, by the year 1804, Sir John had become something of a Nelson supporter and was now openly expressing admiration for his achievements.

But now Nelson was much wounded, the more so when it was adjudged that Sir John was entitled to £10,000 as his share of the prize money for the Spanish treasure ships captured in October as the Flag Officer now commanding the squadron off Cadiz. And he was to pick up very much more as further prize ships came his way, much to the gall of the much acclaimed but impoverished Horatio Nelson. Clark Russell judged that in the space of a month the Admiral and his officers were enriched for life.[25] Despite this all was not well with Sir John, for he was often laid low with what was thought to be gout. And as for Nelson, misunderstandings and the slowness of communication generated in him a feeling of uncertainty and a sense of unease which manifested itself in letters written in accusatory and hysterical terms.

In a letter to Lady Emma Hamilton on 4 December he wrote,[26]

All my things are on board the *Superb*, and would my successor arrive I could be off in two hours. We have reports that Sir John Orde is the man, which has thrown a gloom over all the fleet, but I hope unnecessarily, for six years upon the shelf may have taught him a little moderation towards officers. I have made up my mind to overwhelm him with respect and attention, and to even make an offer, as Admiral Campbell has gone home, to serve till the Admiralty can send out another flag officer. I have wrote to Lord Melville that I should make such an offer and that I entreated him to send out a flag officer as soon as possible but I dare say Sir John Orde is too great a man to want my poor services, and that he will reject them; be that as it may, you will, I am sure, agree with me, that I shall shew my superiority to him by such an offer, and the World will see what a sacrifice I am ready to make for the service of my King and Country, for what greater sacrifice could I make, than serving for a moment under Sir John Orde and giving up for that moment the society of all I hold dear in that world. Many here think that he is sent out off Cadiz to take a fortune out of my mouth, that would be very curious. The late Admiralty directed Admiral Cornwallis to send Campbell to cruise at the mouth of the Straits, and he took all my sweets, and now this Admiralty sends and takes all my golden harvest; it is very odd – surely I never served faithfully, I have only dreamt I have done my duty to the advantage of my country, but I am above them, I feel it, although not one farthing richer than when I left England . . .

The following day, 5 December, he wrote from the *Victory* to his old friend, Ball. 'No Sir John Orde, no orders, no letters from England, very extraordinary. I almost begin to think that he is sent off Cadiz to reap the golden harvest, as Campbell was sent off Cadiz by Cornwallis (by orders from England) to reap my sugar harvest. It's very odd, two Admiralties to treat me so.' And then, with a burst of Shakespeare, 'Surely I have dreamt that "I have done the State some service". But never mind; I am superior to those who could treat me so. When am I to be relieved? . . . I shall not trouble you with all my conjectures about Sir John Orde's never communicating with me for the three weeks he has been off Cadiz.'[27] Pettigrew, in his work on Nelson, was to take this up and repeat Nelson's accusation that Orde had failed to notify him of his arrival, but such was not the case. Not only had Este, when carrying Nelson's despatches home, come across Sir John on 18 November on board the *Swiftsure* which was bringing him out, but Sir John had already written to Nelson on 17 November soon after taking up his command off Cadiz,[28] and sent it by the *Anson* but the lapse of time before this could be delivered to Nelson was such that he did not receive Sir John's letter until 15 December by which time Nelson was lying in Pula Bay on the coast of Sardinia. This letter Nelson then acknowledged by letter dated 16 December.[29] Sir John had written, 'Should it be in my power, during my stay, to be useful to your lordship in promoting the King's service, or your particular views, I beg you will command me without ceremony.' Mahan therefore noted in his account of it that 'It seems fair . . . to acquit Orde of a discourtesy.'[30] This was but one of many misunderstandings which were to make the lives of both Nelson and Sir John so miserable that winter. It had been a tactless move on the part of the Admiralty to have arranged things so, but then they had assumed that Nelson was coming home on leave, as requested, not knowing that he had by then learned of Orde's arrival and the reduction of his command and had then changed his mind. Thus Nelson wrote to his old friend Hugh Elliott on 19 December, 'I have learned not to be surprised at anything; but the sending an officer to such a point, to take, if it is a Spanish war, the whole harvest, after all my toils, (God knows unprofitable enough! for I am a much poorer man than when we started in the *Amphian*) seems a little hard; but patienza. I suppose Sir John, in the end, will command here . . . Sir John Orde has three cutters, and four or five fire Brigs attached to his squadron; but, no; not one for me . . .'[31]

That same day he wrote to Lady Emma reporting the arrival of 'the great Sir John Orde,'[32] and complaining that 'he has threatened my ships a little harshly but never mind he will get all the money and your poor Nelson all the hard blows, am I to take this act as a proof of Lord Melville's regard for me, but I submit patiently . . . is Sir John after he has got riches to come here and get glory . . .' And he complained by letter to Captain Malcolm also that same day that 'To my surprise I am not yet relieved for Sir John Orde is for the present placed in command of a squadron outside the Straits which is for the present occasion lost from my Command, when there was nothing to be got I had it, when the prospect of money comes forth it is given to another. Adam Campbell had it at the beginning of the french war and now Sir John the beginning of a

Spanish war . . .'[33]

On Christmas Day the *Swiftsure*, which had brought Sir John Orde out, now joined Nelson's squadron bringing with it mail for Nelson, including the Admiralty's formal written grant of his request for leave! It was then, on 26 December, that he wrote to Marsden acknowledging his letter dated 26th of October which told him officially of the creation of the Cadiz Squadron and in his reply repeated Marsden's orders, pointedly, that he was 'not to consider my command as extending without the Straits of Gibraltar', and promising obedience.[34] Three days later, on 29 December, he penned a letter to Sir John Orde, writing that it was 'unnecessary for me to point out to you, that the convoys, either to or from England, are not safe, unless taken in charge from twenty leagues to the westward of Cape Spartel, and seen safe to an anchor in Gibraltar Bay; or from Cape Spartel as far to the Westward.' By the same letter he reported that he had, on 26 December, found the enemy's fleet still in port at Toulon.[35] Then, on 30 December, he wrote to the effect that he thought it right that he should await a replacement for Campbell who had suffered a nervous breakdown and gone home on leave, before he himself returned home. In two letters to Elliott dated 13 January, Nelson wrote that '. . . he [Orde] is to wallow in wealth, whilst I am left a beggar . . .', and, 'Sir John Orde brought my leave and many supposed that the moment I had passed the straits he would take upon him the command . . .'[36]

At about this time, Samuel Taylor Coleridge, the poet, then Secretary to Nelson's friend Ball at Malta,[37] and taking Nelson's part in all this, wrote in *The Friend* in histrionic, exaggerated and inaccurate terms that,

> when the resolution was taken of commencing hostilities against Spain, before any intelligence was sent to Lord Nelson, another Admiral, with two or three ships of the Line was sent into the Mediterranean, and stationed before Cadiz, for the express purpose of intercepting the Spanish prizes. The Admiral dispatched on this lucrative service gave no information to Lord Nelson of his arrival in the same sea, and five weeks elapsed before his Lordship became acquainted with the circumstance. The prizes thus taken were immense. A month or two sufficed to enrich the Commander and Officers of this small and highly favoured squadron, while to Nelson and his fleet the sense of having done their duty, and the consciousness of the glorious services which they had performed, were considered, it must be presumed, as an abundant remuneration for all their toils and long sufferings! . . . Of all the wounds which were ever inflicted on Nelson's feelings (and these were not a few) this was the deepest! This rankled most![38]

The entry of Spain into the war had indeed caused great excitement in some quarters, and, despite the presence of Sir Richard Bickerton as his second in command in the absence of Rear Admiral Campbell, Nelson remained with the Fleet, deciding not to take up his grant of leave.

As soon as he arrived off Cadiz, Sir John proceeded to mount a most efficient and comprehensive blockade with his small squadron of ships which was to keep the Spanish Fleet in harbour throughout that winter until the arrival of Villeneuve. Indeed, *The Times* of 18 April 1805 reported that:

The last letters received by the Lisbon Mail from Cadiz state that Sir John Orde continued the blockade of that port with the utmost vigour; vessels freighted with corn only were allowed to pass unmolested. His refusal to permit neutral vessels to leave the port of Cadiz, had produced several applications from the Neutral Consuls. The following is Sir John's answer to the American Consul on the subject: 'His Majesty's Ship *Glory*, at sea, March 11th, 1805.

Sir, Imperious circumstances compel me to order the blockade of Cadiz to be strictly enforced from this time, which deprives me of the gratification I should otherwise have had in complying with your request. You would oblige me by communicating this information to all whom it may concern as speedily and generally as convenient, in order that none may suffer from their own imprudence.

J. Orde.'[39]

So effective was Sir John's blockade that even British ships passing through the Straits were intercepted and questioned so that intelligence could be gathered and collated. This too led to further misunderstanding with Nelson who assumed, when a ship of his was intercepted perhaps carrying his despatches for London, that Sir John was seeking to exercise some control over Nelson's command.

PARKER INCIDENT

Indeed, so irritated did he become so soon after Sir John's arrival that on one occasion, on New Year's Day of the year 1805, he resorted to subterfuge in order to deceive Sir John's squadron. Here Nelson recruited the assistance of one Wilfred Parker, a nephew of the ominous St Vincent and Captain of the frigate *Amazon*.[40] According to Parker himself he was ordered to carry Nelson's letters for London in the *Amazon* slipping past Orde's squadron in the straits at dead of night as if they were Frenchmen, and then putting in at Lisbon so that the despatches could then be sent overland to London unbeknown to Sir John Orde. Should he have the ill luck to be intercepted by a ship of Orde's squadron, then, according to Parker, his orders were to obey whatever orders the Admiral gave if the squadron carried an Admiral who was senior to Nelson, but, if not, he was to show the Captain Nelson's instructions which were to proceed on his way.[41] Again according to Parker himself, Nelson further ordered, 'But . . . if you cannot weather that fellow, I shall think that you have not a drop of your uncle's blood in your veins.' For a young officer to be thus taken into the confidence of the celebrated Admiral was flattering to say the least and he accepted the challenge with enthusiasm. However, although he then took care to give Orde's squadron a wide berth, creeping up to Gibraltar, he failed to 'weather that fellow' and was spotted and intercepted by an ever-vigilant frigate in Orde's command which had been lying out. However, fortunately for Parker, and, indeed, for Lord Nelson, the Captain who then boarded the *Amazon* was one Captain Hoste, a devoted admirer of Nelson who owed all his advancement in the service to him. Hoste's father, like Nelson's, was Rector of a Norfolk Parish. Hoste had entered the Navy in the care of Nelson as a Midshipman on the *Agamemnon* and had gone with him five years later when Nelson transferred to the *Captain*, and then to the *Irresistible* and finally to the *Theseus*. Nelson treated him as a son and had promoted him after the Battle of the Nile to the command of a brig in his own squadron. So attached was he to Nelson, that, when Nelson returned to the *Eagle* in 1801 and Hoste transferred to Lord Keith's command, an officer not known to him, he considered himself neglected, and, with the encouragement of Nelson, looked upon Keith as an enemy. However, in September of 1805, Nelson had found a place for him in the *Amphion* off Cadiz, one of those ships so recently transferred to Sir John Orde's squadron. It was therefore good fortune indeed for Parker that the officer who stopped him should have been Hoste. When Parker explained the orders he had received from Nelson and then added, 'Do you not think it would be better if you were not to meet the *Amazon* this night?' Hoste was persuaded to disobey orders and quietly left, leaving Parker to proceed on his way.

With full press of sail, Parker now ran for Lisbon. He arrived there offshore on 26 January 1805 just as an English packet was coming out, and so Nelson's despatches were delivered and Parker's mission had been accomplished. For Parker the matter did not rest there for Nelson had promised him that, if successful, he would have two week's licence to hunt the waters west of Gibraltar for prizes. That promise Parker now redeemed. And his luck held, for, the second day out the Spanish vessel *Gravina* hove into view carrying riches indeed including 300,000 dollars in cash. It was lamb to the slaughter and Parker returned to the Fleet flushed with success and almost £20,000 the richer in prize money. And Nelson as his Flag Officer received a further £10,000 as his share.[42]

That winter Sir John was to escape the stormy weather which drove most of the Channel Fleet off station. The blockade continued successfully and according to orders, thus preventing any junction of the enemy fleets or threat of invasion. Only one escape was possible and that could be put down to stormy weather which allowed one squadron of French ships under the command of Admiral Missiessy to slip out of Rochefort one evening in January unseen by Sir Thomas Graves, and head for the West Indies with orders to damage British commercial interests there – a mission which was accomplished, but only to a very limited extent.

In the Mediterranean Nelson perceived his role to be very different. So far from seeking to keep the French Fleet in harbour at Toulon, he sought to lure them out by lying at anchor just over the horizon out of sight, whilst leaving but one or perhaps two frigates to keep watch on the harbour. By this means he hoped to lull the French into a sense of security in the hope that they would then venture out and into confrontation with Nelson's Fleet which would then annihilate, or at least seriously cripple them. Well into the New Year complaint was still emanating from Nelson about Orde's run of the Straits. To Collingwood he wrote on 13 March 1805, '. . . We are in a sad jumble with Sir John Orde off Cadiz; but let him do as absurd things as he pleases about blockading the Ships under my command – even to be angry at my sending ships to Lisbon with my dispatches, and angry at my sending ships to a part of the Station under any orders, before I knew of his arrival to take that lucrative part of my Station from me – I shall never enter into a paper war with him, or anyone else.'[43] To Radstock on the 15th he wrote of Orde's Command '. . . I think whoever has [it] should have this . . . so much did I expect Orde to relieve me in toto that all my things were sent to the *Superb*, where they still remain . . .'[44] Then, in a letter dated 14 March 1805 to Captain Sutton of the *Amphion*, he wrote, 'If Sir John Orde condescends to ask after me, make my respectful compliments . . .'[45] Then, in a letter dated 29 March to Ball at Malta he wrote:

Fox has called upon Sir John Orde, who tells him he must refer to me, which he has done, and I have been forced to answer him that I regretted the Officer at the Straits mouth was not junior to me, when I should order him to take care of Gibraltar. But this cannot go on. I have, on January 17th, wrote home of what would happen; and I dare say, Orde has a trimmer before this time. He will not be suffered to remain much longer; he will go to the Channel; he will be the richest Admiral that England ever

160

had and I one of the poorest . . .'[46]

And to Radstock on 1 April he wrote '. . . Report says that Sir John Orde will be the richest Admiral that England ever saw . . . I would have made as much good use of a large fortune as Sir John Orde, or any other Admiral. I should like to have tried . . .'[47] Even when writing to his sister Mrs Bolton on 9 May he wrote '. . . I should have been a very rich, instead of a poor man, if Lord Melville had not given the Galleons to Sir John Orde . . .'[48]

But events now began to move apace.

Notes

[1] N Walder, p. 457.
[2] N Hol, p. 287.
[3] Warner, p. 45.
[4] NN, VI, p. 162.
[5] NN, VI, p. 191; N Kerr, p. 205.
[6] N Mah, p. 614.
[7] Terraine, p. 55.
[8] NB, p. 234.
[9] NJR, p. 317.
[10] Bowles, p. 19.
[11] NJR, p. 327.
[12] NN, VI, p. 250.
[13] Terraine, p. 53.
[14] N For, p. 228.
[15] Cornw, pp. 162-3.
[16] Cornw, p. 474.
[17] NB, p. 234.
[18] Terraine, p. 53.
[19] Letters of George III, Para 2959.
[20] *Blockade of Brest*, II, p. 114.
[21] Terraine, p. 53.
[22] N Mahan, pp. 625, 627, 628; N Brad.
[23] Orde Papers.
[24] Orde Papers.
[25] NJR, p. 245.
[26] N Pet, II, p. 438.
[27] NN, VI, p. 285.
[28] NN, VI, p. 288.
[29] NN, VI, p. 288.
[30] N Mah, p. 623.
[31] NN, VI, p. 289.

[32] N Pet, II, p. 443; in Monmouth.
[33] Monmouth.
[34] NN, VI, p. 299.
[35] NN, VI, p. 305.
[36] N Mah, p. 626; NN, Vol VI, pp. 319-20.
[37] N Brad, p. 173.
[38] Essay vi, p. 358 quoted by Pettigrew; N Pet, p. 445.
[39] *The Times*, 18 April 1805.
[40] N Wi, p. 272.
[41] NN, VI, p. 308.
[42] N Phil, p. 125; N Mah, p. 628; N Fitch, p. 251.
[43] NN, VI, p. 308.
[44] NN, VI, p. 362.
[45] NN, VI, p. 362.
[46] NN, VI, p. 382.
[47] NN, VI, p. 391.
[48] NN, VI, p. 429.

CHAPTER XIII

VILLENEUVE REFUSES TO PUT TO SEA BUT THEN SAILS FOR THE WEST INDIES PAST SIR JOHN ORDE

Throughout the winter of 1804/5, Napoleon was formulating and reformulating plans for the invasion of Great Britain, all of which involved the squadrons at Brest, Rochefort, El Ferrol and Toulon breaking out through the blockade of British ships, forming a junction, and then sailing for Boulogne to give cover in the Channel for the invasion force. As before, most involved sailing for the French-held island of Martinique in the West Indies, thus drawing off Nelson's Mediterranean Fleet, and, hopefully, some of the Channel Fleet as well, before doubling back to protect the French invasion flotilla. 'On their successful arrival,' Napoleon was to say, 'hang the destinies of the World.'[1] But at every turn he was met by the refusal of Villeneuve to take his Fleet to sea. The January plan envisaged the combined Fleet sailing for the Caribbean to damage and pillage British interests there. The February plan involved the Spanish Fleet. Each time the Naval Minister, Decrés, was met with a plea from Villeneuve that the time or the weather was not quite right. Indeed Napoleon, ever a man of precision, reckoned without the vagaries of the weather on which the success of the planned crossing so depended for weather was one factor which could not be forced to respond to his commands. Lack of breeze was of course fatal to the movement of ships under canvass and could sink the best laid plans. It was Villeneuve's constant report either that the weather was bad or that the British were alert to their plans or that supplies were inadequate – whatever the reason Villeneuve refused to budge however much the Emperor cursed his name. He did emerge momentarily on 18 January but soon limped back into harbour in the face of bad weather but also because of the presence of two British frigates lying out to sea. His next move was to ask Decrés that he be relieved of his command rather than face the humiliation of defeat at the hands of an enemy numerically inferior.[2] It is clear that here was a commanding officer who did not know how to command.

Reports of Villeneuve's emergence from Toulon on 18 January filtered through to Nelson, but not of his return to harbour. This news sent Nelson into a frenzy of activity. For several weeks he searched every corner of the eastern

Mediterranean whilst all the while Villeneuve and his Fleet snuggled safe and secure in port, the last place Nelson thought of looking for him. The Emperor had met with similar reluctance from Vice Admiral Ganteaume, albeit he was a much more robust and seasoned campaigner who had also been present at the Battle of the Nile. But he too steadfastly refused to put to sea with the Brest Squadron.

The March plan involved the Brest, Rochefort, Cadiz and Toulon squadrons sailing for the West Indies and then returning to Boulogne as a combined force of forty ships or more in time to escort the *Grand Armée* across the Channel in June or July. Ganteaume in particular was to call at Ferrol on his way to the West Indies and capture the seven or eight vessels of the English squadron there present, and, at the same time, release the French and Spanish ships there held in port before sailing for Martinique where he was to assume command of the combined fleet before sailing for Boulogne. Villeneuve's appointed task was to take the Toulon Squadron and those ships at Cadiz together with 3,140 troops and set sail for Martinique where he was to land those troops under the command of General Lauriston before placing his Fleet under the command of Ganteaume for the return journey to Brest, and, finally, Boulogne. In fact the Emperor produced yet another plan for the invasion late in March which did not involve the West Indies at all, but that was not issued until after Villeneuve had set sail, whilst yet another order, issued on 13 April, reverted to the original plan and did involve the West Indies in the hope of drawing off the Channel Fleet. Surprisingly this final plan placed Villeneuve in overall command of the French Fleet. The Emperor then planned to leave a naval presence at Cadiz to take the attention of the British and to send a force to Toulon to give Nelson the impression that an expedition was heading for the Mediterranean.

On 30 March 1805 the weather was set fair and the sea was clear of Nelson's ships. So Villeneuve at last weighed anchor, slid out of Toulon and set sail for Cadiz and the West Indies with four 80-gun ships, seven 74-gun ships, six 40-gun frigates and two brigs together with a cargo of 3,332 troops, whilst Nelson, oblivious to the escape, was watering his fleet in Sardinia. Hugging the Spanish coast Villeneuve reached Cartegena unmolested, where, for reasons best known to himself, he declined the offer of six Spanish ships of the line. Some reports suggest that they were either not ready or not offered and certainly Villeneuve was to so claim.[3] From there, on 9 April, he slipped quietly through the Straits of Gibraltar and, again hugging the coast, sailed for Cadiz and the waters where Sir John Orde lay at anchor with his squadron of six ships, including his flagship the *Glory* of 98 guns, the *Renown* which had reported in, the *Defence* of 74, the *Polyphemus*, the *Ruby* and the *Agamemnon*, all 64s, and the *Amphion* and *Mercury* frigates which had rejoined the Squadron with transports from Gibraltar that same morning.[4] The game was now afoot. In fact Villeneuve's passage through the Straits had been spotted both by Lord Mark Kerr, Captain of the frigate *Fisgard* of the Mediterranean Fleet whilst refitting at Gibraltar, and also by the sloop *Beagle* of Sir John Orde's Squadron which then went off in search of Sir John. In fact it was Captain Sir Richard Strachan in the *Renown* who brought a report of the sighting to Sir John as he was taking on provisions from transports and refitting in the Bay of Cadiz. Realizing then that Villeneuve was hard on his heels, Orde took action. The report which appeared subsequently in *The Times* of 8 May,[5] which caused such a furore in some quarters in London, was grossly misleading where it claimed that Sir John promptly sent the transports away, threw his stores overboard and then quickly ordered his squadron into formation for battle, whilst at the same time slowly withdrawing from the bay in the evening of the day that Villeneuve sailed for Cadiz (9 April).[6]

Fortunately a report independently made by an officer serving on Sir John Orde's flagship at the time has survived, and it is the report of one who did not owe his position there to Sir John. In fact, before that time he had been a total stranger to Sir John Orde. The probability is, therefore, that it is an impartial and more accurate version of events. His written report was that:

> . . . Almost every ship had a transport alongside with water etc. The *Agamemnon* had her main-yard down, unrigged, and I believe alongside. The *Glory* with two cables on end, and every deck full of empty casks; the people at dinner, and nearly a calm. About half-past twelve or one-o'clock, the signal officer reported to me a ship in the Gut firing guns, with signal-flags flying everywhere. We at last distinguished, at her lower studding-sail-boom rigged out, one for an enemy's fleet of superior force to the eastward. This ship proved to be the *Renown*, Sir Richard Strachan. So soon as the enemy were distinctly seen, bringing up a breeze. Sir John ordered the signal to be made to cast off the transports, and prepare for battle. When Sir John communicated these orders to me, he did it in the most cool and collected manner; and my reason for making this observation is, that the squadron at that time was in a state of perfect non-preparation, and the French Fleet running down fast, with a strong Levant wind. The *Renown* soon came out, catching the breeze; and I being the person who received Sir Richard on his coming on board, can bear witness to his observing, 'How coolly we took it, considering the force that was near us.' At this time we were heaving in (no cutting and slipping, indicating hurry and confusion), the French fleet coming round Trafalgar, with a strong wind, shewing a force of twelve sail of line and eight frigates.

There was another French line-of-battle ship at the entrance of Cadiz, and three Spanish ships of the line in the harbour, all ready to come out; and the wind being easterly, was of course quite favourable for their forming a junction with the French fleet. The exertions of the squadron under Sir John were very great, and in a short time the breeze reached us. At half-past four o'clock, the transports having been ordered to Lagos, where they were seen in safety, the *Amphion*, which had kept her station to the last, and in danger of being cut off, recalled, and the *Mercury* dispatched to the West Indies, the squadron weighed. Thus unexpectedly and critically situated, in the face of an enemy more than treble the force of our squadron, possessing the advantage of being to windward, and indeed one might say, having the power of overwhelming us, Sir John, instead of making a 'runaway' of it, as has been maliciously reported, ordered the signal to be made to form the larboard line of bearing, steering to the W.N.W. under easy sail. Evening came on, and the enemy were lost sight of. The *Amphion* was left so stationed as to be best enabled to obtain further intelligence of the enemy, as well as to give to any vessels of ours which might be approaching, due notice of where they were. Sir John's reasons for joining the Channel fleet were these: On the same evening he sent for me into his cabin, and whilst walking up and down, without asking advice, or leaning for any support of opinion, as his mind was firm and made up, he observed that the appearance of the enemy was very unexpected, and he could not account for it, adding, 'I must now make up my mind where to go. In the first place, the enemy may proceed to the West Indies, perhaps to the East: but no, that man Napoleon is not a man to trifle about islands and settlements – England is his object; and as at this time the French army is all ready at Boulogne, and the Brest fleet anchored in Camaret Bay, blockaded by Lord Gardner with a very inferior force, to join him is my duty and object, and there I will go.' . . . Subsequent events have proved the correctness of Sir John's judgment, for in the publications of Warden, Las Casas and O'Meare, it appears that such were the intentions of that extraordinary man, if Villeneuve had acted up to them . . . it would have been an act of madness in him, had he encountered an enemy's force of twelve sail of the line out, one at the entrance of, and eight ready in the harbour, in all twenty-one sail of the line and eight frigates, with his inferior force of five sail of the line (three of which were only 64's) and two frigates.[7]

It is a measure of Villeneuve's timidity that, even though he outnumbered Sir John by at least three to one, he chose to slip quietly into harbour rather than confront Orde's Squadron which he obligingly allowed to withdraw intact.

What was Sir John now to do? For he judged, rightly, that Villeneuve would emerge again fairly soon. Take on the eighteen or nineteen Frenchmen, augmented as they would undoubtedly be by the six Spanish ships of the line under the command of Admiral Gravina which had been lying in harbour? Had it been the intrepid Nelson, always more than ready for high risk, the answer would have been clear and simple as would the result – annihilation with glory, although not before Villeneuve's Fleet had suffered many crippling blows. But Sir John was a good deal more cautious and circumspect and less suicidal, for he knew full well that the real danger now lay in the possibility of a conjunction between Missiessy's Fleet which was still at sea, Ganteaume's Squadron under orders to break out of Brest, and Villeneuve's Mediterranean Squadron, strengthened as it now was by the Spanish ships. Whereas Nelson had waited impatiently and long for the French to emerge so that he could confront, and, hopefully, annihilate them, and so by such offensive tactics remove the threat of invasion once and for all in a more effective and permanent way, the orders which governed the Channel Fleet of which Sir John's Squadron was a member, were otherwise and more cautious. Their role for two years or more had been to mount a defensive blockade and so keep the French in harbour so that Napoleon would lack the cover necessary to escort his invasion flotilla across the Channel. And, in the event of an escape, it was Cornwallis's standing order that the Channel Fleet should withdraw to the Channel and concentrate there to protect the shores of Great Britain from invasion. This, after all, had been the broad policy for very many years. This Napoleon had consistently failed to understand in the succession of plans which he produced that spring and summer, most of which had but one central object, the escape of the Toulon Fleet to the West Indies drawing off the menace of Nelson in pursuit, coupled with the escape of the French Fleet at Brest and Rochefort in the hope of enticing away a part of the Channel Fleet as well, followed by a quick return of a combined Fleet to overcome the remainder of the Channel Fleet and provide cover for Napoleon's invasion flotilla. All he needed was protection from the British Navy for a matter of hours. In all this he counted on the very high commercial value which the British placed on the rich sugar export, especially from Jamaica but also from other British possessions in the West Indies, and therefore the need to protect those interests from French invasion. Sugar convoys at this time were rich prizes indeed. So much so that the British Government had, over the years, poured troops into the area to guard British interests. Indeed, in the year 1796, no less than 40,000 soldiers had been carried off by yellow fever in the West Indies alone.

And so, when Villeneuve ventured out on 10 April, Sir John was in no doubt as to the course which he should take, namely a quick report to the officer commanding the Channel Fleet followed by withdrawal to join the Fleet off Ushant, thus adding his squadron to those protecting the Straits of Dover. Of course Nelson has left a legacy of boldness and risk in his constant determination, not just to defeat the enemy but to annihilate him. But if the actions of lesser men were to be judged by the same standard and Flag Officers were expected to rush into battle whatever the odds, failing which censure would follow, few naval actions would ever have succeeded involving as they did, men of lesser genius.

In fact the French emerged at 2 a.m. on the morning of 10 April without the Spanish Fleet which followed several hours later when eventually ready to put to sea. Sir John and his squadron had by then withdrawn. Back in London he was castigated for not engaging the enemy, not by the Admiralty or by those who understood naval tactics, but, somewhat unfairly, by those merchants in the City who were concerned that their commercial interests in the West Indies now stood at risk from the threat of French invasion followed by marauding and pillaging. Nelson was to suffer similar criticism on more than one occasion from that same quarter. However, with hindsight, at the very least Orde should perhaps have detailed off one or two ships to shadow Villeneuve's Fleet in order to know of their destination. But perhaps the complaint made by Nelson had greater validity for when he later heard of Villeneuve's departure westward, he complained bitterly that Sir John had not sent him so much as a frigate to tell him of it, thus preventing a hot pursuit. But in that criticism there may perhaps have been a note of irritation with himself for having allowed Villeneuve to escape from Toulon for there were those too in London who were currently censuring Nelson for just that. In fact Sir John had been quick to report what he had seen, not, it is true, to the officer commanding the Mediterranean Fleet, of which he was not a part, but to the officer commanding the Channel Fleet of which his Squadron was a member, and indeed to the Admiralty. And he did at least make some attempt to inform Nelson on 11 April of Villeneuve's position.[8] And in fact, after sending the sloop *Sophie* to London on 12 April to inform the Admiralty of these developments, Orde spent two days on 14 and 15 April in the waters to the south of Cadiz in search of Villeneuve's Fleet which had by then sailed for the West Indies. It was not until the 18th that he turned north for the Channel Fleet. Of course had he known Villeneuve's timid state of mind he may have done better to stand his ground and fire a few warning shots which could just have been enough persuasion to keep Villeneuve in harbour at Cadiz!

By letter to Lord Robert Fitzgerald at Lisbon dated 10 April Sir John had written that:

> I send a merchant ship near me with this, to acquaint you that while at
> anchor yesterday off Cadiz, I had nearly been brought to action by the
> Toulon Fleet of 20 or 24 sail, 11 to 12 clearly of the line, possibly having
> some Spanish ships from Carthagena with them . . . 7 or 8 sail of the line
> are in readiness to join them from Cadiz, and in 24 hours, perhaps 2 or 3
> more. Where their destination may be after this junction (which I am not
> astonished at) I cannot tell, but I judge westward. Where Lord Nelson is I
> cannot hear but I am told he is likely to return to Egypt on hearing of the
> French fleet being at sea. Pray forward this intelligence in all directions,
> with every possible despatch.[9]

In this Sir John showed remarkable prescience both as to the intentions of
Napoleon and Villeneuve to sail westwards which he judged correctly, but also
in guessing the possible reaction of Horatio Nelson.

Two days later, on 12 April, he reported to Lord Gardner, then commanding
the Channel Fleet or Western Squadron, whilst Cornwallis was on leave, that
he had been 'induced to quit my station before Cadiz with the Squadron under
my command . . . by the sudden appearance of the Toulon Fleet which joined
the Spanish force in Cadiz the same evening . . . What the destination of this
force may be I cannot ascertain, but I judge westward – in any case I think it
would not remain long in Cadiz.' He then provided a detailed list of the Spanish
vessels, their armaments and a not entirely accurate description of the officers
commanding, reporting also that he had

> not heard from Lord Nelson since December last nor can I positively
> ascertain his actual position and movements. I have directed the commander
> of the ship who will deliver you this, and my dispatches for the Admiralty
> and for Ireland, to follow your orders for his further proceedings, thus
> leaving it to your lordship to detach him on for England with my Admiralty
> letters, or to send them by any other means your Lordship may judge fit to
> ensure their earliest delivery to the Admiralty, it being of the greatest
> consequence their Lordships should receive them without delay. I shall
> with the remaining ships of my Squadron make the best of my way to
> submit them to your disposal, so soon as a distribution of provisions and
> water is made, of which we are very short.[10]

The author John Terraine in his book *Trafalgar* cites a letter written by Orde
in which he writes 'I think the chances are great in favour of their destination

being westward where by a sudden concentration of several detachments, Bonaparte may hope to gain a temporary superiority in the Channel, and availing himself of it, strike his enemy a mortal blow.'[11]

In fact it was not until 26 April that Gardner sent a copy of Sir John's letter to Lord Robert Fitzgerald and to Marsden at the Admiralty,[12] with the comment that, 'Whether it is their intention to proceed to the northward or to the southward is very uncertain, but Sir John Orde is inclined to think their destination is westward,' and, by a further letter to Marsden on 27 April he pointed to the possibility of the Toulon Squadron of eighteen or nineteen sail of the line combining with the Squadron of thirteen sail of the line and six frigates lying off Ferrol. 'I therefore hope that the two squadrons to the southward under Sir John Orde and Sir Robert Calder, will endeavour to join the fleet under my orders consisting of seventeen sail of the line, and that their Lordships will take such measures for my being reinforced as they may judge necessary.'[13] In that letter the commander of the Channel Fleet clearly hoped that Sir John would take the course which in fact he did take when withdrawing his Squadron of ships to the Channel Fleet.

The sloop *Sophie*, detached from Orde's Squadron, delivered his despatches to the Admiralty on 29 April. By now, unbeknown to Orde, Barham had succeeded Melville as First Lord of the Admiralty on 2 May. He quickly laid Orde's despatches before William Pitt and both then gave anxious consideration to the dangers which now presented. Not surprisingly Pitt described Orde's assessment that Villeneuve could be under orders to sail post haste for the north-west coast of France after his return from the West Indies, as 'of the most pressing importance' especially since a contingent of British troops under Sir James Craig had, only a few days before on 19 April, set sail from Portsmouth for Malta and were now on the high seas – or so they thought – bound for the Tagus with no cover but two ships of the line to escort them.[14] In fact they had by then reached their destination and were safely on shore but Pitt and Barham were not to know this. More information as to Villeneuve's movements then arrived on 2 May by the sloop *Beagle*, one of Orde's cruisers.[15] Barham now acted with speed and with the sure touch of a man with years of experience in naval strategy behind him. He immediately saw the importance of maintaining the strength of the Channel Fleet off Ushant in case of invasion. His orders to Cornwallis were that 'all other orders should be interpreted in terms of the necessity to keep the Western Squadron in strength of not less than eighteen sail of the line.'[16] At the same time Admiral Lord Keith's ships of the North Sea Fleet were concentrated at the Nore.

Despite the criticism made at the time of Orde's withdrawal on 9 and 10 April, some biographers of Nelson have since dealt with it more fairly. Walder, in his biography of Nelson, judged Orde's logic to have been 'impeccable', and the path he took as 'the correct one', albeit a path of extreme caution.[17] (It has however to be conceded that Walder may have been persuaded to this view in discussions of many years ago with the author.) Terraine's conclusion was that Orde 'took guidance from the tried tradition, given that "Everything pointed to a great and dangerous French combination."'[18]

And in his prediction as to Villeneuve's destination and purpose, Terraine considered that Orde 'deserves full credit, since no-one else had yet reached it', when he reported that 'I am persuaded the enemy will not remain long in Cadiz, and I think the chances are great in favour of their destination being westward where by a sudden concentration of several detachments, Bonaparte may hope to gain a temporary superiority in the Channel and availing himself of it strike his enemy a mortal blow.'[19] In this, Terraine writes, 'Orde was the first to penetrate Napoleon's plan. Orde has been blamed for not pursuing them, and cutting off their stragglers, but it is hard to blame him for not foreseeing that Villeneuve's stay at Cadiz would only last six hours!' Bradford, in *Nelson – The Essential Hero*, describes Orde's withdrawal as 'in accordance with normal strategy to join the fleet off Ushant'. When the enemy's intentions were unknown, it was always wisest to concentrate forces so as to guard the approaches to the Channel.[20] Corelli Barnett wrote that 'the genius of Bonaparte (had) thus been rumbled at the outset by a run-of-the-mill English flag officer whose name few of his countrymen now remember.'[21]

J. Steven Watson described Orde's action as 'prudently' hurrying north.[22] Beresford, on the other hand, condemned him out of hand in round terms, claiming that

> he laid hands on Nelson's frigates, paralysing Nelson in his arduous watch off Toulon; he omitted to send Nelson information of the enemy's doings and proceedings . . . finally, in a critical moment, he went off in a dudgeon to England with his fleet. It is no exaggeration to say that at every point Nelson's work was doubled by the intrusion of this jealous, incompetent, meddlesome superior, and we cannot wonder that he felt bitter at the way in which he had been treated. It was not that he himself lost money, it was rather because the country and the service suffered, because the escape of the French was facilitated.[23]

But no other commentator has ever seen fit to question Orde's competence or indeed to criticize him in such an extreme and intemperate way. Indeed Beresford went on, 'Orde's command was a national debt due to Nelson . . . He made his ignoble escape and fled north . . . such was the shameful issue of a political job. Had Nelson or Collingwood been there . . . they would have thought first for the honour and greatness of England . . . and not for their own ships.'[24]

Admiral Lord Radstock had written on 21 May to his son, then serving under Nelson's command, that 'The City people are crying out against Sir J.O., and, as usual, are equally absurd and unjust. Some are so ridiculous as to say that he ought to have captured some of the Toulon Squadron, whilst others, more moderate, think that he might at all events, have so crippled the enemy as to have checked the expedition.'[25] Rear Admiral Mahan, that much-respected American naval historian, agreed with this assessment with the comment, 'To fight eleven ships with six could only be justified by extreme circumstances.' However, he censures Orde for not keeping better track of the enemy's movements in such a moment of national emergency and for not sending word on to Nelson at Gibraltar. Forester's opinion was that:

He had acted in uninspired fashion; having got his ships out of serious danger he went straight northward to join the fleet blockading Brest – the obvious concentration at the vital point. But he made no attempt to ascertain Villeneuve's further course; he had not clung to him for a day or two, as any good officer might have done, and he had left no news for Nelson following after . . . public clamour turned against him venomously, not for losing touch, but for not fighting Villeneuve which he was quite right not to do. The agitation ended in Orde's resigning the command . . .[26]

In this latter respect, Forester was incorrect for Orde's resignation had gone in before Villeneuve ever set sail from Toulon. Even Southey, in his uncertain but very readable biography of Nelson, wrote that 'Sir John Orde necessarily retired at his approach.'[27] *The Times* reported on 4 May,

It is reported with great credibility that Sir John Orde has brought his squadron from Cadiz to Lord Gardner off Brest. It appears a very wise and prudent step and best calculated to defeat the junction of the squadrons assembled from Toulon and the ports of Spain, from making a final junction with the grand fleet in that harbour. Lord Gardner will doubtless be powerfully reinforced from home; and enabled to protect us from insult in the Channel, if it be really the intention of all these junctions to cover an invasion from Boulogne and the Texel.[28]

And it is to be noted that Lord Gardner highly approved of the step taken.

Indeed, if Ralfe be correct, Lord Barham, First Lord of the Admiralty, afterwards told Sir John's brother that '. . . it was fully known the Admiralty approved of Sir John's conduct' and expressed the hope 'that he might have employment again, if such a measure would be acceptable to him.'[29]

SIR JOHN ORDE'S REQUEST FOR RETIREMENT

An assumption has since been made by many biographers of Nelson including the Cambridge Modern History that Sir John Orde, whilst at Cadiz, was, because of his performance on 9 April, summarily ordered to return to Plymouth and there strike his flag.[30] Such, however, was not the case as correspondence at the time serves to demonstrate. As Nelson had predicted would be the case, the winter spent by Sir John Orde policing the waters off Cadiz was a strenuous one. In March of that year he had begun to find the dual role which had been required of him difficult to fulfil and as irritating as clearly Nelson also found it to be. And so, on 27 March, he had written to Marsden acknowledging receipt of two letters from the Admiralty dated 7 and 26 February in the following terms:

By your letter of the 7th I perceive your lordships have authorised Lord Nelson to appoint an agent for the disposal of certain parts of the Spanish property detained by *my squadron* and now at Gibraltar, and for sending home the remainder of it from that place, detained before the 11th of January, of which I shall acquaint the officers more immediately concerned.

By your letter of the 26th February, I observe their lordships are of opinion it is an essential part of the duty of the squadron under my orders to protect the trade from England to Gibraltar, a circumstance I could not foresee being positively directed by their lordships not to employ any part of the force under my command within the Straits, an order I must disobey if I comply with the other. Besides, I must beg you to acquaint their lordships with the impossibility of my affording a force, under actual circumstances, from that at present under my command, to protect vessels going to Gibraltar, without exposing to immense peril the safety of my whole squadron, and the total failure of the main object for which I judge I am placed here by their lordships – risks that I shall not think myself justified in running without their lordships' more positive commands for the purpose.[31]

By a letter of the same date he wrote to Lord Melville to much the same effect, referring again to the authority given to Nelson to appoint an agent, adding that it was 'an arrangement I should have thought myself entitled to complain of had I been junior to his Lordship'. And, as to the order to protect the trade into Gibraltar, he added, 'I must confess, I was not prepared to have notified, not only because of my general orders, but also because of the insufficiency of my squadron for this duty in addition to the many others it is called upon to perform.' There then followed in this letter a clear request for permission to retire, this a good twelve or thirteen days before the events of 9 April.

> Some other officer may possibly feel these circumstances less mortifying than I do; and possessing greater abilities, may be able to perform all that seems expected by the Admiralty from me, with the small force entrusted to my command; no one, I will venture to say, can have shown more zeal and industry than I have done in the execution of an arduous duty, which, I am sorry, notwithstanding to say I now feel myself unequal to perform with satisfaction to my employers and to my own feelings, extremely hurt by recent treatment.
>
> May I then request your lordship permission to retire from a situation I owe to your goodness, and which to hold any longer would prove me unworthy the protection I have received. In resigning my command into abler hands, possessing the confidence of the Admiralty, I shall have the satisfaction to believe I am promoting His Majesty's service at the same time that I am discharging a duty I owe to my country and to my own character. I remain, my lord, with the strongest sense of obligation, of consideration and esteem, Your Lordships Most faithful and obedient servant,
> J. Orde.[32]

Whether Sir John had in truth found it impossible to perform the dual role given to him with the resources put at his disposal, or not, it is difficult to know, for the suspicion must be that, crippled with gout,[33] and exhausted by the need for eternal vigilance, he had grown weary of his task, especially since there was ever the prospect of petty bickering at the Gibraltar margin of his jurisdiction where it overlapped with that of the Mediterranean Fleet. But, clear it is that, long before Villeneuve came over the horizon, he had decided to go. In itself this effectively answers the accusations of his critics, including Nelson, that he had only come out because of the prospect of riches from prize money on the station. If that had been so, he would not have been quite so anxious to quit his command after only six months in post, as he undoubtedly was.

Although his letters to Melville and Marsden were written in tactless, ungenerous and somewhat petulant terms, he did make his wish and intention clear and so left the Admiralty little room but to accept. Indeed, on 30 April, whilst off Ushant, he pressed the matter to conclusion with a letter to the First Lord, 'When the present alarm is over should it be convenient to allow me to go into port and repair to town for a few days, I would be thankful for the indulgence, having some matters to communicate to your lordship and the Board which I cannot so well convey in writing.'

Accordingly, by a Minute dated 6 May, the Lords Commissioners acknowledged receipt of his letter to Melville and then notified Sir John that they were pleased to grant his request for permission to retire and directed him, upon the *Glory*'s arrival at Spithead, to strike his flag and come on shore.[34] This they then confirmed in a letter to Lord Gardner.[35] Thus ended Sir John Orde's service at sea.

He arrived at Portsmouth on 10 May, and then, on 15 May *The Times* reported that Sir John had demanded a court martial as a vehicle which would enable him to explain his withdrawal, but that this request had been refused.[36] Although he had sought relief from the impossibility of his role on the Cadiz Station, he was nonetheless somewhat taken aback by the speed with which the Admiralty had accepted his request. He was not of course to know when making it in his private letter to Lord Melville that Melville was then on his way out of office to be succeeded, on 2 May, by Middleton as the newly created Lord Barham. Barham clearly viewed matters in a different light and after he had come home Sir John began to regret his somewhat impetuous request for a transfer. He therefore went to see Barham at the Admiralty on 18 May and there followed what *The Times* described as 'a long interview'. And then, by letter dated 20 May, Sir John thanked Barham 'for the flattering manner in which you were pleased to mark your entire approbation of my conduct', and repeated that he had not foreseen that his private letter to Melville of 7 March would be shown to the Board, still less that it would be made the ground of an order for him to strike his flag. He expressed the hope that he may be pressed into active service again without delay to 'rescue' him 'from the advantage taken of my present situation, to calumniate and disgrace me in the public estimation' and because it was his 'highest ambition to be honourably employed at any time . . .' By letter dated 21 May Barham wrote to Sir John that 'If it is your wish to be re-employed, I would recommend your making it known to the Board'! In fact Sir John was never to go to sea again although he was advanced to the rank of full Admiral of the Blue in the Trafalgar promotion later that same year.[37]

Now he had to occupy himself in other ways. One of his first acts was to honour a long-standing promise to himself to erect a tablet in memory of his first wife Margaret Emma, who had died fifteen years before. This now survives on the south wall of the Parish Church of Hanwell in Middlesex.[38]

Notes

[1] Terraine, p. 79.
[2] Schom, p. 198.
[3] N Bry, p. 100.
[4] Blockade of Brest, p. 225.
[5] *The Times*, 8 May 1805.
[6] Terraine, p. 70.
[7] Ralfe, Vol II, pp. 75-7.
[8] Terraine, p. 74.
[9] Blockade of Brest, letter No. 475, p. 225.
[10] Blockade of Brest, letter No. 476, p. 225.
[11] Terraine, p. 71.
[12] Blockade of Brest, p. 240.
[13] Blockade of Brest, letter No. 490, p. 240.
[14] Terraine, p. 75.
[15] Terraine, p. 88.
[16] Terraine, p. 89.
[17] N Walder, p. 464.
[18] Terraine, p. 80.
[19] Barnett pp. 103-4; Terraine, p. 71.
[20] N Brad, p. 317.
[21] Barnett, p. 103.
[22] Watson, p. 428.
[23] NB & W, p. 180.
[24] NB & W, p. 185.
[25] N Mahan, p. 651.
[26] N For, p. 228.
[27] NS, p. 285.
[28] *The Times*, 4 May 1805.
[29] Ralfe, Vol II, p. 77.
[30] *Cambridge Modern History*, Vol IX, p. 224.
[31] The Barham Papers, III, p. 301.
[32] The Barham Papers, III, p. 301.
[33] NN, VI, p. 258.
[34] The Barham Papers, p. 304.
[35] Blockade of Brest, p. 257.
[36] *The Times*, 15 May 1805.
[37] The Barham Papers, p. 308.
[38] *Gentleman's Magazine*, Vol 75(2) for Sept 1805, p. 822.

CHAPTER XIV

NELSON IN PURSUIT

Whatever the truth may have been, the French and Spanish fleets were now at sea after many months of containment. The prospect now was of junction with the Brest Squadron of twenty-one ships and a further contingent of Spanish ships emerging from El Ferrol. The balloon had gone up, the storm clouds were now looming and alarm was great in London as Napoleon waited impatiently the arrival of the Fleet and his opportunity to sail his armada across the waters of the English Channel. Although Sir John had divined, correctly, the probable course of events, namely a run for the West Indies to draw off Nelson and some of the ships of the Channel Fleet followed by a junction of fleets in the English Channel for escort duties, this development had caught Admiral Cornwallis at home on leave, with Lord Gardner assuming command in his stead, whilst Lord Nelson and the Mediterranean Fleet lay off the coast of Italy, oblivious to developments for the moment. Given the difficulty of communication over such great distances, news of Villeneuve's breakout did not reach Gardner until 26 April by which time Villeneuve was well on his way to the West Indies. The moment he received this intelligence he immediately put the Fleet on standby and stepped up the vigil off Brest fully expecting the Fleet under Ganteaume to break out in order to draw off the Channel Fleet and link up with Villeneuve on his return to home waters. In fact there was in truth no cause for alarm, for, to the amazement and fury of the Emperor, Ganteaume had steadfastly refused to sail. Almost beside himself with rage Napoleon could but fulminate against his naval commanders and then amend his plans yet again, giving a new instruction that if Ganteaume had not set sail by 20 May he should not set sail at all but should remain in harbour, for he, Napoleon, would be on the coast at Boulogne in July as planned waiting for the return and for the protection of the Fleet which had sailed for the West Indies. Thus would his plan for the invasion of Great Britain proceed with or without the Fleet in harbour at Brest. For their part the Admiralty now ordered Vice Admiral (as he had become) Cuthbert Collingwood to sail for the West Indies with a newly formed squadron of ships in order to protect British interests there.

There followed what has come to be known as 'the long chase' which was perhaps more remarkable for the seamanship it demonstrated than for anything it may have achieved. Nelson first learned that Villeneuve had left Toulon on 4 April when the cruiser *Phoebe* brought him the information as *Victory* lay in Italian waters. But there was no indication as to where they had gone. His first thoughts, as always, were of Egypt and the need for his protection there and at Sicily. And so he spread his Fleet across the waters south of the island of Sardinia and scoured the Mediterranean. It was not until 18 April that Nelson learned that Villeneuve had left the Mediterranean altogether. Yet still, as a Mediterranean Fleet, he regarded it as his prey. The day following he wrote to Lord Gardner that he felt 'vexed at their slipping out of the Mediterranean, as I had marked them for my own game . . .'[1] To Melville he wrote that he intended to abandon the Mediterranean Station since there was now no other French Fleet of significance which remained there. Although Villeneuve had eight days start on him and he was becalmed he wrote that he intended to set off in pursuit in the hope of bringing them to battle. His decision to do so met with much criticism in the London press which regarded it as both an act of disobedience and an act of folly leaving these shores unprotected in his absence.[2] After all Collingwood had already been appointed in the task and what if the Channel Fleet had also decided of its own volition to sail in pursuit? Nelson's belief was that Villeneuve must be headed for Brest and a junction with the squadron there in harbour, or perhaps even for Ireland.

As he left the Mediterranean he put into Gibraltar for victualling to cater for the journey, impatient to be on his way the moment he detected a change in the wind. That impatience was later to be described by Dr Scott in these terms. 'Off went a gun from *Victory*, and up went the Blue Peter, whilst the Admiral paced the deck in a hurry, with anxious steps and impatient of a moment's delay. The officer said, "Here is one of Nelson's mad pranks." But he was nevertheless right, the wind did become favourable, the linen was left on shore, the fleet cleared the GUT, and away they steered for the West Indies.'[3] It was not until he had reached Portugal and was anchored off Lagos Bay that he learned from the crew of ships which had been supplying Orde's Squadron, and then from a British officer serving in the Portuguese Navy, Rear Admiral Donald Campbell, that it was believed that Villeneuve was headed for the West Indies. For imparting that information Campbell was dismissed his command at the insistence of the French Ambassador at Lisbon,[4] to whom the Spanish naval commander at Algezeros had complained.[5] The Ambassador regarded his act as a breach of Portugal's neutrality. On 9 May the Captain of one of Orde's frigates reported to Nelson that Villeneuve had not been spotted heading for the English Channel by ships coming out from Spithead or across the Bay,[6] and so, after taking on board further provisions, Nelson set sail for the West Indies on 12 May.

More than a month had now gone by since Villeneuve had emerged from Cadiz. Collingwood, poised with fourteen ships of the line, ready to pursue Villeneuve's Fleet, now learned of Nelson's expedition and therefore judged it better to remain where he was, patrolling the waters off Cadiz which had been vacated by Sir John Orde, sending two of his ships only to the West Indies to help there with the protection of British commercial interests. No doubt the yellow streaks and the black surround for the portholes, customary to Nelson's ships, were painted on to accord with his wishes. With an even greater insight than even Orde had shown earlier, that other Northumbrian, Collingwood, now read the mind of the Emperor accurately when he wrote to a friend, 'I believe their object in the West Indies to be less conquest than to draw our force from home. The Rochefort squadron seems to have had nothing else in view . . . If with the Spaniards they can cause a great alarm, and draw a great force there from England, they will have so much less to oppose them in their real attack, which will be at home in harvest time.'[7] And, for his part, on his return at the beginning of July, Cornwallis immediately put the Channel Fleet on full alert, expecting that after two years of watching and waiting the enemy Fleet was eventually about to break out of Brest, Rochefort, El Ferrol and Cadiz the moment Villeneuve's Fleet arrived back in the English Channel. He anticipated a junction of almost sixty French and Spanish sail of the line which would then be placed at the disposal of the Emperor to protect his flotilla of 2,000 or more invasion craft as they negotiated the waters of the English Channel. In those dark thoughts, Cornwallis was fully justified, although, in truth, the danger was not as great as it seemed, for, as with Napoleon, he had reckoned without the timidity of the French Naval Command which had not the slightest intention of putting to sea in the face of the Royal Navy, if that could be avoided. Nelson crossed the Atlantic and back in record time. *Victory*, which he had acquired in 1803, had been St Vincent's flagship six years before. A magnificent first rater, she was tall masted with a vast spread of sail and carried 104 guns and over 800 officers and men. His own quarters immediately below his Captain's beneath the poop at the stern of the ship, were spacious indeed. Although now fifty and more years old, she had recently undergone an overhaul and was now capable of great speed[8] Unknown to him he passed close to Villeneuve in the waters of Antigua and but for incorrect information from one General Brereton, he would have caught him. But his pursuit served British interests nonetheless, for, the moment he heard that Nelson was on his heels, Villeneuve promptly abandoned Napoleon's orders for the invasion of British territories in the West Indies and in his panic turned tail for Europe with Nelson in hot pursuit, landing the troops, arms and supplies which had been sent out for the protection of French-held islands, indiscriminately. On 1 June Villeneuve wrote to Decrés, 'The enemy is on his guard, having been warned by the *Mercury*,'[9] a ship which had been sent by Orde. In fact Nelson had also sent the brig *Curieux* on ahead to carry the news to Lord Barham at the Admiralty.[10] Again luck was not with Nelson, for, as chance would have it, he took a route back to the south of that which Villeneuve had taken. And so Villeneuve eluded him.

CALDER AND THE BATTLE OF EL FERROL

In fact the return of Villeneuve to European waters had been spotted on 22 July by Sir Robert Calder then lying some 117 miles off El Ferrol at the order of Lord Barham. Calder, then a Vice Admiral of the White, was an excessively arrogant and opinionated officer who had generally been counted one of Nelson's enemies ever since the Battle of St Vincent at which he had openly criticized Nelson's disobedience of orders. But he was nonetheless intelligent, skilful, experienced and resourceful enough to take on the Franco-Spanish Fleet and they were evenly matched in numbers, Calder with fifteen sail of the line as against nineteen or twenty in the Combined Fleet. But, as chance would have it, fog descended on that hot July day and visibility was reduced almost to zero. Ships moved silently in and out of view on a slight breeze like ghosts passing in the night. Nonetheless Calder stood towards the French, and then, at noon, formed his ships into single line ready for battle. After some hesitation which lasted two or three hours Villeneuve decided to take up the challenge. As the two fleets moved towards each other so the first shots were fired at about 5.15 p.m. by Admiral Gravina's Squadron of Spanish ships. There followed an intense exchange of fire, chiefly between the British and the Spaniards who took the brunt of the fighting, although three ships of the French Fleet also played an active and courageous part. So the battle raged for three hours or more in confused and chaotic conditions until failing light, fog and the smoke of gunfire reduced visibility to almost nil and prompted Calder to discontinue the action with the 'night private signal' to his Fleet. Such were the conditions that it was another hour or so before the order had been received by all of his Captains by which time two Spanish ships, the *San Rafael* and the *Firma*, badly damaged by gunfire, had surrendered to the British and their crews taken prisoner. Thirty-nine British officers and men had been killed in the engagement. Villeneuve had lost 149, most of them Spaniards who had shown great determination and courage. Dawn the following day found the two fleets still in a position of confrontation, and, as the fog began to lift, so the wind picked up slightly. And yet, for reasons which have never been explained adequately, no movement came from either fleet. Each stood its ground but no move was made on either side to renew the engagement. So too, on the day following that, 24 July, it was a case of waiting and watching, the British Fleet in particular seemingly reluctant to press home their advantage. And then, on 25 July, both fleets silently withdrew, quitting the battlefield, sailing off in opposite directions. There can be no doubt but that if Nelson had been present at that moment, the Battle of Trafalgar three months later would never have taken place for the French Fleet would have been in no shape to fight it. Although Villeneuve was never at any time called to account for his actions off El Ferrol, in December of that year a court martial which Calder had himself demanded was convened by the Admiralty to enquire into what was described as 'the humiliation' and Sir Robert Calder's responsibility for it. At that hearing he sought to justify his decision to stand away and his failure to pursue the enemy on the grounds that he had believed that Villeneuve was about to be reinforced with a fleet coming out of El Ferrol which would have made his, Calder's, position impossible, but also because he had been most anxious to safeguard his own damaged ships, together with the two Spanish ships which had been captured. Calder escaped with a 'severe reprimand' but he was never to be employed at sea again, although five years on, he was appointed C-in-C at Plymouth and subsequently became an Admiral of the White.[11] For his part Napoleon characteristically concealed the truth of the fiasco from the French public and dressed it up as a victory! As for Villeneuve, he put in to the nearest harbour at Vigo Bay on 27 July before proceeding to El Ferrol on 31 July where the junction with two other French squadrons increased the overall strength of his Franco-Spanish Fleet there in harbour to twenty-nine sail of the line. Calder withdrew to join Cornwallis off Ushant as Villeneuve lay in harbour and England breathed again. Although he was to be condemned for it, Calder had thus prevented Villeneuve from sailing to join Napoleon. Nelson meanwhile, having sailed almost non-stop over a distance of several thousand miles, had missed the possibility of action, and so now, judging that he had earned a rest after more than two years at sea, he sailed for home. On 19 August he struck his flag, went on shore and headed for Merton, Lady Hamilton and his daughter Horatia.

St VINCENT AND MELVILLE

Throughout that momentous year, and even though the enemy was at the door, and despite the success of the Admiralty in keeping the Fleet at sea, Lord St Vincent nonetheless pestered, pursued and harried the First Lord of the Admiralty from the opposition benches without mercy, much to the delight of Napoleon Bonaparte. The target for his bombardment was the extravagance of the Navy Board in years gone by, for it was permitted to issue its own bills for the supply of stores and for the construction and repair of ships without the need for Parliamentary or Treasury authority. As Admiralty Treasurer between the years 1782 and 1801, Melville had been a member of the Navy Board, albeit the treasurership had been something of a sinecure held whilst he was successively Home Secretary and then Secretary of State for War. But it had produced emoluments amounting to £4,000 per annum.[12] St Vincent had assembled a lot of ammunition for his attack, which had been gathered for the most part by his devoted follower and secretary, Tucker, who had been planted on the Navy Board as a member by St Vincent himself.[13] St Vincent's main discovery had been that the Paymaster of the Navy, one Trotter, had speculated with public funds drawn on the Bank of England on a large scale in the ten years leading up to the year 1801. So much so that St Vincent had insisted that a Commission of Naval Enquiry be set up. It had spent two long years in deliberation but then reported in February 1805, during Melville's tenure of office as First Lord, that there was indeed truth in the allegation. Although every penny of the amount involved had by then been repaid, it had been a gross misuse of public funds and it provided ammunition enough for St Vincent in his private war with Pitt and Melville, and enabled him to allege negligence on the part of Melville in his monitoring of public expenditure in years gone by. Indeed it went further for Melville admitted that he had, very foolishly, obtained loans from Trotter himself in those earlier years for purposes which he refused to identify, although it was supposed that these had been borrowed in order to finance a secret service. The irony was that, as Treasurer of the Navy back in the year 1785, Melville had himself put a Bill on the Statute book under which the duties of the office were prescribed and regulated precisely so that the possibility in the future of public fund embezzlement could be eradicated.

In those difficult early months of 1805 therefore, whilst Pitt and Melville exhausted every effort and every waking hour prosecuting the war with France, at their back was always the figure of St Vincent, sniping and accusing and urging the House to impeach Melville. Eventually it was Samuel Whitbread, the brewer, a supporter of St Vincent, who moved the impeachment of Melville for 'gross malversation and breach of duty'. The House rejected that motion by a large majority, only to replace it with another, which asked for a criminal prosecution by the Attorney-General, one Piggott, in a court of law, and that second motion was carried by a narrow majority. But rather than see their friend exposed to a jury and judge and the probability of a prison sentence if convicted, several Melville supporters now switched their votes in favour of a further motion for impeachment which was then carried, and, accordingly, all criminal proceedings were stayed.

Whitbread duly presented himself to the House of Lords and there impeached the Viscount Melville. However, at his trial in Westminster Hall, which did not take place until the following year, 1806, and which lasted but fifteen days, refreshingly short by the standards of today, he was acquitted on all counts. But he had by then been driven from office by a Vote of Censure early on in April 1805, carried by but one vote, the casting vote of the Speaker. His resignation had followed on 9 April, for, although there had been no question of embezzlement on his part, he recognized that he had not been as prudent or diligent as he should have been in his enforcement of his own Act of 1795.

Many then turned on St Vincent, accusing him of using this affair as a cover for his own neglect whilst First Lord of the Admiralty. Melville, a just and honourable man, then withdrew to his estates in Scotland and there lived out the five or six years of life which remained to him. Recognized in his time as the greatest man in Scotland, his portrait had been painted by the three fashionable portrait painters of the day, Romney, Raeburn and Reynolds. And it was only appropriate that the statue of Melville which surmounts the column raised in the very heart of St Andrew's Square in Edinburgh, should have been presented by officers and men of His Majesty's Royal Navy, for his contribution in rebuilding the strength of the Navy which had been so sadly reduced by the Earl St Vincent, and so his part in the success of the blockade and the subsequent Battle of Trafalgar, had been immense.

Not surprisingly Napoleon lost no time in exploiting the Government's embarrassment, ordering his Finance Minister to 'Have a little pamphlet prepared on the Melville affair to show the immorality of the English Government',[14] whilst Pitt reluctantly set about finding a replacement. It was to be a relative of Melville's, Sir Charles Middleton, then in his seventy-ninth year. He was raised to the peerage as Lord Barham. This appointment infuriated St Vincent, but Barham proved himself to be an inspired choice, surprisingly hard-working and extremely efficient. His work as First Lord was to vindicate Pitt's choice entirely.

Barham, then Captain Charles Middleton, had gone to the Navy Office as Comptroller of the Navy back in 1778. He was an immensely hard-working, seagoing, professional naval officer used to working long hours. In the years which followed he targeted for his attention the efficiency of the dockyards for which he had responsibility. In the result he achieved a remarkable improvement in productivity. This was recognized when he was charged with the supervision of all business done by the Navy Office, which was then located at Somerset House in the Strand. But it seems that with his new and larger responsibility he became somewhat tyrannical and would brook no interference. It was not surprising therefore that he should have resigned the moment that a proposal of his that the functions of the Board be split among three committees, was rejected. But with the Declaration of War in 1793 Pitt had remembered Barham and the value of his services and so had brought him back as a Lord Commissioner to advise on Admiralty affairs.[15] There he came under the control of Lord Spencer, First Lord of the Admiralty, a somewhat aloof man not given to seeking advice or the opinions of others. Almost inevitably therefore he soon became irritated with Middleton and his habit of bombarding him with written opinion on every conceivable subject where it concerned Admiralty matters, and so resolved to get rid of him.[16] For his part Middleton complained more than once about Spencer's arrogance in refusing to take his advice. And relations between St Vincent and Middleton were even worse for St Vincent seemed to harbour a great contempt for all Scotsmen, and not just Melville, for reasons which he never explained, telling Nepean that 'They are only fit for drudgery.'[17] And describing Middleton as a 'Scotch packhorse'. But when Melville departed the Admiralty, hounded out of office, it was to Barham that Pitt turned, recognizing, as he did, the past achievements in naval administration which were his, and wanting now to employ his talents which were still very evident at the age of seventy-nine, for a sure hand was now required. And in Barham he did indeed find a safe pair of hands, born of years of experience, for he was to be one of the few Ministers counted a success in Pitt's Administration, apart from Pitt himself, who largely carried the Government with his brilliant debating skills and prodigious hard work.

EVENTS LEADING UP TO TRAFALGAR

The Navy was quick to appreciate the support it had received over the years from Pitt's Government, and so, in the few days which remained to him on shore, Horatio Nelson found his way to Downing Street, not just to Lord Castlereagh's Colonial Office where the celebrated encounter with Wellington occurred but to No. 10, there to spend many a long hour with the politician he admired most in this world, William Pitt. On the face of it, these two men had very little in common. The one proud, reserved, aloof, patrician, articulate, alone. The other flamboyant, vain, boastful, excitable and ambitious. And yet there was much which united them – an integrity, a sense of honour, an openness, a warmth and humanity, a generosity of spirit and a sense of duty coupled with genius which had converted many a sceptic into a devoted follower, for, unusually for the time, there can be no doubt that Nelson was adored and respected by those who served under him. Each in his own way was prepared to lay down his life for his country and each in his mid-forties had but a few more weeks to live. Nelson of the two had the reassurance of faith. Son of a clergyman he got down on his knees and knelt in prayer every day of his life both when he rose in the morning and before going to bed. Pitt had not before this time troubled to know Nelson, but now, after the last briefing on 6 September, he paid him a compliment he had accorded very few others when he escorted him to his carriage for the final farewell.[18]

The threat of invasion loomed large that summer as the *Grand Armée* stood poised on the northern coast of France waiting only for a fair wind and the arrival of the Combined Fleet to descend on these shores. Alert to the danger Pitt now warned Nelson to be ready at any moment to rejoin the Mediterranean Fleet, now lying off the coast of Spain, as its Commander-in-Chief, a fleet which had been enlarged and strengthened by the ever-watchful Cornwallis now that Cadiz came within its responsibility. After his clash with Calder in July, Villeneuve had kept the Combined Fleet at El Ferrol at the entrance to the Bay of Biscay. Orders then arrived from Napoleon at Fontainebleau to sail north to cover a crossing by the *Grand Armée* which had been placed on a 24-hour alert. It was on 3 August that the Emperor arrived at Boulogne for the final push and there reviewed his troops. But it was not until 16 August that Villeneuve ventured forth and he then turned south rather than north and sailed for Cadiz, ostensibly to take on board water and supplies! In this he was spotted by Collingwood, now a Vice Admiral of the Blue,[19] who wrote to Cornwallis that same day, 'This morning the combined fleet of 36 ships came down upon me when I was before Cadiz with three, and obliged me to abandon my station.'[20] This decision, unlike that made by Sir John Orde some four months earlier, escaped all criticism or censure by the merchants of London, for the French Fleet was not then, of course, sailing out to threaten British commercial interests in the West Indies so much as returning to harbour which is where Barham wanted them to be, pending arrangements for the final encounter. On 22 August Napoleon once again ordered Villeneuve to 'Put to sea and sail here. We will avenge 6 centuries of insults and shame.'

It was on 2 September that Captain Blackwood, bringing home despatches for the Admiralty from Collingwood, brought word to Nelson from Collingwood that the Combined Fleet had assembled in the harbour of Cadiz. Now, with a series of masterful strokes, Barham set the stage for the Battle of Trafalgar by relaxing the blockade at both Brest and Cadiz in order to entice the French Fleet out and into battle with the Mediterranean Fleet, whilst at the same time maintaining the strength of the Channel Fleet lest the southern shores of England should stand unprotected. Thus was the squadron off Rochefort sent to reinforce Calder off Ferrol whilst Cornwallis was ordered to draw back from Brest where he had been keeping watch on Ganteaume. All of England now looked to Nelson for deliverance and put their trust in him.

On 6 September he wrote to his friend Alexander Davison, 'I much fear that I shall not have the pleasure of seeing you before my departure, and to thank you for all your kind attentions. I wish you would name anyone to settle my long term Account; for, although I may not be able to pay off at this moment the balance due to you, still it would be a satisfaction to me to have it settled; and then I could give you a Bond for the amount, until I may be able to pay it, which I still hope to be able to do in spite of Sir John Orde . . .'[21] After leaving instructions in London with his upholsterers to prepare and engrave the coffin which had earlier been made from wood salvaged from the French Admiral's flagship at the Battle of the Nile,[22] and then presented to him by Captain Hallowell, Nelson left Merton on the evening of Friday, 13 September for 'The George' at Portsmouth, traditionally the resort of senior officers in that very crowded town. Then, in the early hours of the following day he walked from the hostelry a backway down to the seafront in the hope of avoiding the crowd and then through the short tunnel which survives to this day, before crossing the moat which leads onto the front where his barge lay waiting for him. And so he left England for the very last time, seen off by George Canning, Treasurer of the Navy, together with George Rose, another Minister in the Government and a large crowd of well-wishers, many of whom cheered him to the echo and wished him God speed, others of whom sank to their knees in silent prayer. On 15 September the *Victory* weighed anchor and set sail for Cadiz and the Cape of Trafalgar.

In fact, and unbeknown to the British, the immediate danger of invasion had by now passed for Napoleon, despairing of both the timid Villeneuve and also Ganteaume who was likewise refusing to leave harbour and asking to be relieved of his command, had finally accepted that naval cover for a crossing of his invasion force, was unlikely to materialize. His patience now exhausted and faced with a mounting bill for the flotilla which had been built and the exorbitant cost of provisioning the *Grand Armée* which was rapidly becoming demoralized with inactivity, Napoleon abandoned the whole enterprise. On 26 August he ordered Marshal Soult to break camp at Montreuil, St Omer and Bruges and to force march the *Grand Armée* east to the Danube as General Mack advanced into Bavaria and as the Czar was moving down through Poland. He himself quit his own headquarters at Boulogne on 2 September to take command of the Army and with a series of lightning strokes won great victories at Ulm in October, where Mack surrendered 27,000 Austrian soldiers, and at Austerlitz on 2 December where the Russian and Austrian armies were both routed. It was probably the greatest victory of his career. These and other victories elsewhere gave France full-scale territorial expansion on the mainland of Europe and resulted in the dissolution of the Holy Roman Empire and the creation of the Confederation of the Rhine. Meanwhile, in an exercise of saving face, for he had boasted of victory over the British for so long, he lost no time dressing up the presence of the *Grand Armée* on the northern shores of France for two long years between 1803 and 1805 as a charade played out simply in order to deceive and frighten the British, claiming that he had never had any real intention of mounting an invasion. If in truth a pretence, it must have been one of the most costly pieces of play-acting known in history.

Nonetheless, so long as the Franco-Spanish Fleet remained in being, the possibility of invasion and the threat to British commercial interests in the West Indies and in the East, would remain. The nation therefore had much to thank Lord Nelson for in the weeks that followed which culminated in the Battle of Trafalgar and the virtual annihilation of the Franco-Spanish Fleet. It was in large part his inspiration and his determination which brought victory, supported as it was by the courage and loyalty of the men under his command. To some extent chance had persuaded the Combined Fleet out of harbour. Having by now lost all interest in his Navy, as a parting shot before moving east with his Army, on 16 September Napoleon ordered the French Fleet to return to the Mediterranean, to Genoa and Toulon. Then, at last, on 17 September, he ordered that Villeneuve be removed from his command to be replaced by Admiral Rosily, at the same time directing Villeneuve to return to Paris to explain himself. Paradoxically it was this order and the prospect of the impending humiliation and disgrace which would inevitably follow which had finally stirred Villeneuve into action and which drove him out into the Atlantic, albeit now far too late to be of any assistance to his Emperor.

Thus did Napoleon's own order make possible the Battle of Trafalgar and the destruction of the French Fleet of ships for Villeneuve found himself trapped uncomfortably between the wrath and displeasure of his Emperor inland and the ferocity of Horatio Nelson lying out at sea! In fact these orders did not reach Villeneuve until the end of September although Rosily had not by then arrived at Cadiz to take over the command. And when his orders did arrive, Villeneuve and several of his officers still refused to sail for the Mediterranean, pleading lack of trained men and shortage of supplies, although the real obstacle was Nelson's Fleet offshore, even though the French now outnumbered the British. The news of his successor reached Villeneuve on 18 October.[23] He learned then also that Rosily had, on 14 October, set out from Madrid for Cadiz, on his way to take up the command. Now rather than await his arrival and then suffer the inevitable loss of face, Villeneuve at last ordered

Lord Nelson at prayer before Trafalgar

the Fleet to weigh anchor and set sail for the Mediterranean without further delay, believing, wrongly, that some of Nelson's ships had by then been detached to Gibraltar, thus giving him an even greater numerical advantage. Because there was no more than a slight breeze it was the 19th before the entire Fleet came out, to the undisguised astonishment and delight of Horatio Nelson.

Superceded in command by Collingwood, then ordered to strike his flag and return home, Sir Robert Calder had by now set sail for England and he took no part in the Battle of Trafalgar which was fought two days later. Sir John Orde, the while, languished at home, unemployed whilst the Earl St Vincent, at his most difficult, continued to harry the Pitt Administration. Fortunately Nelson remained oblivious to all that.

Although the French and Spanish fought tenaciously and with great courage at the battle which followed on 21 October, the Combined Fleet was indeed so severely crippled, with twenty ships taken or sunk, that the strength and the will of the French Navy was broken irrevocably and Napoleon's plans for the invasion of Great Britain could never thereafter be resurrected. After Trafalgar the British Navy was to reign invincible and supreme on the high seas for a century or more, although, in the eyes of almost every true Englishman, the loss of Nelson in the very hour of victory, and many more under his command, had been an awful price, almost too much to pay. Thus ended eight of the most glorious years in the long history of the Royal Navy.

In the months which followed, Napoleon established the 'Continental System' designed to exclude Great Britain from all European trade, and, to a large extent and for a time, it worked. But the greater loss was to be to Europe itself which lost not only the British market but also markets elsewhere in the world as the British Navy continued to blockade European ports and so prevent exporters from sailing, whilst at the same time developing new markets of their own overseas.[24] Although Napoleon's thirst for territorial expansion continued apace for almost a decade or more until the defeat of his armies at Waterloo, it was in the years 1803, 1804 and 1805 that Great Britain had been most at risk of invasion. Nelson had appreciated this well enough, as had William Pitt who was woken at 3 o'clock on the morning of 5 November to be told of the great victory off Trafalgar, but also of the sad death of Horatio Nelson, news delivered by the Captain of the frigate *Pickle*. The King too recognized full well that a great danger had passed when he was woken with the news at 7 o'clock and read aloud the noble despatch written by Cuthbert Collingwood, modest of the part he himself had played, 'The ever to be lamented death of Vice Admiral Lord Viscount Nelson, who, in the late conflict with the enemy, fell in the hour of victory . . . the loss of a hero whose name will be immortal . . . I beg to congratulate their lordships on a victory which I hope will add a ray to the sun

of His Majesty's Crown, and be attended with public benefit to our country . . .'
Visibly moved by the awful news of Nelson's death and by, also, the grace and
sweetness of Collingwood's majestic language, the King was unable to find
words for a while as the tears rolled down his old cheeks. But then after a little
he said, 'Where did this sea-Captain get his admirable English?', going on, 'Oh
I remember he was educated by Moises!' recalling what his Lord Chancellor,
Eldon, had earlier told him, that the two had sat together some forty-five years
before at the feet of the celebrated Moises, then headmaster of the Royal
Grammar School in Newcastle upon Tyne.[25] Although not the large and
nationally reknowned private independent day school of today, feeding students
to Oxford and Cambridge Universities almost as a matter of course, the
Reverend Hugh Moises was, nonetheless, a schoolmaster and Cambridge-
educated scholar of high repute with such a love of classics and an enthusiasm
for books that no pupil of his could fail to be infected by it. And Collingwood,
perhaps not the most gifted of boys academically, had been no exception, for a
love of books and the written word was to be his support and joy over many a
long day spent at sea. The King remembered all this now, coupled with the
name of Moises. He had learned a little of that distant academy many years
before from the Poet Mark Akenside who had been there long before, and who,
as Chief Physician at St Thomas's Hospital in London, had become Physician
to his Queen in the early years of his reign. He seldom lacked employment for
the King fathered a large family, and whilst Akenside tendered to his family, so
that originally more humble man of Northumberland, Capability Brown, tendered
to his gardens as Royal Gardener with a grace and favour house at Hampton
Court. Unlike the brothers Eldon and Stowell, who moved on so easily and
naturally to Oxford University and the highest echelons of the judiciary,
Collingwood had gone to sea. But the probability is that he gained just as much
from that remarkable teaching as had either of those two most eminent judges.

On the night of Saturday 9 November Pitt was toasted at a Guildhall
banquet as 'The Saviour of Europe'. In reply he chose his words with care. 'I
return you many thanks for the honour you have done me; but Europe is not to
be saved by any single man. England has saved herself by her exertions, and
will, I trust, save Europe by her example.' With but a weak team of ministers
to rely on, he had himself taken much of the burden of the Exchequer, Foreign
Affairs and War upon his own frail shoulders and he was now all but spent.
The nation started then to dismantle its coastal defences and stand down the
voluntary militia in preparation for a return to normal life and for the return
also of HMS *Victory* and the body of its hero. It was to be a long delay for the
crew of *Victory*, devoted to the memory of their commander, rightly insisted
that he be brought home in his own battle-damaged ship and by his own crew.[26]

Notes

[1] Terraine, p. 70.
[2] N Walder, p. 464.
[3] N Mahan, p. 654; N Brad, p. 318; *Life of Revd. A.J. Scott*, p. 171.
[4] N Brad, p. 318.
[5] NC & M, II, p. 406; also at NJ, p. 333.
[6] N Bry, p. 104.
[7] Schom, p. 217.
[8] Warner, p. 9.
[9] Schom, p. 226.
[10] N Mar, p. 36.
[11] ND, p. 70.
[12] Parkinson, p. 8.
[13] Gardiner, p. 196.
[14] Schom, p. 151.
[15] Gardiner, p. 188.
[16] Gardiner, p. 188.
[17] Gardiner, p. 195.
[18] Ehrman, Vol III, p. 790.
[19] Barnett, p. 104.
[20] Schom, p. 279.
[21] NN, VII, referring to VI, pp. 283 and 289.
[22] N Whi, p. 8.
[23] Schom, p. 304.
[24] Preston, pp. 97-8.
[25] CW, p. 3; CR, p. 5; CM, p. 193.
[26] N Wh, p. 7.

CHAPTER XV

ORDE AT NELSON'S FUNERAL

It was on 4 December that *Victory* arrived home. Five weeks later, on 9 January 1806, following a complete autopsy of a body which had been preserved in brandy, and then, at Gibraltar, in vinegar wine, for the journey back to Portsmouth, and after it had lain in state at Greenwich Hospital for two days so that the British public, in deep mourning for the little Admiral, could pay its last respects, the funeral procession set out from the Admiralty in Whitehall bound for St Paul's Cathedral and Nelson's last resting place. Unrivalled though the British may be in mounting grand processions on great occasions, the sure grandeur of this occasion was matched only by the terrible grief felt by those who saw it. None had ever witnessed a spectacle quite like it before. It was to be the last act and final curtain of a Greek tragedy.

Led by General Sir David Dundas with detachments of Light Dragoons, Light Infantry, Royal Artillery and Grenadiers, the procession set off at 12 noon. There followed 48 pensioners from Greenwich Hospital, 48 seamen and marines from Her Majesty's ship *Victory*, trumpeters, drummers and bandsmen beating out Handel's 'Dead March' in Saul, then mourning coaches which carried Rouge Croix, Pursuivant of Arms, Blue Mantle, naval officers, servants of Nelson, representatives from the City, clergy, chaplains to Nelson, the banner of the deceased as a Knight of the Bath, Knights Bachelor, Sergeants at Law, Knights of the Bath, baronets, Nelson's trophies, his friend and treasurer Alexander Davison, Charles James Fox, Privy Councillors, the Rt. Hon. Sir Evan Nepean, the Rt. Hon. Sir William Scott MP (Judge of the Admiralty Court), William Windham MP, countless peers of the realm, representatives of the Government including Viscount Castlereagh, the Earl Marshal, the Earl Camden KG (Lord President of the Council), the Archbishop of Canterbury, all the Dukes of the Blood Royal headed by the Prince of Wales attending in a private capacity, and then, mourning coaches which carried officers of the Royal Navy, Nelson's knightly accoutrements and coronet, followed by two coaches in which rode the six Admirals who were to bear the canopy. Finally came a mourning coach which carried four Admirals who were to support the black velvet Pall, followed by the funeral car itself and the body of Lord Nelson. Then came the Chief Mourner, old Admiral of the Fleet Sir Peter Parker, now eighty-five years of age, the assistant mourners and members of Nelson's family.[1]

As General Dundas ascended the steps of the Cathedral and entered by the great west door, so the tail of the procession was still leaving the Admiralty, such was its length. When the funeral car eventually reached the great entrance at two in the afternoon, the body was taken from it, covered with the Pall, and borne by twelve seamen from *Victory* to within the gates where it was received by the supporters and Pall Bearers.

From all contemporary accounts, as the procession moved down the Strand and up Fleet Street to Ludgate Hill, streets densely packed with silent mourners, heads bared in silent homage, it was the contingent of sailors from *Victory* who most caught the public eye as they bore their Union Jacks and the St George's Ensign brought from the ship, perforated and torn as it was by enemy shot. It was a tangible and direct link with the battle itself and a moving reminder to those lining the route that as well as Nelson many others had fallen for their country at Trafalgar. And as he entered the Cathedral, Nelson's old friend, the Duke of Clarence, sobbed uncontrollably.[2]

Inside, greeted by the organ which had begun to play, the coffin was placed in the choir. The Chief Mourner and his two supporters, Admiral William Lord Radstock and Admiral Samuel Viscount Hood took their seats beside the coffin, around which sat the four bearers of the Pall. Amongst the congregation sat the commander of the French Fleet, Admiral Villeneuve, together with Captain Magendie of the *Bucentaure*, now both in captivity, but paroled by the Admiralty for the day to allow them to attend.[3] War at this time was indeed conducted according to a more chivalrous code. Absent, tragically, was William Pitt the Prime Minister who had but days to live. He was a dying, broken man for the French victory at Austerlitz and so the end of the third coalition had destroyed all the plans he had so carefully laid. It had taken away his will to live just as surely as a sniper's bullet had put an end to Horatio Nelson. So changed now were the boundaries of Europe by Napoleon's expansion that he had said of a map lying on his desk, 'Roll up that map, it will not be wanted these ten years.' The country was now in financial straits and taxation was high and the menace of France remained unchecked on the Continent of Europe. Pitt was to die a sick and lonely man, worn out by his exertions, on the 23rd day of that same month. He was but forty-seven years of age. The whole of his adult life had been sacrificed to work and duty. He had missed the ordinary pleasures of a family or home life even more so than had Horatio Nelson. Each in their different ways had given their lives for their country. But Pitt had indeed been a

Nelson's Interment at St Paul's Cathedral

great Prime Minister, and, had he known it, he had by now guided the country through the worst of the storms and steered her on a course which was to end in the defeat of the French at Waterloo. In his place now at the funeral stood the Earl of Camden. Absent too was Lady Hamilton, for this was an all-male occasion. Vice Admiral Lord Collingwood, as he had now become, second in command at Trafalgar and the first into the battle, remained on the high seas keeping watch for his country at Cadiz, as the new Commander-in-Chief of the Mediterranean Fleet, appointed at the insistence of his sovereign. His secretary wrote:

His Majesty considers it very fortunate that the command, under circumstances so critical, should have devolved upon an officer of such consummate valour, judgement and skill as Admiral Collingwood has proved himself to be, every part of whose conduct he considers deserving his entire approbation and admiration. The feeling manner in which he has described the events of that great day and those subsequent, and the modesty with which he speaks of himself, whilst he does justice, in terms so elegant and so ample, to the meritorious exertions of the gallant officers and men under his command, have also proved extremely satisfactory to the King.

With Collingwood out at Cadiz were most of the Captains who had fought at Trafalgar. The Duke of Clarence had earlier applied for the command, but the choice of the King and the Admiralty had been Collingwood. It was a doubtful reward for it meant that he was never to set foot on shore again.

As for the ever dutiful Cornwallis, he too was at sea, lying off Torbay, watching the Channel, not invited to the funeral. But the Earl St Vincent, who had been invited, and who had claimed for himself so much of what had been achieved by Nelson and the Royal Navy, was absent this day, his seventy-second birthday, pleading ill health. The true reason for his absence was never to be explained.

But the final irony was that, of the four Admirals appointed to support the Pall, and who therefore rode in the procession closest to the body of Lord Nelson and then sat and stood nearest to him in the Cathedral in the final moments before he was laid to rest, one was Sir John Orde, now an Admiral of the Blue. Rear Admiral Eliab Harvey and Vice Admiral Thomas Taylor stood at the foot of the bier whilst Vice Admiral James Hawkins Whitshed and Sir John Orde stood at its head.

And so, at thirty-three minutes past 5 o'clock in the evening and in failing light, when the coffin was finally carried by the Admirals from the choir to the centre of the great dome to an enclosure which had been erected there for the occasion, and as the thin and emaciated Bishop of Lincoln and Dean of St Paul's, Sir George Pretyman Tomline, Pitt's tutor at Pembroke College, Cambridge and one-time Secretary and friend, who had been appointed to that elevated position by Pitt himself,[4] raised his arms to the heavens and gave voice to the final rites, 'We therefore commit his body to the ground; earth to earth, ashes to ashes, dust to dust . . .',[5] it was in the presence of those four officers of the Royal Navy that it was lowered through the floor to the crypt below.

In spite of their differences Sir John had continued to demonstrate his admiration for Horatio Nelson, although in fact his presence as Bearer of the Pall had only come about by chance when one of the four originally nominated, Vice Admiral Henry Savage, had pleaded indisposition also. Sir John had then been invited to stand in his place.[6] He too had been unwell but such was his regard for Horatio Nelson by this time that, with determination, he rose from his sick bed in order to be at Nelson's side in his very last moments.

It was not until 1824 that the custom of holding a dinner each year on board *Victory* on Trafalgar Night, 21 October, was established.[7] And it was not until the 1920s that, with the help of public subscription, repairs were undertaken to preserve the ship for posterity on dry land at Number 2 Dock in Portsmouth dockyard. Not surprisingly HMS *Victory* and Nelson's tomb at St Paul's Cathedral are the subjects of frequent visits by the tourist and patriot alike to this day, and the memory of Nelson, hallmarked by Collingwood as 'immortal' in his Trafalgar despatch, is still toasted each year by naval officers high and low even now, one hundred and ninety-two years after his death at Trafalgar.

Notes

[1] *The Naval Chronicle* for 1806, Vol XV, Chapter 15, p. 138; *The Times*, which is not as accurate on this occasion.
[2] Fulford, p. 120; NCR, p. 314.
[3] Preston, p. 98.
[4] Ehrman, Vol I, p. 13.
[5] *The Naval Chronicle* for 1806, Vol XV, p. 232.
[6] *The Naval Chronicle* reporting the *London Gazette* of 18 January 1806; Ralfe, p. 79; Marshall, p. 73.
[7] Preston, p. 98.

CHAPTER XVI

THE AFTERMATH

Not only were the fortunes of the British nation destined to change with the death of Nelson, so too were those of many named in this account who had been associated with him. It was something of a watershed. Within a matter of weeks Pitt lay dead, and the decline and fall of Lady Emma has been told often enough.

After the death of Pitt so soon after Nelson's funeral, Spencer returned to government as Home Secretary in the Greville/Fox Administration, but for one year only after which he retired to his Northamptonshire estates and to more literary and scientific pursuits.

The new First Lord of the Admiralty was Captain Grey's older brother, Charles. Although still the member for Northumberland to which he had succeeded after a member of the Duke of Northumberland's family, Lord Algernon Percy, had vacated it, he now used his father's new courtesy title, Lord Howick. With the death of Fox, Grey became leader of the Whig section of the Government and Foreign Secretary. The following year his father died and he succeeded to the title as the second Earl Grey. But in that same year the Government was dismissed and Grey went out of office for no less than twenty-four years, which suited him well, wedded as he was to his distant Northumberland. It was in the year 1830, as leader of the opposition to the old Duke of Wellington's Government that he was to take under his wing reform of the franchise. As Prime Minister, and, of course, after a monumental struggle, the Reform Bill was put on the Statute Book in 1832 and the monument erected to him to mark that achievement which stands high at the top of Grey Street in the very heart of Newcastle upon Tyne and which bears an inscription by Sydney Smith, continues to tower over and dominate that city to this day. So ended the age of 'rotten boroughs', bribery and corruption and so too began the

197

emancipation of householders. In the fullness of time Captain George Grey's great-grandson, Sir Edward Grey was to become the celebrated Foreign Secretary in the First World War and the 1st Viscount Grey of Fallodon, the old family house in Northumberland where both he and Grey of the Reform Bill had been born.

Nelson's Treasurer, Alexander Davison, had by this time amassed a large fortune from Government contracts and was living in great splendour in London in St James's Square and at Swarland Hall in Northumberland. Yet within two years he was standing in the dock in the Court of King's Bench facing charges of fraud. After the Battle of the Nile he had been appointed by the Government buyer of barrack supplies for the Army. This was a contract of increasing importance and size at a time when the military was being concentrated in larger and larger numbers in barracks up and down the country to meet the threat of invasion. Davison's remit had been to obtain whatever was required at prices in the market most favourable to the Government in return for a commission of 2½ per cent. Regrettably he took advantage of the position to supply from his own warehouses at his own prices and then compounded the offence by manufacturing bogus invoices for the eyes of the authorities in order to conceal the deception whilst all the while continuing to take his 2½ per cent – or so the jury found. By Christmas Day of the year 1808 he was behind bars in Newgate Prison starting a twenty-one months' sentence imposed by Lord Ellenbrough. Testimonials as to his character from officers in high places and the fact that the commission improperly paid, amounting to some £8,000, had been reimbursed, had not saved him, for he had milked the public purse. In fact he had earlier served a short term for a more technical offence involving election irregularities when contesting the Ilchester constituency. Yet, looked at in the round, he had rendered Nelson long and faithful service over many years and was destined to live on quietly for a further twenty-three, long enough to see one son become a Major General and another an equerry to the Duke of Cambridge.[1]

Three months after he had attended Nelson's funeral, Villeneuve, released by the British, was found dead in a hotel room in Rennes, stabbed by his own hand or that of another, it was never discovered which.[2]

As for Collingwood, of medium height and thin, described by Eldon as a 'pretty and gentle boy' when at school, now that command of the Mediterranean Fleet had devolved upon him he maintained his vigil standing off Cadiz and was never to see his wife, daughters or home at Morpeth in Northumberland again. Although he had never had independent command of a fleet in battle, he was now something of a hero for the major role he had played in the three battles of 'The Glorious First of June', Cape St Vincent and finally Trafalgar, where, as second in command to his close friend Nelson, he had been the first to break the French line, attacking at the centre with his ship the *Royal Sovereign,* drawing from Nelson the comment, 'See how that noble fellow Collingwood takes his ship into action! How I envy him!' The Royal Sovereign was manned for the most part by men from his native Northumberland labelled by him 'Tars of the Tyne', and commanded by one Captain Rotherham of Hexham in the Tyne Valley whose father was for many years senior physician at Newcastle's Royal (later Victoria) Infirmary.[3] Indeed he had been showered with honours by a grateful nation, raised to the peerage as Baron Collingwood of Caldbourne and Hethpole in the county of Northumberland, made a Freeman of the City of London and granted a pension of £2,000 a year for life, with a reversion of £1,000 to his wife and £500 each to his two daughters. He was to write to his wife '. . . I never dreamed that I was to be a Peer of the Realm. How are my darlings? I hope they will take pains to make themselves wise and good, and fit for the station to which they are raised.'

But now the need and opportunity for further naval action with the French had largely gone and his years of command were spent, for the most part, dealing with all those administrative matters involved in keeping a fleet at sea. He was a martyr to duty, unable to delegate, and, without his guide and mentor, Nelson, to lead the way, his mistake was to make his ship his headquarters and his cabin his office and there he spent the rest of his days, desk-bound for much of the time. Such a sedentary, lonely existence did little for his health and well-being. In fact it wore him out and was finally to kill him less than five years after Nelson's death in action. However, Napoleon was to say after Waterloo that the downfall of his Empire could be laid at the door of what he described as 'the Spanish Ulcer'. Collingwood in the Mediterranean in the five years after Trafalgar had made no small contribution to Wellington's success in the Peninsular.

In 1809 his most faithful friend and closest companion, his dog Bounce, died at sea, and then, eventually, in 1810, he was finally persuaded to come home on medical grounds, his only thought now for Morpeth, his wife and his two daughters, but, alas, he was by then too feeble to survive the journey and he died at sea four hours out of Port Mahon on 7 March at the age of sixty-one.

After an impressive public funeral he was laid to rest in St Paul's Cathedral alongside his old friend and comrade-in-arms, Horatio Nelson, buried by old Admiral of the Fleet Sir Peter Parker who had been a father to the two of them,

Cuthbert, Baron Collingwood

yet outlived each to be chief mourner at both of their funerals. Present too on this occasion was Lord St Vincent, his old commanding officer, and, of course, Lord Eldon, almost uncontrollable. But his request that his title should survive by passing to his elder daughter had been refused him.

Trafalgar had been the climax of his career. Known as 'Cuddy' to his friends from the name given to donkeys in Northumberland,[4] Collingwood was a quiet, modest and unassuming man which some, including Nelson's friend Gilbert Elliot, read as coldness. But rather it was a diffidence, a shyness and a carefulness, for, although he was a strict disciplinarian, beneath it all there was a purity, an honesty, a warmth, a kindliness, a decency and a strong sense of justice and fairness. There was too an intense love of country. Well grounded in Latin and well read thanks to old Moises, duty was his watchword, loyalty his habit. With a firm belief in the Almighty, throughout his life he had been a perseverer, steering a steady and consistent, albeit unremarkable course, and so it was that both the Admiralty and his King recognized in him a man they could trust. By the standards of his day, he had been something of a humanitarian. So much so that his men, when out of earshot, called him 'Father'.

Warner, in his *Life of Collingwood*, relied upon Thackeray's judgment of the man fifty years on. '. . . I think since Heaven made gentlemen, there is no record of a better one . . . than that of brighter deeds. I grant you, we may read performed by others; but where of a nobler, kinder, more beautiful life of duty, of a gentler, truer heart?' And Algernon Charles Swinburne, proud of his Capheaton, Northumbrian ancestry was to end his poem 'Northumberland' which began with,

> Between our eastward and our westward sea
> The narrowing strand
> Clasps close the noblest shore fame holds in fee
> Even here where English birth seals all men free – Northumberland,

with,

> Our Collingwood, though Nelson be not ours,
> By him shall stand
> immortal, till those waifs of oldworld hours
> Forgotten, leave uncrowned with bays and flowers – Northumberland.

He was not a rich man when he died but then he was very far from being poor. The product of an old Northumbrian landed county family, he belonged to a branch of it which had lost its land and so his father had moved into Newcastle from Dissington and turned to trade, and not with very much success. But they were comfortably off. Living on the side where a large block of offices known as Milburn House now stands, a steep road which tumbles down to the river Tyne, little material advantage had been passed on to him before he went to sea, and little came to him after he did so. But then, in 1806, his cousin Edward had died leaving Collingwood his estate at Chirton, near North Shields which lay on the outskirts of Newcastle. This, when realized, for he had no wish to move near to town from his country home at Morpeth, provided him with an income, which, taken together with his service pay and the pension which had been granted him by a grateful nation in that same year, yielded an income assessed at more than £10,000 per annum. Ever a close man in money matters he now had little use for this new-found wealth for he was never at home, and, anyway, had no interest in society or the usual avenues of expenditure. Moderate in his eating and drinking habits,[6] unlike Nelson, he disliked and almost disapproved of luxury, feasting or excessive merriment. When at home in Morpeth where his heart lay, or at his small estate at Hethpole, his greatest obsession had been planting acorns which he carried in his pockets that they may in future years be felled as oak trees for use as ship's timber! Plainly, if such rumours have truth and from the time spent at sea, he was first and foremost a sailor. When he died his eldest daughter was barely out of her teens for he had not married until forty-three years of age.

After his death his beloved wife Sarah and the two small daughters to whom he was so devoted erected a cenotaph to his memory in Newcastle's St Nicholas Cathedral, and then, thirty years on, a monument was put up by public subscription at the mouth of the river Tyne.[7] Of the fifty years he had given to the Royal Navy, forty-four had been spent away from home. He was perhaps the noblest sailor of them all.

Old Sir Peter Parker, patron of both Nelson and Collingwood, lived just long enough to see them off before he too died in the year 1811 at the age of ninety.

Collingwood's old headmaster, The Reverend Hugh Moises, lived just long enough to be able to bask in the reflected glow of his pupil's success. A gifted classical scholar of some renown and a fellow of Peterhouse College, Cambridge, he employed in the classroom the twin persuasions of birch and bible, but he was essentially a kind man and a born teacher with a passion and an enthusiasm for his subject which never failed to infect and win over his pupils. He made extensive use too of the sermon,[8] its construction and composition, so that his boys might acquire a clarity of thought and a felicity of expression. And it is recorded that he had such a presence about him that he took his seat at his desk with as much dignity as a judge takes his seat on the bench.[9] As a tribute to his teaching Clark Russell in his *Life of Collingwood* was to write of Collingwood, 'No youth ever profited more from his school . . . in general knowledge there was probably not a man in the service that could have matched him . . . was a student of everything good in English literature, and had such an art in expressing himself with his pen . . . as brings many of his letters . . . very close to some of the happiest compositions of Addison'. But he too died in the year after Trafalgar on the fifth day of July. A mural monument was afterwards erected in St Nicholas Cathedral, Newcastle in his memory by Stowell, Eldon, Collingwood and others of his grateful pupils.

On the death of Pitt soon after Nelson's funeral, Lord Eldon of Eldon in the county of Durham, where he had purchased an estate, surrendered the Great Seal to Erskine, but then, on the return of Pitt's friends to office soon after, he was reinstated as Lord Chancellor. He was to sit on the Woolsack for a total of twenty-five years, and was for much of that time Steward of Oxford University.

Although fond of broadcasting his supposedly modest origins, in fact his father had been '. . . an enterprising and prosperous man. He started in business as a coalfitter for the Bowes family, owned keels, kept a Public House on the quay to supply the keelmen in his employment with the beer which formed part of their wages, speculated in shipping and marine insurance, owned a sugar-house and supplied timber, waggon wheels and rails to the collieries.' Hence the name given Eldon by the Prince of Wales, 'Old Coal Bags'. At his death in 1776 when Eldon was twenty-five years of age, his father '. . . left to his family, including what some of them had already received from him, property to the value of between thirty and forty thousand pounds',[10] which included an estate at Usworth. Hence the substantial property in Love Lane on the Quayside, Newcastle upon Tyne, where Eldon was born and grew up, shown on many an old print of the town. His future wife lived nearby at Millbanke House, which had at one time been the home of the Millbanke family before they moved to the house in County Durham where lived Anne Isabella Millbanke, the unfortunate wife of Lord Byron.

With his earnings as a member of the Bar travelling the Northern Circuit and then as a tenant in Chancery chambers in London together with his stipend as judge, then Lord Chancellor, augmented by a legacy from his father and judicious investment, when Eldon died in 1838 he left almost a million. He had received his Earldom when the Prince of Wales ascended the throne.

His older brother William, known as Harry, a man with a large and serious appetite for food and drink and a lifelong friend of Dr Johnson, continued to preside over the Admiralty Court and went on dispensing judgments until the ripe old age of eighty-two. Thoroughly dishevelled but ever courteous, he was blessed with a powerful intellect and an easy eloquence and was a truly outstanding judge in an age of naval warfare when so much of international complexity was brought before the Maritime Court for adjudication.

In the year 1812 when presiding at the Admiralty Sessions held at the Old Bailey, he had occasion to pass sentence on the Marquis of Sligo for enticing two seamen to desert their ship. The upshot was a second marriage between Sir William and Sligo's mother, the Dowager Marchioness, who was the daughter of old Admiral Howe. It was a tempestuous marriage and a disaster which ended five years on with her death. In 1822, on the Coronation of George IV, he was raised to the peerage as Baron Stowell of Stowell Park in the county of Gloucester, a property he had purchased but seldom lived in, living for most of the time at Earley Court in Berkshire which was his principal home. The following year his daughter married Viscount Sidmouth, the former Prime Minister Henry Addington. Stowell died in the year 1836, two years before his younger brother and almost as wealthy. Indeed Addington profited greatly from the will, so much so that he resigned a Crown pension which had been granted him in 1817.

The Bowes family referred to in the account of the father to Stowell and Eldon was the family which traded as John Bowes and Partners, colliery owners. By marriage to a Lyon of Glamis, the name Bowes-Lyon emerged, hence the connection of the Queen Mother with the County of Durham and Bowes magnificent museum.

The health of Sir John Orde's brother, Thomas, which had so concerned Sir John over the years, finally broke in the year following Nelson's funeral. He died at the age of sixty-one at the southern home which his wife had inherited at Hackwood Park, Basingstoke.[11] It had been built by the 1st Duke of Bolton on the site of an older house long in the Bolton family. He was buried at Old Basing.

Born in Morpeth in the year 1746, he had, whilst a student at Cambridge, developed a rare talent as an etcher and cartoonist. His caricatures were so admired that many were exhibited subsequently, including one of his younger brother John. Indeed this brought him into contact with Romney in the year 1775 and they afterwards remained friends, so much so that Romney painted his brother John in Captain's uniform when little more than twenty-seven years of age, although it flatters him as a man much younger. A portrait of Thomas Orde followed which was engraved in Mezzotint. It was the practise of Thomas to donate any profit from the exhibition of his works to the sitter.

But his talents elsewhere were less obvious. Although called to the Bar in 1775, he never practised but stood for Parliament instead, representing first the town of Aylesbury and then the port of Harwich. He served as a Member of Parliament for a total of sixteen years from 1780 until 1796. Although not a man obviously destined for high office, the work which initially brought him to the attention of his political masters was a well argued fifth report of the secret committee on Indian affairs of which he had become a member. As the author he won high praise from Henry Dundas, its Chairman, which set him on the road to junior office which was achieved in 1782, when, to the surprise of some, he was appointed Under-Secretary of State for Home Affairs to Lord Shelburne and then Secretary to the Treasury when Shelburne went there. In order to be close to his minister he took a house in Park Place off St James's Street, but then, within months, saw Shelburne go out of office and Orde went with him.[12] Thorne's *History of Parliament* assesses him at that stage of his career as 'Hardworking, able and persevering, he was valued by his chiefs, but was not popular, and like the typical civil servant, ill-suited for the Parliamentary arena.[13] Nevertheless when Pitt came in he invited Orde to take up his former position at the Treasury, but Orde, loyal to Shelburne, refused.

However he was soon afterwards appointed Chief Secretary to the Lord Lieutenant of Ireland, the Duke of Rutland, and in the years that he was in Dublin between 1784 and 1787 he did much good work. There he became 'the first instrument of Administration' and its main spokesman in the Irish Parliament.[14] This was really where his strength lay for he was more of a diligent and dependable staff officer than a General leading his troops into battle. But the work in Ireland, although largely successful, was very demanding. A bill brought forward at the request of Pitt seeking commercial equality between the two countries but then amended to give advantage to London, had to be dropped by Orde in the face of considerable opposition in Dublin.[15] Eventually the pressure of work broke his health and ended his political career. When an opportunity arose with the death of Rutland in 1787, he retired from government altogether before he had ever reached full ministerial rank, 'suffering from extreme relaxation and nervous affliction'.[16] Hence the concerns expressed by Sir John Orde for his brother's health when writing home from Dominica to which reference has already been made. In Prior's *Life of Oliver Goldsmith* it is noted that he gave 'a snug little place in the licence office to Maurice Goldsmith in honour of his brother's literary merit, in April of 1787'. Sir Jonah Barrington was more censorious. Orde was, he said, 'a cold, cautious, slow and sententious man, tolerably well informed, but not at all talented, with a mind neither powerful nor feeble'.[17]

In the *Rolliad*, he was lampooned, somewhat unfairly in the following words:

> Tall and erect, unmeaning, mute and pale,
> O'er his blank face no gleams of thought prevail:
> Wan as the man in classic story fam'd,
> Who told old Priam that his Ilion flam'd.
> Yet soon the time will come when speak he shall,
> And at his voice another Ilion fall!
> Caesar, we know, with anxious effort try'd
> To swell, with Britain's name, his triumph's pride:
> Off he essay'd, but still essay'd in vain;
> Great in herself, she mock'd the menac'd chain.
> But fruitless all – for what was Caesar's sword
> To thy all-conquering speeches, mighty Orde!
> Amphion's lyre, they say, could raise a town:
> Orde's elocution pulls a nation down.[18]

In his book on Pitt, Lord Ashbourne judged Orde's term of office in Ireland more objectively as successful on the whole, 'He appears not to have excited any hostile or bitter feelings, and to have enjoyed consideration and respect. His correspondence suggests that he was able, prudent, circumspect and cautious; a man who knew how to keep his own counsel. The notes of his speech in the House of Commons in the commercial resolutions are very full and suggest that his speech was most conciliatory, able, well-reasoned and clear.'[19] Indeed, judging by the many letters which passed between Pitt and Orde in this period, clearly both he and the Duke of Rutland thought well enough of him to induce him to stay on when he first expressed a wish to retire. Certainly he was a very industrious man who kept up a copious correspondence. A modern historian has portrayed him as a man of 'exceptional ability . . . who could be relied upon to judge from evidence, to record with accuracy and to negotiate with patience . . . upon which Pitt relied greatly in Irish matters.'[20] Four years after he had gone Pitt rewarded him with a post more appropriate to his delicate condition, when, in 1791, he appointed him Governor and Vice Admiral of the Isle of Wight in place of his father-in-law, the late Duke of Bolton and Marquis of Winchester, whose family had held the position for several generations.[21] It carried a stipend of £1,200 per annum. Perhaps it was nepotism but Orde gave it all his attention. He set about the repair of the Governor's official residence at Carisbrooke Castle and he built a delightful mansion at Fernhill, near Wooton. He was now extremely well off thanks to a judicious marriage to the illegitimate daughter of the Duke of Bolton, Jean Mary Browne Powlett, born to Mary Browne Bankskin, represented as Mary Browne Banks in Thorne's *History of Parliament*.[22] The Duke's Yorkshire estates in their entirety had been entailed to this daughter in default of male issue of his younger brother and heir. When that brother died on Christmas Eve, 1794, leaving only female children, the property passed to Thomas Orde in right of his wife. Two weeks later, by royal licence, he assumed the additional surname of Powlett. Two years later, in October of 1797, he was raised to the peerage as Baron Bolton of Bolton Castle in Yorkshire. Then in 1800 when the Lord Lieutenancy of Hampshire fell vacant, Orde wrote to Pitt asking to be considered. 'You know my principles and my uniform adherence to them, and you cannot, I trust be insensible of my steady feelings for your success and that of your administration.'[23] It achieved its object and to Governorship of the Isle of Wight was added the Lord Lieutenancy of the county of Hampshire. Having built Fernhill with its impressive watchtower, he sold it in 1804 and for the three or so years of life which remained to him he was a constant resident at Carisbrooke Castle. It was reported in a magazine at the time that 'His Lordship's recovery . . . from a deplorable state of health to that of convalescence and a new constitution has been effected from the natural and powerful causes which this situation affords.'

In one of her letters, dated 19 December 1798, Jane Austen wrote from Godmersham Park, Faversham, that 'My father is glad to hear so good an account of Edward's pigs, and desires it may be told, as encouragement to his taste for them, that Lord Bolton is particularly curious in his pigs, has had pigstyes of a most elegant construction built for them, and visits them every morning as soon as he rises.'[24] And then by a letter dated the 24th of that same month she set out in a letter a list of those who had partnered her at a ball, including one 'William Orde, (Cousin to the Kingsclere Man)', reckoned to be William Orde of Nunnykirk in Northumberland, the older half-brother of Thomas and John, and cousin of the Reverend John Orde of Weetwood Hall, Northumberland,[25] then vicar of Kingsclere in the county of Hampshire.[26] On the other hand, in a letter dated 9 January 1799, she wrote that 'one of my gayest actions was sitting down two Dances in preference to having Lord Bolton's eldest son for my partner, who danced too ill to be endured,'[27] although, twelve years later, the marriage of her cousin Margaret Beckford to Lieutenant Colonel Orde of Weetwood Hall, Northumberland, drew the comment from her in a letter dated 29 May 1811 that 'The papers say that her father disinherits her, but I think too well of an Orde to suppose that she has not a handsome Independence of her own!'[28]

St Vincent and Sir John Orde both lived on.

After the death of his old adversary William Pitt, and the advent of the Grenville/Fox Administration, St Vincent hoped for a recall to the Admiralty as First Lord.[29] But none came. However he was given command once more of the Channel Fleet, taking over from Cornwallis. Accordingly, in March 1806 he hoisted his flag in the *Hibernian* lying off Ushant. Although now weak in health, there he remained until the following year, when, at his own request, he retired home. He was then seventy-one years of age. His declining years he spent in peaceful retirement at his home, Rochetts near Brentwood in Essex, making occasional journeys to the House of Lords to make his contribution there. A final honour was bestowed upon him in July 1821 at the time of the Coronation when George IV appointed him Admiral of the Fleet and presented him with his gold baton. It was a tribute to his eminence and seniority for it involved a departure from an age-old tradition that no more than one should ever hold that ultimate rank at any one time. Back in 1811 after the death of Sir Peter Parker, as Prince Regent he had appointed his brother, the Duke of Clarence, to that exalted position at the tender age of forty-one, thus blocking the way to others for many a year. But now he allowed that St Vincent too could hold that rank.

St Vincent died on 14 March 1823 at the age of eighty-eight. At his own wish he was buried in Staffordshire near to his childhood home at Stone, although a more elaborate monument was later erected to his memory in St Paul's Cathedral in London. He died without issue and the Earldom died with him, although his sister's son, Edward Jervis Ricketts, then changed his surname to Jervis in order to succeed to the Viscountcy of Jervis.

Although he remained a very cautious and careful man, especially so in matters financial, in his last few years he was always ready to help sailors who had served under him who had since fallen on hard times. But he died with no word of apology or regret to Sir John Orde who survived him in that knowledge until he too died eleven months later in February of 1824.

But since Nelson's funeral Sir John Orde had sailed in calmer waters. That year had brought sadness on 25 October when his small daughter, Jane Emma, died. She was but five years old and lies buried alongside Sir John's first wife in the crypt at Hanwell Church. When his brother died in 1807 his son succeeded to the barony and took his seat in the House of Lords, thus vacating his position as Member of Parliament for the Yarmouth Division of the Isle of Wight. Sir John, then a full Admiral of the Blue, was nominated his successor and so represented that constituency for the rest of that Parliament although he made no attempt to return to the House of Commons after 1812.[30]

It is recorded that he supported the Government of the day, defending their Copenhagen expedition in 1808 with the words, 'The gentleman opposite seemed to wish that we should give the sword to the enemy and content ourselves with the scabbard.'[31] His allegiance to the Government seems to have continued for he spoke and then voted in favour of the Government's action over the Scheldt expedition in the year 1810, which drew from the ever cynical Canning a report to his wife that 'Many people will vote as Sir John Orde has just now consumed an hour and a half in telling me he intends to do – with the Government . . .'[32] Orde's brother-in-law, John Hookham Frere, had been best man at Canning's wedding in the year 1800. But Sir John's contributions in Parliament seem to have been unremarkable otherwise.

On 25 October 1809 he was promoted Admiral of the White in a general promotion,[33] and finally became an Admiral of the Red on 4 June 1814. In his final years charity was close to his heart. He became Vice-President of the Naval Charitable Society,[34] which was a busy organisation in the years following the Napoleonic Wars with so many claims being made upon its resources by disabled and destitute old sailors and their families. And in the local registers at Bognor he and his wife are listed as subscribers to the Bersted and Bognor National School built next to South Bersted Church.[35] In those early years Bognor was a small, new and fashionable resort by the sea striving to compete with Brighton for the favour of society. Dignitaries such as the Marquis of Lansdowne, who, as Lord Shelburne, had been Prime Minister, were attracted enough to the town to acquire properties. Others included Count Stanhemburg, the Austrian Ambassador to London, Lord Tenterden, one-time Lord Chief Justice,[36] and, of course, the much-loved Princess Charlotte, daughter of the Prince Regent, who fell in love with the town and it with her. She spent much of her time there from the year 1808 until her untimely death in childbirth a few years later. Sadly little of Georgian Bognor has been allowed to remain.

It seems too that Sir John provided maintenance at the rate of five shillings a week for a child born to one Mary Ann Stewart in the town and christened John. In his will Sir John made further provision for the boy so that his support should continue for a further five years, but then, it seems, when those five years were up the solicitor to the parish had difficulty placing the boy in employment, even when he appealed to Sir John's former constituents on the

Isle of Wight. It is not known what happened to him.[37] It is reported that, shortly before his death, Sir John took stock of his chequered life with these words, 'I have had a great many political enemies, few men more; but those who have gone before me, and those whom I may not outlive, I have long, long ago forgiven; and in private life, I do believe none ever wished to shove me off the stage.'[38] Thus, implicitly, did Sir John finally withdraw the challenge he had issued to St Vincent. And then having made his peace with this world he died at his home in Gloucester Place, London on 19 February 1824 after a long and painful illness, reportedly borne with great courage and composure. He was by then in his seventy-third year and stood eighth in the list of naval officers. Of the five issue by his second wife, a daughter, who never married, and a son survived him.[39]

Without doubt the last twenty-five years of his life had been clouded and poisoned with controversy and unhappiness, some of it of his own making but much of it not for it had stemmed for the most part from a high-handed decision taken back in the year 1798 with little thought for the welfare of its victim. There can be no peace in the world until we learn to suffer through the flesh of others – do unto others as you would be done by. But then if we expect too much of life we will most certainly be disappointed by it. It can at least be said of Sir John Orde that his life had been one of truth and honour. Pray God we may do as well.

Notes

[1] DNB.
[2] Ralfe, p. 350.
[3] CR, p. 142.
[4] CM, p. 19.
[5] CW, preface (xvii).
[6] Ralfe, p. 351.
[7] CM, p. 278.
[8] N Hol, p. 313.
[9] CR, p. 5.
[10] Welford, III, p. 360.
[11] *Gentleman's Magazine.*
[12] Namier, p. 233.
[13] Namier, p. 233.
[14] Namier, p. 233.
[15] Namier, p. 234.
[16] Namier, p. 234.
[17] *Rise and Fall of the Irish Nation*, pp. 320-1.

[18] Welford, Vol III, p. 243.
[19] Ash, p. 78.
[20] Reilly, pp. 120-1.
[21] Thorne, p. 696.
[22] Thorne, p. 696.
[23] Thorne, p. 696.
[24] Austen, p. 25.
[25] Austen, p. 559.
[26] Austen, p. 29 and Index.
[27] Austen, p. 35.
[28] Austen, letter 29 May 1811, p. 187.
[29] Ralfe, Vol I, pp. 314-15.
[30] Thorne, p. 696.
[31] Thorne, p. 696.
[32] Thorne, p. 696.
[33] *Gentleman's Magazine* 1809.
[34] Welford, Vol III, p. 243.
[35] Young, p. 72 and notes to his book at Bognor Regis Library.
[36] Young, p. 43.
[37] Young, p. 91.
[38] Ralfe, Vol II, p. 81.
[39] Ralfe, Vol II, pp. 79, 81.

BIBLIOGRAPHY

(Letters/names in brackets after each entry are those used in the footnotes)

Manuscript Collections, Newspapers and Periodicals:

The Keith Papers (Navy Records Society) 1927 (Keith).
The Barham Papers (Navy Records Society) 1907 (Barham).
The Naval Miscellany (Navy Records Society) Vols 1, 2 and 3, 1902.
The Orde Papers at the National Maritime Museum, Greenwich (Orde).
A Correspondence between the Admiralty, Earl St Vincent, Earl Spencer and Sir John Orde (R. Faulder) 1802 (Orde Corr.).
The Letters of Lord St Vincent (Navy Records Society) (JN).
The Letters of Admiral Lord Collingwood (Navy Records Society) (CL).
The Blockade of Brest (Navy Records Society) (Brest).
The Spencer Papers (Navy Records Society) (Spencer).
The Dillon Narrative (Navy Records Society) (Dillon).
The Journal of Rear Admiral James (Navy Records Society) 1896 (James).
The Llangattock Papers at The Nelson Museum, Monmouth.
The Public Record Office, Kew.
The *Naval Chronicle*, 40 vols, 1799-1819 (TNC).
The Annual Register (AR).
The *Gentleman's Magazine* (GM).
The Times (Times).
The *Morning Chronicle.*

Published Nelson biographies:
Nelson The Commander by Captain Geoffrey Bennet (Batsford) 1972 (NB).
Nelson and his Times by Lord Charles Beresford and H.W. Wilson (Eyre & Spottiswoode) 1897-8 (NB & W).
Nelson – The Essential Hero by Ernle Bradford (MacMillan) 1977 (N Brad).

Nelson by Arthur Bryant (Collins) 1970 (N Bry).

Southey's Life of Nelson edited by Sir Geoffrey Callender 1922 (NC).

The Life of Admiral Lord Nelson by Revd. James Stainer Clarke and John MacArthur (Cadell & W. Davis) 1809 (NC & D).

Lloyd's Nelson Collection edited by Warren R. Dawson (MacMillan) 1932 (ND).

Horatio Nelson by George Edinger and E.J.C. Neep (Jonathan Cape) 1931 (NE).

Nelson and his Captains by W.H. Fitchett (Smith, Elder) 1902 (N Fit).

Nelson, a biography by C.S. Forester, 1929 (N For).

Nelson the Sailor by Captain Russell Grenfell (Faber and Faber) 1953 (NG).

Nelson by Roy Hattersley (1974).

Nelson: A Personal History by Christopher Hibbert (Viking) 1994 (N Hibb).

Horatio Nelson by Richard H. Holme (Sir Walter Scott Publishing) 1905 (N Hol).

The Immortal Memory by David and Stephen Howarth (Dent) 1988 (NHH).

Trafalgar, The Nelson Touch by David Howarth (Collins) 1969 (N How).

The Durable Monument – Horatio Nelson by Admiral Sir W.M. James (Longmans Green) 1948 (NJ).

Nelson's Band of Brothers by Ludovic Kennedy (Odhams Press) 1951 (NK).

The Sailor's Nelson by Admiral Mark Kerr CB MVO (Hurst & Blackett) 1932 (N Kerr).

The Nelson Memorial: Nelson and his Companions in Arms by Sir John Knox Laughton (George Allen) 1896 (NL).

The Life of Nelson: The Embodiment of the Sea Power of Great Britain, by Alfred Thayer Mahan, 1897 (N Mah).

What's left of Nelson by Leo Marriott, (Dial House) 1995 (N Mar).

Nelson's Letters to his Wife by G.P.B. Naish, 1958 (N Naish).

The Dispatches and Letters of Vice-Admiral Lord Nelson edited by Sir Nicholas Harris Nicolas, 1844-6 (NN).

Nelson by Carola Oman (Hodder and Stoughton) 1947 (NO).

The Memoirs and Life of Vice-Admiral Lord Nelson by Dr Thomas James Pettigrew (T. & W. Boone) 1849 (N Pet).

The Last of Nelson's Captains by Sir Augustus Phillimore, 1906 (N Phil).

Horatio Nelson by Thomas Pocock (Bodley Head) 1987 (N Po).

Remember Nelson by Tom Pocock (Collins) 1977.

Horatio Nelson and The Naval Supremacy of England by W. Clark

Russell (G.P. Putnam's Sons) 1896 (NCR).
Nelson and the Hamiltons by Jack Russell (Anthony Blond) 1969 (NJR).
The Life of Horatio Lord Nelson by Robert Southey 1813 (NS).
Nelson by David Walder (Hamish Hamilton) 1978 (N Walder).
A Portrait of Nelson by Oliver Warner (Chatto & Windus) 1958 (PN War).
Nelson by Oliver Warner (Weidenfeld and Nicolson) 1975 (N War).
The Nelson Companion by Colin White (R. Naval Museum Publishing) 1995 (N Wh).
Nelson by Clennel Wilkinson (George G. Harrap) 1931 (N Wi).

Published Jervis biographies:

Life of John Jervis, Admiral Lord St Vincent by Captain W.V. Anson (John Murray) 1913 (JA).
Nelson's Dear Lord by Evelyn Berckman (MacMillan) 1962 (J Ber).
Life of Earl St Vincent by Edward Pelham Brenton (Henry Colburn) 1838 (J Bren).
Old Oak, The Life of John Jervis, Earl of St Vincent by Sir W.L. James, 1950 (JJ).
Life of Lord St Vincent by O.A. Sherrard (Allen and Unwin) 1933 (J Sher).
Memoir of Admiral The Rt. Hon. the Earl of St Vincent by J. Tucker, 1844.

Published Collingwood biographies:

The Life of Admiral Lord Collingwood by Geoffrey Murray (Hutchinson) 1936 (CM).
The Life of Admiral Lord Collingwood by W. Clark Russell (Methuen) 1891 (CR).
The Life and Letters of Vice-Admiral Lord Collingwood by Oliver Warner (Oxford University Press) 1968 (CW).

Miscellaneous Published:

Ralfe's Naval Biography, 1828 (Ralfe).
Royal Naval Biography by Lieutenant John Marshall (Longman) 1823-1835 (Marsh), 8 vols.
Men of Mark 'twixt Tyne and Tweed by Richard Welford (Walter Scott Ltd) 1895 (Welf).
History of North Durham by Reverend James Raine (John Bowyer Nichols & Son and George Andrew) 1852 (Raine).

A History of Morpeth by John Hodgson (1832).

Bell's Pedigrees (Bell).

The Dictionary of National Biography (Oxford University Press) (DNB).

The History of Parliament by R.G. Thorne (Secker and Warburg) 1986 (Thorne).

The History of Parliament by Namier and Brooke (HMSO) (Namier).

A History of Bognor Regis by Gerard Young (Phillimore) 1983 (Young).

Winston Churchill 1914-1916 by Martin Gilbert (Heinemann) 1971 (Gilbert).

The Later Correspondence of George III edited by A. Aspinall (Cambridge University Press) 1963 (George III).

The Reign of George III by J. Steven Watson (Oxford History) (Watson).

Pitt: some Chapters of his Life and Times by Lord Ashbourne (Longman's Green) 1898 (Ash).

Pitt The Younger by Robin Reilly (Cassell) 1978 (Reilly).

The Younger Pitt by John Ehrman (Constable), 3 Vols, 1969-1996.

Jane Austen's Letters (Oxford University Press).

The Great Mutiny by James Duggan (André Deutsch) 1965 (Duggan).

Sea Law and Sea Power by T. Gibson Bowles MP (Bowles).

The Impress Service in North-East England by Norman McCord (McCord).

Life of Lord Chancellor Eldon by Horace Twiss (John Murray) 1844 (Twiss).

Tarnished Coronets by M. Nelson D'Auvergne (T. Werner Laurie) (D'A).

Trafalgar by Alan Schom (Michael Joseph) 1990 (Schom).

Trafalgar by John Terraine (Sidgwick and Jackson; Purnell) 1976 (Terraine).

Britannia Rules by C. Northcote Parkinson (Weidenfeld and Nicholson) 1977 (Park).

Fighting Sail by Oliver Warner (Cassell) 1979.

Navy and Empire by James L. Stokesbury (Robert Hale) 1984 (Stoke).

The Oxford Companion to Ships and the Sea.

Britain's Naval Heritage by Gregory Clarke (HMSO) 1981.

Command at Sea by Oliver Warner (Cassell) (Warner).

History of the Royal Navy by Antony Preston, (Hamlyn Bison) 1983 (Preston).

Life and Letters of Admiral Cornwallis by G. Cornwallis-West (Holden) 1927 (Cornw).

The Royal Navy in The American War of Independence by Gerald S. Graham (HMSO) 1976 (Graham).

Cassells Biographical Dictionary of The American War of Independence (Cassells).

American Naval History by Jack Sweetman (Naval Institute Press 1991) (Sweet).

Royal Sailors by A. Cecil Hampshire (William Kimber) 1971 (Hampshire).

The British Admiralty by Leslie Gardiner (William Blackwood & Sons) 1968 (Gardiner).

Royal Dukes by Roger Fulford (Collins) 1933 (Fulford).

Bonaparte by Corelli Barnett (Book Club Associates; Allen and Unwin) 1978 (Barnett).

Letters from the Lower Deck.

INDEX